Eric Two Crowns (Supercabbie)
A Memoir by E.J.B. Comoretto

Eric Two Crowns (Supercabbie)
© 2018 E.J.B. Comoretto

All rights reserved. The use, reproduction or transmission of any part of this publication that is not covered under other individuals' copyright, in any form or by any means electronic or mechanical, including photocopying or recording, without written consent from the author is prohibited.

All photos in this book are from the author's collection, except where noted.

ISBN: 978-1-7750844-1-9

Cover Design by Jodi Howey and E.J.B. Comoretto
Edited by James Bow
First Edition printed by St. Jacobs Printery, St. Jacobs, ON
This edition printed by Lulu.com

A portion of the proceeds, of this book, will go to support Big Brothers Big Sisters of Waterloo Region

Table of Contents

Introduction — 3
   May 6, 1976 — 5
Kidnapped from Canada — 15
   Because This to Me is Paradise — 16
   The Barber Shop — 21
   Petersburg — 31
   Birdman Dad — 36
   My First Real Hunt — 39
   Dreams Come True — 43
Running to Italy — 47
   Living in Italy — 49
   The New Home — 50
   Leaving for Lignano — 54
   Predator — 60
   Mona — 65
   Biker Gang — 69
   Meesha — 73
   The Last Time — 81
Going to England — 85
   Touchdown — 86
   Die Hard — 91
   John Virgo and I — 95
   Pay up or Else — 103
Marylyn — 109
   For Better or For Worse — 110
   The Burford Bridge Hotel — 115
   By Hook or By Crook — 120
   Insurance — 125
   Brothers Again — 133
   Opportunities Knock — 140
   Down the Drain — 149

Returning to Canada — 157
- Finding Old Friends and More — 158
- East End Madness — 162
- The Break-Up — 168
- Neutraceuticals and TW — 174
- Forgiveness — 181
- Kill the Beast — 183

Coming Home — 185
- Returning to Les Escoumins — 186
- Pastel Coloured Friends — 192
- My Cousin Serge — 195
- Chief Joseph Moreau — 202
- Paying the Piper — 204
- A Father's Duties — 209

The Reasons I am Here — 213
- Supercabbie — 214
- For the Love of Golf — 223
- My Buddy Graham — 236
- Lightning Strikes Twice — 240
- Soccer Days — 244
- A Final Message — 248

Acknowledgements — 250

Dedicated to my Mother, Alberta Moreau.

Also the abducted and abused children of this world.

Introduction

My story is one of hard fought mental battles with belonging from a European and Native background. Having lived both lives and both cultures I became lost. Lost in Metis identity. I have been compelled to write this memoir through a promise. This promise was to my Mother. She wanted me to share our story, to help others.

Shortly before she passed, she shared her sorrows. The hurt of being stripped of us, her children. Through the selfish actions of a desperate husband and father. I and my siblings taken to Italy, a place I had visited a few times as a child, and then lived there as a teenager. She needed through me, a way of leaving her legacy. A legacy of Love yet anguish. She was the daughter of a "Chief" and knew her duties as a mother, instilled in her, from her mother. She is my Hero. The intermixing of two different cultures with different ideals that would eventually collapse.

My role, is to explain the aftermath of abduction, and my journeys as a youth leaving home at 15 to eventually discover after many years, my being, belonging, and purpose to my life. Follow me through my life's journey thus far, and my visions of the future.

Chapter One
May 6, 1976

The first time I felt the earth move was in Italy, on May 6, 1976, around 8:45 p.m.

I was fifteen. I was staying in Lignano with my friends Roberto and Lino, helping them open their restaurant. My family was back in Osoppo, about an hour or so away.

Roberto and Lino, as well as their father, were meeting with an electrician to discuss where to put in power sockets for the kitchen equipment, when we felt the first tremors.

I was sitting on the couch, watching television, when suddenly I felt the couch shaking back and forth. I thought Rob was maybe farting about, but when I looked around, he wasn't there. Instead, everybody started shouting *"Schampait! Schampait! Terremot!"*

Though my father was Italian and I'd been living in Italy for about a year or so, I'd never heard the word "Terremot". I could feel the panic behind it, though. Rob ran towards me, grabbed me by the arm, and we jumped off the porch onto the grassy ground seven feet or so below. All the while, the brothers' father was screaming, "Earthquake! Earthquake! Run!"

My heart was pounding like crazy, now that I understood what was happening. Feeling the ground shake was terrifying. Rob and I looked to our left and saw a few people milling about at the entrance of the driveway, well away from the building.

The tremors had stopped. As I looked around, I could see Robert's mother walking towards us. The people were talking to Rob in German and he translated to me that they'd felt the building shake a few minutes before as well and had gotten out as quick as they could. We'd felt the second one.

Eric Two Crowns (Supercabbie)

We all waited a bit in case another tremor hit. People talked, a bit nervous, but in good spirits, because everybody was okay, and there was no damage around us. Then Robert's mother made a remark which I'll never forget. She said, "Tomorrow, you'll have to go and make sure your Nonna's (Grandma's) crockery isn't broken!"

We were in Lignano, a tourist resort on the Adriatic coast in the northeast of Italy. Nonna was my grandmother. The family home, where I'd been living for the past year or so, was an hour's drive inland to the north, in the foothills of the Alps. I was bewildered. Why should the earthquake have affected them there?

We re-entered the apartment. The TV was still on and we huddled around it as a newscaster announced they were getting reports of a strong quake in the "Friuli" region, where our home was. Now we were worried. The earthquake's epicenter was near there.

I was apprehensive, but I told myself that it would all be okay. Robert said we should leave early, to make sure we would be back in time for lunch session that day. Really, we all just wanted to make sure things were well back home.

We left Lignano at about seven the next morning and drove north towards Osoppo. I felt more and more anxious the further we went. Lino was pushing our little Autobianchi car to the limit, going pedal to the metal.

Not much was said as we sped along the road. The back roads heading towards Osoppo had few houses, initially none of them looked damaged. However, I don't recall much traffic along the way, which was strange.

Finally, we came to a crest on the road approaching "Colloredo Di Mont'Albano" and saw an image I'll never forget. This was a small village we often passed through between Osoppo and Lignano (as kids on the bus going to the beach). I knew it by a beautiful blue and gold clock steeple that was one of the tallest buildings in town.

Except part of it wasn't there anymore. The beautiful clock tower had partially collapsed. I could see part of the clock face as we passed, but the left side of it from (one o'clock to seven o'clock), was gone.

There was a haze of dust all around the town. As we descend-

Introduction

ed, we could see the *"Carrabinieri"* police directing people onto a path alongside the vineyards and cornfields as an alternate route through town. Something was wrong with the road ahead. My apprehension and panic grew as I realized that the epicenter was farther north, closer to where Osoppo was.

The engine was roaring but we were all silent, in fear of what might be. My family was back in Osoppo. My thoughts were filled with Nonna, my sisters Dina and Lydia. I thought about my brother Jack. He was in Arta Therme, in culinary school, even higher up in the Alps. I was even worried about Dad.

Jesus, I thought, *please let them be alive!*

We sped through small towns and villages and saw more and more houses with cracks in their walls. The farther we went, the worse the damage got. Then, when we arrived in Osoppo, we saw a *Carabinieri* police officer putting up a wooden barricade across the main road into town.

Lino brought the car to a halt, rolled down the window, and shouted at the officer to let us through.

The policeman shook his head. "It's a mess! You'll have to go to the train station, park your car, and go in by foot. All the roads have been blocked off!"

Tires squealing as we sped off towards the station, skirting the town. We parked at the station and got out, not a word between us, just tears and terror. We ran as fast as we could through the back streets, towards the centre of town...

As we came to the intersection, I glanced to the left. There were Red Cross tents in "Piazza Alighieri" with rescue workers busily taking in the injured and the dead. A military helicopter hovered above, and dust was flying everywhere. People were shouting and running around, looking for loved ones, or learning that they had perished. By now, I was sure I'd lost my family.

I broke away from Robert and Lino and started running towards a street that was guarded by two soldiers. There was rubble piled high in the middle of the street, blocking the entrance. Beside it was a half-crumbled building that I could see inside. I saw a woman in her nightgown lying on a bed, obviously dead, covered in dust. The bed was teetering on the edge of a floor about to collapse.

Eric Two Crowns (Supercabbie)

Rendering aid after the earthquake. Image courtesy the Italian Civil Protection Department

The soldiers were not going to let me into the street, but before they moved to stop me, something pulled their attention away, and I ran for it. I climbed the rubble and scurried towards *Via San Danielle*, the street we lived on. The soldiers turned back, saw me, and shouted, "Stop! Get back here! Come back immediately! They were on edge, anxious about thieves who would soon be stealing jewelry and items from the dead bodies (*Sciacalli*).

But I wasn't going to stop for anything. I needed to get to my house.

The soldiers didn't chase me, I kept running. On my left, our street was full of rubble, totally inaccessible. Damaged roofs looked about to fall. On the next street, I saw rescue teams digging for someone in the middle of the rubble. Someone was buried under there, but still alive, moaning for help (It turned out to be the local pharmacist's young son). So, people were still alive. That gave me hope.

I ran up a side street and doubled back to where I'd started, when I spotted Marissa Missana. She'd been my classmate at school when we were younger. I was elated to see a familiar face, but it did nothing to sooth my panic. I ran up to her and, gasping, said, "Have you seen any of mine?" *Please, please, say yes!* I was thinking.

Marissa shook her head, and my heart throbbed. I gasped for air, and was trying to control myself when she said, "Try your cousin Ivo's place! The town is being evacuated, and maybe they're gathered there."

That made sense to me as my cousin's family were close by. They had a house attached to their restaurant and gas station just down the road, safely away from the town.

Introduction

I began to run again, but after a few minutes, I had to slow to a walk. My legs couldn't pull me any faster, I was exhausted.

I made it to my cousin's place and arrived to see my sisters Dina and Lydia, dust-covered sitting beside Grandma Irma (Nonna), on the front lawn.

Lydia and Dina then saw me, and began to scream, "Eric! Eric!" They ran towards me with arms outstretched. Tears made dark streaks on their dust-covered faces. Dina flung herself into my arms and Lydia hugging my waist. We sobbed and embraced with all our strength.

I asked where Jack was, and the girls said he was still not home. I quickly went over to Nonna, who was laying down on a blanket, on the lawn beside a small tree. She woke and just said, "Look at this mess boy ... look at this mess!"

That sent me into another panic. I pulled away from the girls and looked around for some sort of transportation to go and search for him.

He would have been in Arta Terme. It was a town further north, right in the middle of the earthquake zone, but I had to get there somehow. I spied our motorcycle under the bar patio. Shouting that I would be back, I jumped on and took off towards Arta.

I cried as I rode, fearful that I had lost my only brother. I went full throttle over the Ledra Bridge on the road towards Gemona, not knowing what I would find. I would have to take the Pontebbana Road, which takes you north towards Austria. The trip would be close to an hour.

All of a sudden, I saw a figure in the distance. Could it be him? I couldn't tell. Closer and closer the figure got, and then, *euphoria*! I could see that it was Jack just by his walk. He realized that it was me and began to wave me down with both arms.

I pulled over. Both of us cried as we embraced each other, tears streaming. We took a moment and then he asked me if anyone was hurt.

I told him that Dad was hurt, but that everyone was alive and waiting for him. That was the best moment of the day. There were few such good moments, but they were vital to me. There were many terrible moments too, and what followed after I dropped Jack back with my family was perhaps the worst of all.

Eric Two Crowns (Supercabbie)

Aerial view of Gemona, one of the cities damaged by the Friuli Earthquakes. Image courtesy the US Air Force.

Leaving Jack, I went back into Osoppo to look for my friends. The obvious place to go was Missana's bar. As I approached, I could see the place buzzing with people from the town, and lots of military personnel.

Servicemen had come to assist with the disaster. I could see flags on uniforms: Americans from local bases, Poles, Yugoslavians, Germans and Austrians. There were Swiss soldiers with sniffer dogs. There were even Canadians!

My heart thudded when I saw that Canadian flag on their uniforms. I could have told them that I was Canadian too. They could have taken me home, away from Dad, back to my mother.

I didn't say anything. I still don't know why.

Then, all of a sudden, Enrico, a friend of mine, in his twenties, who'd been studying at the University of Toronto in Canada, came into the bar, distraught, asking about his family, if anybody had seen them alive.

There were still many people unaccounted for. Nobody knew anything that could help Enrico. He looked horrible, tired and drained. He began begging for someone, anyone, to go to his place to try and find his family.

Introduction

The kids were all refusing to go with him. Then he saw me, and immediately plucked me from my chair and pulled me towards the door. *"Veng, picile! Veng!"* he pleaded. "Come help me!"

The kids didn't want to go with him because they were afraid of what they would find. So was I. But Enrico was such a nice guy. He had come back from Canada on the first available plane to Venice, and then somehow had gotten to Osoppo. He was desperate, and he was my friend. So, I went with him. I told him that we would have to go the back way as the soldiers were guarding the main thoroughfare through town, keeping people away for their own safety. His house was right on that thoroughfare.

As we passed the Albergo Pittis, the only hotel in town at the time, I looked over and saw a dead man in green overalls, pinned between a collapsed roof and an ice cream freezer. His neck was exposed, and I could see the colours purple and yellow from his hairline to the shirt collar... I looked away.

Enrico was now in front of me as I hesitated. I quickly took another look back at the dead man.

I can remember thinking, was this what lay ahead for Enrico? I was getting more and more scared as we approached his house. He began scuffling over the rubble that was all over the place, moving stones and masonry, calling out family members names. "Help me!" he cried. *"Picile!* Help me!" (*Picile* was our family nickname)

His home had been completely destroyed. I just stood there frozen. If his family had been home at the time of the earthquake, they were probably dead. There were no cries of help. There were no moans from the rubble. There was just hope vanishing away.

Again, Enrico begged me to go with him.

"Where do you want me to go?" I asked.

"Come, come to the cemetery! Please! *Picile!* Help me look for them!"

It was gut wrenching. I followed him to the west side of town where the cemetery was. I was deliberately slowing down as we approached because a stench suddenly hit me.

It was a smell I had never encountered before; the odor was choking. The heat, unusual for that time of year, was decomposing the bodies already. I pulled my shirt up to my face to cover my nose and mouth, it was so bad. As we walked up the grey stoned

Eric Two Crowns (Supercabbie)

walkways, Enrico stopped and stood by the white row of sheets the dead had been wrapped in. There were many, all their faces covered. The row was long, and he begged me as he stopped beside a little body "Eric, lift the sheet from the face!"

"Please don't ask me to do this!" I cried.

Again and again he begged, with me just ready to run away. Finally I agreed, looking the other way as I exposed each face. "No," he said, and moved to the next body where there were two little feet showing.

Suddenly, he started to scream. "It's him! It's him! I know it's him! Uncover the face! Please uncover his face!"

I knew that I had to eventually do it, so I bent over.

His brother was 9 years old, I believe. Dust covered his eyes. His angelic little face was at peace.

Enrico went out of control. As I stood there shaking, he began to punch the Roman style stone column beside him, like a boxer. I swear I could hear his knuckles breaking. His hands bleeding, he screamed to the sky, *"Why Lord? Why him?"*

I couldn't take any more and ran back to Missanna's. To this day, this horrible experience still sends me to tears.

I know that the quake killed 989 people. I know that it injured over 3,000, damaged over 75,000 homes and destroyed 18,000 more across 137 towns. However, these numbers don't tell you about all the lives that were affected, not just the injured and the dead.

Jack and I took a big chance that day, going to check out our house. The outer walls were bowed, you could see inside through all the cracks. The place would have to be torn down. It had been there for hundreds of years; Osoppo was founded in 330 AD.

We realized how lucky Dina was to be alive. Normally, she would have been in bed by nine but, by pure fate, she was returning home with the rest of the family after visiting an aunt and was in the car when the earthquake struck. A large piece of ceiling broke off and fell on Dina's bed. It would have crushed her if they hadn't been late.

Of my father, I remember seeing him lying beneath a pine tree, sleeping, while Nonna sat on the lawn. After hugging Nonna for a minute, I asked her if he was all right.

Introduction

"Leave him be," she replied. "He's been up all night, searching, trying to dig people up from the rubble. He's exhausted. Just let him sleep."

Still, I went over, and moved the blanket to cover him properly. I couldn't help but notice that his hands were all bloody from pulling rubble, trying to get to all the screams and voices of the people beneath the masonry. Dina later told me that he'd saved her, Lydia and Nonna, herding them to safety, and had borne the brunt of some falling bricks from the house next door.

My father had brought me to this place against my will. However, for once, I felt proud of him. He could be strong when it mattered, and it had helped him through that awful experience. These experiences may also have been a contributing factor to my future decisions.

Part 1:
Kidnapped from Canada

Chapter Two
Because This to Me is Paradise

I was born of an Italian father and a Metis mother on the west bank of the St. Lawrence River, 300 kilometres east-northeast of Quebec City. I was born (in 1961), along with my brother Jack (in 1957), in Forestville, just 61 kilometres east of the reserve, at the closest hospital.

My grandfather, Joseph Moreau was Chief for 22 years. My mother, my siblings and I are Metis. Of the Montagnais tribe, to be exact.

Things had changed when I returned there in 1992, after nearly twenty years of absence. The roads are paved now, and there are more modern houses. It's become a summer vacation destination for tourists. However, the winters can still be treacherous. The wind blows off the St. Lawrence, cold and full of snow.

Dad once told me that snow from a single storm would reach nearly to the top of the screen door, and you'd have to shove the door open to get out. He would also say that you'd have to remember where the car was parked in case you had to dig it out.

My uncles, aunts and many cousins still live there. When I asked Uncle Bertrand, after I returned, why he would live in such a cold, snowy place all his life, he would answer in French, "Because this to me is paradise."

I came to understand why my uncle said this after burying my mother there a few years ago.

This place is called Essipit, Les Escoumins.

Les Escoumins is married to the Laurentian mountains. As cold as it can be, it is truly spectacular. There are chalets, which are beautiful and maintained to the highest standards. The St. Lawrence River spans out towards the Gulf of St. Lawrence, with

Kidnapped from Canada

the Gaspe Peninsula on the south side of the mouth. Huge cargo ships pass by, blowing their horns. Beluga and Humpback whales are often seen dancing around them. There is so much beauty to see. But strangely, it was only a year ago that I went whale watching for the first time, out in one of these big powerful Zodiac boats. I had never been before.

My cousin Yannick captained a fleet of five Zodiacs. He was the guide, letting me ride in the back while he steered and monitored the radar. All five boats would take off at once, each holding a maximum of twelve passengers, all looking for pods of these whales that came to feed in the fresh water coming down from the Great Lakes. Yannick knew how to get as close as possible without disturbing them.

The exhilaration of seeing my first humpback was heavenly. I wanted to jump in and swim with these magnificent creatures, to touch one, to talk to it. I was numb watching their thrusting spouts of spray, thirty-to-forty feet high. Their huge, black and white tails. They'd breathe one-by-one, yet act like an orchestra, surfacing and diving in perfect timing. They'd appear, and we would laugh and cheer, then disappear, and there was sudden silence.

A seal even appeared, checking us out with its huge whiskers, curious as a cat, before disappearing into the water.

"This side! This side!" A passenger pointed, and there it was again, hovering on the starboard side. It was playing with us.

The whole trip was about 2 hours long. You have to wear a special rubber suit to keep warm and dry as the cold water, spraying at 60 or 70 kilometres an hour, really cuts into you. If you have to go to the bathroom, and if you've got really good balance, there's a space in the control area and a bucket. Most make sure they go before departure.

I remembered my cousins years before coming up from the bay with fresh clams in a steel bucket. Water was boiling, ready for us to soon feast on the river's abundant crustaceans. I also remember on one visit a freshly skinned black bear pelt fixed to the wooden shed beside the home, drying out. I'm sure it had a purpose other than being a trophy.

My uncle once gave me a traditional handmade beaver hat. He also gave me a necklace made of leather and beaver teeth. I wish I still had them today, as they were beautiful.

Eric Two Crowns (Supercabbie)

A humpback whale breaching. Image courtesy Whit Welles

On my most recent visit, Marylyn and I went across the street to a sanctuary full of other interesting artefacts on display. The tools that were used over centuries bring to mind the ingenuity of the peoples at different stages of their existence. We saw many different styles of tents from giant teepees for gatherings, smaller ones that accommodated families to single person hunting tents.

Long ago, my grandfather was Chief of the reserve. I can feel his spirit in me. Maybe it was part of that, and my friendship with Jesus that has helped guide me through the turmoil I've endured so far in my journey through life. If so, let me thank both for their strength and guidance.

I've been on a long road. It's been a rough road and a winding one, and it's stretched back past my birth, connecting me to my father and my mother, grandparents and my Native forefathers, I think about that often. How did the road bring me to here? Sometimes looking back can be painful but looking back at all of the memories and the history, good and bad, tells us where and who we are, and can help us decide where we are going.

If you made a list of priorities when you are eighteen years of age, I guarantee you that by age forty, they'd be upside down. Look back at the road, and you'll see. If only I could have seen the road ahead to forty when I was eighteen, but that's just not possible.

Twenty-five years ago, I returned to Canada after being kidnapped by my father to Italy, growing up there, and then making

Kidnapped from Canada

Marylyn on the shore at Forestville.

a prosperous life for myself in England, before losing it all to a bad economy. By the time I came back to Canada, my desire for financial success had become less important. Instead, I needed a spiritual fulfillment, and that meant I needed to rediscover a part of my heritage that I hadn't explored since childhood. I needed an awakening.

So, I made a quest to deepen my ties with my Innu background. This took me down another long road that I am looking back on — a road I'm still on. It's one with none of the BMWs I had in England, no suits and ties, no briefcase, no fancy restaurants, nor celebrity friends. It's a road where my aunt Lissette read a vision I had and told me I would be amongst powerful people. Today, I still wait for that moment.

But I feel, given the roads I've been on, that I can be a guide to people. And so I'm writing this memoir.

Maybe I can be a liaison or advisor to the Chiefs and leaders whose language I speak, the language of hope. Perhaps I can speak to the plight of aboriginals who still suffer the backlash of being conquered, stripped of their land and their spirit, which was once so strong.

Or perhaps I can speak to the young people of today, telling them that life can be difficult, but it will change. There will be good things and bad things, and they won't happen all at once. You will stumble along and bump into things, places, people at random. But you can still live on to the better things tomorrow brings.

My cousin Nancy often reminds me that I, along with my mother's family, are Innu, which means "the people". On our reserves and in the cities, we are retrieving our past so as not to lose sight

Eric Two Crowns (Supercabbie)

of the future. Essipit, the name of the Innu reserve around Les Escoumins, is bringing back our native language to our schools so our children can carry on knowing that not all is lost. We are reintroducing the skills that our ancestors depended on, and we no longer compromise ourselves to white corruption, nor doubt our relationship with Mother Earth. Unfortunately, some have succumbed to the almighty dollar or have led themselves into a dark hole of iniquity and blurred vision.

We must understand our culture and never forget who we are, because that helps us guide and build on what we've become. I watch in horror as Attawapiskat loses its grip so much that suicide is the cure for too many. Too many youths nowadays have too little respect for themselves and their duty in life. A lack of spiritual leadership. We must pass on the skills and consolidate our knowledge of the creator and all that is good.

I have lived the "white life" for most of my existence. I have lived in Europe, and as an Italian-Canadian here in Canada. The white life is still a part of who I am. So, I have had to look through many worlds, including wealth and poverty, to try and understand myself and where I come from.

The "People of the Mountains", the *Montagnais*, set me on a better path. The moment I inhaled the breath of the whale, my life changed. When I heard my mother's voice asking me to lay her to rest in a place that's pure so that her spirit would be at peace. When I witnessed my cousin Serge cut off his long braided hair and give it to my sister Dina, who collapsed to the ground, screaming in shock as he gave her his power, my life changed again.

The God I was forced to believe in is no more. The spirit of Manitou is now the voice that guides me.

What lies ahead, I do not know, but I have courage in the belief that all is not lost. That Essipit, Les Escoumins has already saved me and set me on another path.

And this is why I am here, writing these words down. This memoir is part of that path, of gratitude for what I have, and a better understanding of who I am. I hope to share this, so that others can have a better understanding of who they are. We can only be the better for it.

So, let me talk about how my story unfolds.

Chapter Three
The Barber Shop

Let's begin with my parents.

My father began his story in Italy. He lived through World War Two and its aftermath. There was a lot of misery after the war, with not much food and very little money. Dad helped with the reconstruction in France, sending money back home to his family.

When I was growing up in Petersburg, Ontario, I'd seen my father do cement work around our house. I could see that he was skilled.

As Dad grew older, more of his friends started leaving for Canada. They told him that life was better there; that there were jobs here. After some coaxing, he decided to join them. As far as I can tell, he found work on one of the railways. He arrived in 1954, under contract to work for the railroad for a couple of years, on condition that, if he broke that contract and quit, he would have to pay some penalty back to the government or his employer.

He worked briefly for the railroad, but it wasn't the job he wanted. He was a barber by trade, and found a job working in a barber shop in Toronto. He paid what he owed to get out of his contract and worked in the city instead.

However, Dad was more of a country person and he jumped at an opportunity to move to Forestville, Quebec, taking over a barber shop from someone who was retiring. Dad made the long journey up to Forestville, bought the shop, and moved in.

The shop was basically a house with a shop front that was split in two, with one side used as a women's hair salon, and the other side a barber shop.

Eric Two Crowns (Supercabbie)

My father (left) meets his future in-laws in Les Escoumins.

That was where he met Mom.

My mother was born in Les Escoumins (Essipit) on November 16, 1937, in the family home, as had her siblings. There were only four bedrooms at the time and things must have been cramped with Grandma, Granddad and 15 children. I figured out that Grandma had been pregnant for at least 135 months of her life.

I can hardly imagine how Grandma coped with 15 kids, with no electricity or running water, but her people had lived off the land for thousands of years, and she made the best from what they had. The family hunted. They ate bear, deer, porcupine, seal and moose. They caught fish from the river. As soon as the kids were old enough to go, they were out working, bringing home what they could to help make ends meet.

For the boys, bush life was normal. They worked with lumber in the forest, trapped or hunted. Most of my cousins on my mother's side were lumberjacks. Kin still labour in the forests of the Laurentian mountains.

Mom was helping Madame Gagne, the owner of the salon, washing hair, sweeping, laundry, et cetera. Dad, seeing this, asked her if she would also do his bits of laundry from the shop. She obliged, and he was smitten.

Dad had told me stories of when he first went to the reserve to be introduced to the Moreau clan. There were seven boys and eight girls, including Mom. Strangers coming in to take a woman away from the reserve were frowned upon, so he got a cold reception, from what I gathered.

My mother as a young woman.

He told me once that he'd gone to the local bar where most of the men would gather after a hard day's work, to enjoy a beer or ten, and he felt he was being stared down by all the locals. They'd heard of his intentions to court Mom, and he wasn't welcome.

On his next visit, he brought his razor with him in his back pocket — the ones barbers use to shave men. When he went to the bar again, he was approached by a guy who challenged him to a fight. My father replied that he was ready to go but warned the guy that if he didn't back off, he'd lose his guts on the floor.

Dad was over six feet tall and a pretty fit guy. He could take care of himself and it was clear to anyone that looked, that he could. Also, others had heard that he was a barber, and the guy wisely connected Dad's words to the sort of razor barbers used. He backed off.

Dad told me that, after that, things changed. He was accepted by the locals, and when he declared his intention to marry Mom, her brothers didn't object. In fact, they began treating him like family, like a brother.

From the stories my cousins, aunts and uncles tell, Dad could party with the best. They pronounced his name Ferruccio as "Faraccio", and he would laugh when he heard them say it. They looked at him as a brother with a damn good weapon.

Mom and Dad married in 1956 and began to make a life together. The chaplain at the time said, "you have come and taken the 'Rose of the Reserve. Go in peace.'"

Eric Two Crowns (Supercabbie)

Mom and Dad's Chapel

I've looked at photos of the chapel where Mom and Dad were married. Aunt Eda took me over to see it in person once. It was little bigger than a shack. I can only imagine getting the bride, groom, best man, bridesmaid and a couple of witnesses inside, though it's nice to imagine such a plain and basic ritual done in that beautifully peaceful surrounding.

There were trees all around, and the St. Lawrence river is in full view. A narrow gravel path leads up to the front door.

My brother Jack was born on October 11, 1957, and I followed on March 20, 1961. We were both born at the hospital in Forestville, the only hospital in reach, 61 kilometres up the road, and one which could be a challenge to get to in the winter.

We moved to Kitchener sometime later (early sixties), then a few years later, the village of Petersburg outside Kitchener, where we were joined by my sisters Lydia (in 1967) and Dina (in 1970). Dad found an opening in a barber shop that still exists to this day in Waterloo Square. For a short time, we lived on Union Boulevard, and then bought a house in the rural village and commuted.

For a time, Dad tried to teach me the trade, wanting to keep it in the family. I learned by watching him sharpening his scissors and clip away at his customers. He had a rectangular stone that was grey on one side and ivory white on the other. The grey side was hard and used to de-burr the sharp scissors. The other side was like ivory, but finer and softer, used to de-burr razors.

Me, at 1 year, in Italy

You needed to watch out with those old-style razors. The first time I picked one up, without my Dad present, I cut myself. That got me a cuff in the head and a scolding when he saw the cut, and I never touched one again.

I was always afraid that Dad would cut someone badly, in spite of his skills. He was known to love his homemade wine and I think he would have a swig or two in the back room some days, although I never saw him do it. One of his old pals told me, however, that he was a better barber drunk than sober!

I was chief hair sweeper, and gofer — Go for this! Go for that! I straightened chairs, cleaned up, fetching whatever was needed, obviously at no pay. I heated up the food Mom had made for Dad. There was a small red metal bucket which he would fill with hot water, and I would put the Tupperware bowl containing leftovers in it – pasta usually – and give it an occasional stir. He would take a quick break when I told him it was hot and gobble it down with some crusty Italian bread.

One day, I was fetching coffee, toast and sandwiches for Dad and the other two barbers, Tranquillo and Vincenzo. I recall it being snowy and cold. The coffee was brewing, and they told me it would take a minute, so I waited, sitting by the magazine stand to read a comic. I'd sometimes sneak a peek at the Playboy too, making sure not to get caught.

All of a sudden, I heard sirens. The coffee was ready, so I picked up the tray and started back, only to be surprised to see an ambulance outside the barber shop. A gurney rushed out with a body on it, and I just stood there, shocked, looking for signs of blood. I thought this was it: Dad had finally screwed up and slit some guy's throat!

Eric Two Crowns (Supercabbie)

The Belmont Village strip where Dad has his shop after his time at Waterloo Square. The shop is just to the left of the Drivers and Vehicles Licenses Storefront.

But there was no blood in sight. The paramedics loaded the body into the ambulance and took off. I walked into the barber shop and saw Dad looking pale and upset. "What happened?" I asked.

Turns out he had given this man a massage with a heavy handheld gadget he used that weighed around three pounds. You fit your hand into the metal band to hold it and, once turned on, the whole thing would vibrate. Dad must have touched a nerve or something, because the guy passed out in the chair. Dad thought he'd had a heart attack and called the ambulance.

Well, he hadn't slit him, but the shock was still there, and even as I and the others laughed about it, Dad stood there, bewildered.

Back in Italy, Granddad and Dad had owned their own barbershop. In Canada, Dad set up his own shop as soon as he could, on Belmont Avenue. Owning a shop was in his blood.

I should have known better about that razor. Dad was a true professional; an artist with the cutthroat razor. He'd shaved thousands of beards and had never once made a mistake. He was a great barber. If only he could have been a better husband and father.

#

As mentioned previously, Dad didn't give me an allowance. I had to be forward thinking if I wanted something.

Dad's tip container was an orange and brown plastic Bassett

hound. It sat right behind him on the shelf near his cash drawer. One day, I was sitting at the barber shop, waiting for hair to accumulate around the two other barbers' chairs as well, so I could sweep up. That's when I heard something interesting.

Dad put a tip in the hound and I realized the coin didn't "clunk" like it did when the hound was empty. It "clicked" instead, in a way that told me the thing was full. Hockey cards were on my mind, like most young Canadian boys, then and now, so I mentioned to dad that it might be time to empty his Basset hound and I would happily count all the coins.

My third birthday party. I'm centre, Jack is on my right, and Dad is on my left. We were living at 104 Union Blvd. at this point.

He stared at me like he already knew what I was thinking.

But after a moment, he said, "Get me some newspaper and come to the back room."

I obliged, and in the back room he told me to pay attention, as he was going to show me how to roll the coins in the old way, with newspaper.

He dumped out the Basset hound, and I got really excited looking at the large pile of potential hockey cards lying on the floor.

Then he showed me how to do it, and with Dad, there was never any messing around. I had to learn fast, and once he showed me the basics, he went back into the front of the shop saying, "Now, don't forget: 40 quarters makes ten dollars, fifty dimes make five dollars, okay?" And he left me to it.

So I began to count out the coins and make the piles. But as I did so, I started counting out some hockey cards for me. Four coins for you, Dad, one coin for me. Four coins for you, one for me. After all, how would he know?

I could feel those hockey cards in my hand already. I rolled up the coins like he asked and finished up after a short while with my

Eric Two Crowns (Supercabbie)

"commission" safely hidden away (in my socks). I stacked all the rolls neatly on a shelf and, when I was done, told Dad.

I remember waiting for the for the next command to go for coffee, as that would be a great opportunity to go down to the variety store and buy my hockey cards!

He never did find out.

That taste of having money in my pocket (or, in this case, my sock) felt like freedom! Before long, I was trying to find ways to get my hands on some more. I couldn't wait for that Basset hound to fill up again, right? That could take months!

So, later, after sitting in my chair at Dad's barber shop, I clicked on an idea as I spotted a blemish on a shoe of the customer sitting in front of me. Though I was only about ten at the time, I thought that I could get a cloth and polish it off. That could be an opportunity for money.

Instantly, I was thinking of having Dad make me a shoeshine box. Just a few pieces of wood, a couple of screws and two hinges would do it. It could hold a tin of brown wax, a tin of black wax, and two brushes (one for each colour, of course), and two polishing cloths (again, for each colour). I remember asking Dad on the way home to Petersberg, "Papa, would you build me a small wooden box?"

"What for?"

"Is it okay if I shine shoes for the customer while you cut their hair?"

He hesitated a moment, and then asked, "Why?"

"I just want to make some money for myself," I replied.

He pondered this, then looked at me with approval. "Okay!" I think it made him happy that I was showing some business savvy at a young age.

Then he started setting down the rules. The first and most important was, "No messing up the socks!!" He told me to practice on some shoes at home before starting.

Dad built me that box, and gave me some money for capital expenses, which I bought at the Zehr's across the road: two wax tins, black and brown (Kiwi brand); two smearing cloths for application; two brushes and two cloths for the final polishing. I was to have everything ready, and then ask whoever was in Dad's chair if they wanted a shoe shine.

We started on a Saturday. Saturday mornings were always busy, so I was looking forward to success. Many of my customers were professionals, doctors and dentists, et cetera. They were all suited up, looking to be groomed. Finally, my heart beating hard in anticipation, the first customer sat down in Dad's chair.

With my box beside me, sitting in front of Dad, watching him start to cut away, I knew my moment was here, but I hesitated. I was too nervous. Dad looked at me and said, in Italian, "*Allora?*" (meaning, "Well?") "Are you going to ask? Yes or no?"

I gulped, then gathered some courage. "Sir? Would you like a shoe shine?"

The man looked down at me and started to laugh. "Is that your box?" he asked.

"Yes, sir! Dad made it for me!"

He laughed some more, but he was impressed. "There's a budding businessman for you," he said. And he agreed to the shine.

Wow! I thought. My first customer!

Carefully remembering Dad's warning, I pulled out my black tin and smearing cloth and began to gently spread the wax. I began brushing, just like I had practiced at home. Out with the polishing cloth, making those shoes shine like a mirror. Finally, I sat back, with the gentleman admiring my work. He got out of his chair, paid my father, and then gave me a quarter for my services.

Yippee! I thought. Five packs of hockey cards!

I made two dollars by day's end, and promptly (and more sensibly) opened up my first bank account. I was well on my way to making my first million (just kidding).

#

A couple of years later, as I attended St. Theresa's school, I came up with a new moneymaking idea that became an instant success.

My friends and classmates were all reaching puberty. With that, music and dancing became interesting to us, and that's when I had my idea. I had a record player at home, as well as some 45s. Maybe it wasn't a big collection, but I figured that, with the help of a couple of friends from school, I could muster up more records.

Eric Two Crowns (Supercabbie)

I also had some money saved up – perfect to provide capital for this next venture. I called the Breithaupt Centre on Margaret Avenue and asked about the cost of renting a hall. It wasn't as expensive as I'd feared. I could also buy boxes of assorted chips and a few cases of pop. The hall also had a dispensing bar and fridges, perfect!

So I convinced my friend Dale Mueller to act as DJ, and another friend to be a bartender. I also bought two rolls of numbered tickets and a small cash box, complete with key and lock. I could charge twenty-five cents to get in, and ten cents for either a pop or chips. Without asking permission, I wrote in the corner of my classroom's chalkboard, "Friday Night Dance! 7:00 p.m. start! Breithaupt Centre!"

The kids were all talking about it when the teacher came in. He spotted the notice and asked who had written it. When I rather nervously said it was me, he didn't seem upset, or to really care. He just advised that, if this was to happen, I should seek out a suitable person or persons to oversee us, who was at least eighteen years of age.

Okay, I thought. Teddy Micher's brother Mike and his girlfriend were both over eighteen. I convinced them to do the honours of supervising. So, everything was organized, and when Friday afternoon came, I was all pumped up, hoping for a good turnout.

I gathered my helpers and we headed down to the Breithaupt Centre, arriving to see a line already forming outside the door! I was elated! We opened up and I started taking in the cash. The kids were having a blast, breaking away from the chains of their parents and letting go. I recall that I cleared twenty dollars on that night! That was huge!

I figured my future as a businessman was my destiny. Ironically, I would go on to other business ventures down the road, until I hit disaster. Nevertheless, as the saying goes, nothing ventured, nothing gained. The worst failure in life is never trying. I don't recall how many Fridays we partied, but it was great fun while it lasted.

Chapter Four
Petersburg

Mom called Petersburg her jail. I could see why. Petersburg is a small village, just west of Kitchener. Back in 1965, the place was considered to be out in the sticks. There were no bus stops or trains into the city. There were no grocery stores or shops to mention; just a gas station, a small convenience store and, of course, the famous Blue Moon Hotel.

Mom didn't drive, so it made it nearly impossible for her to get around, except with Dad at her side. He may have bought the house with that in mind. This was his way of controlling Mom, without having her family nearby, looking over his shoulder. His plan worked for a while, until Mom started to rebel.

We lived on Alice Crescent in its early stages of development. I went to Notre Dame school about two miles north in St. Agatha. I had a park to play in about 400 yards away from the house. There was also the bush, where I spent time with my new friends, discovering nature.

I made friends soon enough. Bored boys out in the country with nothing to do but bind together and get into mischief. When you're a kid growing up in a new town, you want to fit in, so it wasn't long before I had a gang. There was Mark Snyder, our leader. There was Terry and Ronnie Schnaar. There was Gary Beech.

My own image came by accident. The guys all knew my mom was Native and started calling me *Comanche*, then just *Commanch*. I decided that it was a good fit.

At the time, Dad had this white Stetson hat with a huge brim, like J.R. Ewing's hat from the TV show *Dallas*. He wouldn't let himself be seen in it, except as a joke when he was drunk. I tore

Eric Two Crowns (Supercabbie)

My sister Lydia in our back yard at Petersburg.

off the wire that held the brim stiff and wore it all floppy. I took a green marker and wrote 'Comanche' on it. It was so big, it covered my eyes so I could hardly see! The guys laughed at me, but that was okay; I now had my own identity and look.

Mark took me under his wing and protected me like a big brother. He taught me how to shoot a gun, and before long, I had my own, even if it was just a pellet gun. I was now a "brave warrior" and a "great hunter"!

We got up to all sorts of things, the five of us. We hunted squirrels and groundhogs, tracking down the critters in the vast fields around Petersburg. The bush would be one of our retreats. There was a small lake where we canoed. On its shore, we dug a hole, and with a board and some leaves we would camouflage our condiments, for the hot dogs we would cook up on an open fire. We'd cook them using sticks as makeshift skewers that, more often than not, catch fire along with the dog and fall off into the coals. They tasted okay, though, even with some ash on them.

One day, on a warm, late spring day, we huddled in our straw-walled hideout in a nearby barn. It was a place we found on somebody's property, and though I think the owner knew we were there, he didn't confront us about it. It was just boys being boys.

On this particular day, Mark told us about a plan. The next

Jack and Lydia, playing with Mickey the dog in our front yard at Petersburg.

morning, we were all to wear coats with lots of pockets. We would then go down to the local gas station, wait until the owner, a man named Orville, went out to pump gas, whereupon we'd jump the counter and raid the candy and cigarette displays.

My job was to stand by the door and alert them when Orville was coming back in. At the time, I didn't think this was a bad idea; I was just excited to be part of the heist with my friends.

When I got home, I went downstairs to look for Dad's hunting jacket. It had lots of pockets. My Dad didn't ask after it and, the next morning, he left at his usual time. I told Mom I was going out with my friends. She told me just to be careful, warning me to be a good boy. "Don't get in any trouble, okay?" she said. "Off you go."

If she only had known. Dad would have kicked the crap out of me, but by then I was used to his beatings.

We all gathered behind the barn, and Mark said, "Okay, boys, we all know what to do..." My heart was pounding.

We went down to the gas station, me in a coat about five sizes too big, everybody else in similar coats with lots of pockets.

Orville was there, tending to his business, as we walked in, He said, "Hi, kids! What's going on?"

Eric Two Crowns (Supercabbie)

"Not much, sir!" Mark blurted out. "Just want to share a coke with my friends!"

Just then, the gas station bell dinged. A customer had pulled up to the pump.

Orville got up. "Okay, boys, I'll be back in a second," he said, and off he went.

"Commanch!" Mark whispered. "The door!"

I scurried over and watched intently as the boys pounced on the candies and the smokes, filling their pockets, and throwing stuff to me, to fill my pockets with peanuts and the like. My heart pounded even harder. Orville was almost done! I called back, "He's finished! He's coming!"

Quicker than a flash, they all jumped back over the counter, and as he walked in, Terry started handing the bottle of coke around, as if nothing had happened.

Orville hadn't noticed anything yet. I thought maybe it was because of his thick glasses. Mark played it cool, and we mimicked him, bidding good-bye to Orville as we left the station and made our way back to the barn, all the while looking back nervously to see if anyone was chasing us.

I could hardly believe we had done it. We all began to laugh as we emptied our pockets. Mark began to sort out the stolen goods and place them in hiding. There were enough goodies and smokes to last awhile.

To this day, I don't think they ever found out it was us, although the cops started to pull up to Mark's driveway regularly. To me, he was cool, and fearless. I recall he even shot Ronnie and Gary with his pellet gun once (Ron in the butt, Gary in the hand).

One day Mom looked out the window and suddenly shouted, "Eric! Come here! Look! There's a fire over there!"

She was pointing towards the barn. There was smoke billowing into the sky above it.

I watched as the flames engulfed the building. It was soon obvious it wasn't going to be saved. The firefighters arrived too late. Our hideout was gone.

The next day, the cops were at Mark's house, two cruisers in the driveway. Had Mark started the fire? Were they going to take him away in handcuffs? I didn't see Mark much after that. I don't know if he'd been implicated, charged or arrested.

All I know is that if Dad had found out what we'd gotten up to, and that I'd been a part of it, I would have been dead.

That's all in the past, now. Since returning to Canada some twenty-five years ago, I've made no contact with the boys, though not for lack of trying.

#

Dad was always busy and never really paid much attention to me. He never came to the park to watch me. He never picked up a bat and ball to play. He just wanted his space to do what was important to him, like the house, work, garden in the summer, the bottle, and his beloved birds.

One thing Dad liked about his dream home in Petersburg was that the whole property was raw with dirt, gravel, rocks and no trees. This was ideal for him, as he was the ultimate green thumb, with gardening skills passed down to him by Grandma Irma in Italy.

Unlike Grandma and Dad, I can't even grow weeds.

You could see Dad's passion in his work on and around the house. He planted dozens of trees, including poplars, plums, cherries and peaches. He could graft limbs. The vegetable garden yielded tomatoes, asparagus and even grapes. Jack and I laboured beside him, ridding the earth of rocks and debris and laying down new sod.

The last time Jack visited from Italy, we went for a drive and found ourselves in Petersburg. I'd assumed he wanted to see the old house again, and as we stood before it, we both suddenly began to cry. Jack was never a crier, but I could feel the hurt in him. It was a deep cut that still bleeds. I comforted him as best I could, saying, "It's okay, Jack. It's okay."

Personally, every time I visit the old home, there's a feeling of release. It's a type of therapy, I suppose, ridding myself of the pain and trying to understand and accept the past. I think, though, that one can ever totally heal from what happened there.

Chapter Five
Birdman Dad

The bed sheets came off as I woke from my sleep. I saw Dad's belt in his hand, raised and ready to strike when he stopped.

"What's wrong with your leg?" he asked.

He was about to finish off what Mom had started: a true beating. I had gone to the bush that day and forgot the time, which kids do when you're playing and having fun. I had left in the morning to hang out with Mark and the boys as usual, but time had flown, and I was late.

I recall mom waiting for me outside the house as she saw me approaching from a distance. I knew she was angry, which was not her usual style. Mom had always cared and loved me, that I know. I had stepped too far, and she had been worried out of her mind for my safety. This time, however, she did something unusual.

She had a wooden coat-hanger in her hand and, as I got close to her, she hit me in the arm. I ran indoors. She followed me in as I made a beeline for my room. She followed me upstairs and I was trapped. Then, to my surprise, she began to hit me in the legs several times a sting with every blow.

Finally, it was over, with me in my bed, crying myself to sleep, not realizing I was pretty bruised up. She said, "wait till your father comes home," and I knew I would be in for another dose but with Dad's favourite attitude adjuster, the dreaded leather belt.

When he had asked about my legs, I looked down to see them. My left thigh was purple! I told him it was mom, hoping he would not give me another thrashing. He then let the cover go and began yelling at Mom as he went back downstairs. I could hear him telling her that he was in charge of discipline and he then got violent with her.

Dad ruled with an iron fist, controlling everything he could. I had asked Mom once if she loved Dad. She told me she did until the first time he hit her.

I myself had got used to his antics. At the slightest threat of a beating, I would hide in my bedroom closet, huddled up in the corner, shaking in my boots.

It wasn't long before I was taking it out on myself. I began to carve my initials on my upper arms, usually using a pin or a piece of glass, even a bottle cap . I made sure no one could see what I was doing to myself by keeping the scrapes under my arms. The inner turmoil has never really left me, even after all this time.

Now I resort to chewing my fingernails when I'm frustrated, which is constant. Like an open cut that won't heal. Mom would always say in French, "Quit biting your nails, Eric!"

She hated it when I began a session.

#

Dad had a few passions. He was skilled as a barber. He knew how to garden. He loved bicycles. He loved drinking. And he loved birds.

He'd perfected his skills as a whistler. His high-pitched chirps mimicked the canaries, finches and other small birds that he kept in cages. He would come home from the barber shop and immediately go downstairs to see them, opening the cage doors to let them fly out for their exercise. Some would land on his shoulder, or he would raise his hand, so they would land on it.

I remember him puckering his lips to show some saliva and they would drink it like from a mother's breast. He would sing with them as if he was part of their chorus.

He had a friend named Jack from Toronto who was a breeder and had hundreds of these birds in the basement. They would often talk and share stories about their feathered friends. I just watched, mesmerized, at all the birds that sang and flittered about in their cages.

I also remember the smell; a musky odor in the room. Feathers everywhere.

The birds were beautiful with all their colours. They would chirp and sing like crazy.

Eric Two Crowns (Supercabbie)

A neighbour, Mr. Snyder, once asked Dad about some plants he was growing in the garden. Dad explained that when these plants seeds were mixed with other seeds, the birds would sing more. Turns out they were cannabis seeds. No wonder the birds were singing!

On one visit to Italy, I think I was eleven at the time, I was given a room that had been Dad's when he was young. I know now that it was during a break in Dad and Mom's marriage, something was going awry. The room wasn't much to look at, just a bed, an old dresser, a mirror, and a wardrobe to hang clothing in. When I opened the outside window shutters, I noticed a small piece of glass missing from the top right corner of the window.

Later, I went downstairs and told Nonna that the window was damaged, she laughed and explained that it wasn't broken. Dad had simply removed a piece so that the birds he had in his room could get in and out. I didn't know if he had somehow trained them to do so, or if they just loved him so much that they would always return. I thought it was like *Birdman of Alcatraz*, that classic movie with Burt Lancaster.

I wondered what Dad's younger days must have been like, to have those little creatures go their way and return home, and see them waiting for their Poppa, and sing him welcome home.

When we first arrived in Italy, Nonna had a yellow canary in the dining room. It was in a cage on the wall. Cicco was his name. He was quite nasty to me. Every time I went close to his cage, he would puff up his feathers and go silent, ready to bite my finger if I stuck it between the wires. Then he would chirp violently and loudly as if I were an invader on his space.

Perhaps I was. Perhaps he was jealous of me, as I was getting some of Nonna's attention. He would get so upset.

One morning, I came into the kitchen and Cicco was gone. I asked Nonna where he was, and she just shrugged and said she found him "titties up," dead in his cage. I couldn't help but wonder if he'd died of a heart attack due to the stress of us around.

Chapter Six
My First Real Hunt

The black bear was groaning for its mother. It sounded like an injured lamb. *Behh! Behh!* I heard it call out as it slouched forward with its back to the tree. "Vittorio" had shot it and then again as it bellowed. It was now dead. I was in shock as it landed on its backside right in front of me.

I had fallen on my backside and froze as it came down the tree. Like a squirrel it barrelled down towards the ground, I was terrorized thinking I would be its next meal. Vittorio had been walking around 50 yards in front of me as I followed.

It was fall and leaves were semi covering the trail. The rustling of the leaves as I dragged my boots over them made noise and I suddenly noticed that a cloud of leaves was falling down. I was confused as why all those leaves at once?

Bears make hammocks to lay on and catch the breeze up high in the trees. The sound of my scuffling alerted the beast and it became startled. Its descent was rapid and I was panicking shouting out to Vittorio to help me. It was pretty surreal as the scene unfolded with the bear now dead. I got it together and helped Vittorio to tie a rope around each paw and raise the bear between two trees.

He began to cut its belly. Its the guts all dropping out onto the ground. I felt sick to my stomach. I asked Vittorio why he was hanging the bear on the tree?

"His mother is probably close by," he replied

I thought, "WHAT?! Its mother is around?" The cub was big enough in my books (150lbs). Why do we have to hang around here? Was Vittorio was looking to get her as well?

Eric Two Crowns (Supercabbie)

I began to feel anxious and from that point I just wanted to go home.

I had watched Dad shoot rabbits around our house in Petersburg. I had hunted groundhogs and squirrels before, but this was scary. Vittorio was an experienced hunter and very strong man. Rationally, I knew I was safe with him, but beneath it all, the circumstances were still scary. If the cub was 150 pounds then the mother would be a lot bigger!

Moments later as I sat there still in awe, Vittorio begins to eat some food. He asked me if I was hungry. Well, food was the last thing on my mind, so I said, "No."

I didn't say much as he ate. I wanted to go home, but I didn't want to wimp out. I was a young kid, no more than ten years old, and I wanted to "make my bones" and learn something valuable for the future, if I needed it.

Dad had let me go with Vittorio, no doubt to experience what many young men do in places like Canada: hunting and fishing, maybe one day for survival. You never know what life may throw at you.

We waited for a while, but with no sign of the mother bear, we began to collect our things and prepare ourselves for the long walk back to camp. Vittorio took the heavy duty of carrying the creature. He handed me his rifle and back pack. At the time, I weighed in at 80 pounds. The butts of the rifles were nearly dragging on the ground as we began our journey back. They along with the two backpacks on my shoulders made this a true workout for my body. I recall labouring along the paths and falling behind him as he got further away, all the while on high alert for the mother bear that could be lurking. The journey back seemed to go on forever as the gear got heavier with every step.

Finally, as I our car came into view, I began to feel safer. We had a place to hide if we were threatened. Vittorio had told me about other dangers in the forest as well, including wolves. He wasn't lying, either.

We were both asleep in the car when during the night I had woken to noises around us. I cleared some fog from the window with my hand and saw shadows of something outside. I didn't get out to see. The next morning, we discovered that the bear carcass we'd left hanging after sunset had been mauled by wolves. Good thing I'd stayed inside!

Vittorio had shown me how to skin the bear and salt the pelt so it would tighten and not lose its hair. The carcass had to hang, he explained, to deblood itself. That had certainly attracted the wolves.

Vittorio was a little upset that I hadn't woken him to tell him there were wolves outside, but I was half asleep when it had happened, exhausted from the hunt, and we weren't done.

He pulled out a couple of fishing rods and baited them. "Eric, take the rods and cast the lines into the lake" he said. The lake was only a few meters away.

I took the rods and as he requested and cast both lines into the lake. He had mentioned that there were lots of catfish around and would make a good breakfast once cooked. I was famished! I hadn't eaten much the day before, after the kill.

I'd hardly put the line down, when I felt a tug on it. The fish were biting, and I pulled in an average size catfish. The other line also started to shake around and another fish on the line. Now this was more fun, I thought. I called to Vittorio, telling him that breakfast was caught and to come over and de-hook them. I didn't trust myself to take out the hooks. Some fish had stingers, and they could hurt; Vittorio knew this, and obliged.

He then fired up the Coleman, with a small pot and a pan for the bacon which was soon sizzling. But, wouldn't you know it? A few minutes later, and the thing went out with the food half cooked, including the fish. Vittorio had brought the wrong gas canister, which was now empty!

But the next thing that Vittorio did was to throw the half-cooked fish into the pan with the half-cooked bacon, cracked an egg over it, and mix it all up into a slop. He dished this up and handed me the plate, expecting me to eat it! I was ready to puke at the thought. But Vittorio took up the pan and started eating his share of the slop saying, "It's all we have right now, so eat!"

I continued to pass, and he just laughed and kept eating. I took a couple of slices of bread to fill the hole in my stomach, even though watching him eat half-cooked fish, bacon and raw egg had suppressed my appetite.

Eric Two Crowns (Supercabbie)

As you can see, Vittorio was tough all round. I just wanted to go home.

But at least he saw that I'd had enough. We gathered our things and left shortly after "breakfast".

The next Sunday, we were all invited to Vittorio's house for dinner. Our catch was the main meal. Bear stew for all!

The bear pelt was lying in the basement, still drying out. I remember looking straight into the dead bear's eyes, feeling sorry for it. I don't condemn Vittorio for being a hunter, but I did say to myself then and there that I would never kill an animal, unless it was for pure survival.

Chapter Seven

Dreams Come True

In the early 1970s, when Mom and Dad began to have troubles, we found ourselves in Italy again. Mom, the girls and I stayed there for about six months while Dad and Jack stayed in a friend's basement on Blucher Street in Kitchener.

Dad had sold the house and, although I didn't know much, I knew that I was becoming more anxious, lost and insecure.

On our return to Canada, we ended up living in Kitchener on Wellington Street. Divorce was on the cards and Mom had gone to live with the girls on Cedar Street while things were sorted out.

For an Italian with strict beliefs, divorce was frowned upon – basically a disgrace. I had to fend for myself and had to learn how to get on with things as Dad was always at the shop and focusing on his business.

It seemed that I was always on my own because Jack was at school and had a part time job at Dutch Boy. The girls were now with Mom as she was fighting for their custody.

Dad was in turmoil, and when he arrived home at around 7 o'clock, would just eat and then start to drink. Usually he was in bed by 8 or 9, already drunk. I hate thinking about it. All I know is he had less and less time for me.

Hockey, at least, gave me some purpose to my life. I loved playing and longed to share my developing skills with the old man, but to no avail. I started playing like most boys did, on ponds or community rinks, out in Petersburg. Coming home from school and with heart pumping in anticipation, I would make my way down to the rink with my skates on. It was about three hundred yards away and the first to show up would unlock the shed door

Eric Two Crowns (Supercabbie)

and turn on the heater. He would have to grab a shovel to clear off the ice, if needed. I have so many fond memories of the boys in the sticks sharing our lives and having fun playing the game.

After our move into the city, I joined house league hockey. My first team was called the Bisons. I also made the school team at St Theresa's, playing along my new friends, Teddy Micher, Tim Quirke, and Dale Mueller. The next year, I made the rep team, but Dad turned it down, saying it was too expensive. Nevertheless, I tried my best, even with substandard equipment, until I bought my new Black Panthers skates! Then I felt like I could fly. Little did I know that, after I had molded them to my feet with milk-soaked socks, sitting in the living room for hours, that I would learn to fly on foreign ice.

As well as hockey, there was school. I had a shop class on Wednesdays that required me and a couple of other friends to walk a mile and a half to St. Joseph's on Courtland Avenue. I liked this because Mom lived out that way and I could stop in and see her for a few minutes. She always cried when she saw me.

She was also becoming terrified of Dad and his temper.

There was an evening when my Dad came into my room, grabbed me by the hair and pulled me out of bed. "You're coming with me!" he said. He was drunk and angry.

Standing out in the hall, shaking in my boots, I saw him go into his room and come out with his shotgun. He then ordered me into the car and we drove over to Mom's place. We arrived minutes later, he told me to get out and stand on the sidewalk.

He immediately pointed the gun at me and shouted, "Scream out, Puttana!"

Puttana means "whore" in Italian. He wanted me to yell it at the house.

I was terrified and trying not to cry while he poked me with the barrels. Crying would bring on a kick in the ass or a slap to the head for sure. If I didn't do what he said, I knew I could be shot, but I stood frozen for a moment that seemed like a lifetime.

Finally, I began to call out "Puttana! Puttana!" I screamed just out of terror. I would never have disrespected her so, unless I had a gun pointed at me, which I did.

Dad was possessed with rage, but finally he realized that someone had probably called the cops, so he ordered me back to the car and we got in and sped away. When we got home, I went straight to my room and hid in my closet. At least with hits from his belt, the pain would eventually subside, but this time I really thought he was going to shoot me.

I have come to understand that people who resort to that kind of violence are sick or lost in their own world. That does not forgive them.

Somehow nobody reported the incident. However, the divorce proceedings continued, and Mom gained full custody of Lydia and Dina, my sisters. She moved just up the street into a two-bedroom apartment to accommodate them. Jack and I had to keep living with Dad, though Mom kept fighting for my custody.

Dad, in one of his sober moments, asked me whether I wanted to go with her or stay with him. The truth was, I wanted to be with Mom, but I knew that answer would hurt me. His world was crumbling all around him, and his question was asked with a raised hand and a threatening glare. So, under duress, I said I'd rather be with him.

Fortunately, I had my friends and hockey to distract me. I never told them what was really going on. I know now that I should have, but back then I just didn't know what to do. All I knew was that something was coming. I was confused.

#

On one of my visits, I asked Mom if she wanted to come to a hockey game and watch me play. She said yes, and somehow convinced Dad to come out as well. They'd managed to call a truce for one night and I remember saying to Dad that I would score two goals for him, if he came.

We played in the Annex, which was a rink just behind the Kitchener Auditorium. It was a barn-like structure that was a little cold, ugly and uninviting, but I felt so proud that I finally had my family together, sharing something about me. I was pumped up with something to prove to Dad.

The game started, and I scored my first goal quickly. I looked over towards my parents. Mom's arms were raised in excitement as my teammates embracing me. She was shouting with joy, bouncing Dina in her arms. Dad was holding Lydia's hand – she was his favourite of the girls – but showing little emotion.

Eric Two Crowns (Supercabbie)

The first period ended. The second followed, and my team went down by a couple of goals. In the third period, I scored my second goal. Again, there were cheers from the team and the small audience consisting mostly of the other kids' parents.

I looked over, and saw Dad actually clapping, now that I had fulfilled my promise. I was elated. I remember thinking, "There you go! I'm not as useless as you think I am!"

That moment was a huge boost to my pride. Now we were getting to the end of the game, and one of my teammates tied it up. With the game tied at three, and just seconds left on the clock, I took a pass at the centre line and burst past the defencemen.

I raced towards the goalie and, with a couple of nifty moves, deeked past and backhanding the puck to his left side. I remember the puck hitting the goalie's pad and trickling over the line.

I looked towards the referee. He had one hand on the whistle and the other pointing to the net, meaning that I'd made my hat trick. GOAL! I looked up at the clock and saw there was just two seconds to go. I'd scored the game winner!

I looked up at the stands. Mom was screaming her head off. Dad was shouting like crazy, Lydia in his arms. They were jumping up and down.

I was mobbed by my teammates and we rejoiced, yelling and screaming together. I still get excited thinking about it now, that adolescent moment of euphoria you never forget.

Later, in the dressing room, our coach came over to me and gave me a shoebox. I had no clue what was inside, but when I opened it my eyes got wide. All my teammates where standing around me, cheering and clapping. It was a trophy with an engraving saying, "Top Scorer - 1975 Bisons"!

The next surprise was a gift from my Dad: three pucks nailed together to commemorate my hat trick. Although the pucks were a bit mangled, I really didn't care, just the gesture was enough to make me proud. All told, it was one of the best times of my life.

But something was coming. I was unable to finish playing out the year, as Dad came and told me that we were going to Italy for a while.

I remember the day we left, vividly.

Chapter Eight
Running to Italy

Dad, Jack and I had been living on Wellington Street in Kitchener. Mom's custody fight was continuing, and Dad was acting odd. He got our luggage packed and put by the door. I didn't know what he was planning, and I didn't ask him. Then, all of a sudden, he began to move our couch out to the balcony. He called for Jack to help him.

With a couple of heaves, Jack and Dad got the thing over the railing and down to the ground four storeys below. I remember being on the balcony and watching the thing crash and fall apart as it hit the asphalt below.

In hindsight, I can see that it was crazy. It was not only dangerous, it was against the law. But I know now that Dad had gone a bit loopy. However, I went along with things, keeping my mind on hockey.

I had seen an envelope full of money in the kitchen cupboard. I'd convinced Jack to give me some so I could buy some new hockey equipment. I knew Dad wouldn't agree, so Jack and I kept it to ourselves. I don't know whether Dad noticed the missing money, but if he did, he didn't say anything. I wondered if this was so as not to give away too much about his plan.

On that day, Dad had picked up the girls that morning. Under the custody agreement, he had to have the girls back at Mom's place by six o'clock the next evening. We piled into the car and went off to Mississauga to stay with some friends – Ennio and his wife Rosa who, if you live in Kitchener-Waterloo, you may know as the owners of two successful restaurants called Ennio's.

We liked to play with their kids, so this wasn't unusual to me.

Eric Two Crowns (Supercabbie)

We all went to bed that night, with no clue of Dad's intentions. Ennio and Rosa didn't know either.

The next day, Dad packed us into the car and left, but instead of going back to Kitchener, we went to Pearson airport and boarded a plane for Venice.

I remember waking up to the sound of the girls crying in the seats next to me, and Dad sleeping on the floor. I remember the stewardess politely asking him to get back into his seat, but he just waved her off. He'd somehow gotten drunk.

He had also somehow arranged all the paperwork beforehand, including passports for all of us, tickets, the works. He'd sold the barber shop, sold our trailer. He'd made a run for it knowing that the police would be after us if Mom called. Which she would. He'd kidnapped us, and we were now absconding to Italy.

This may seem strange to you today, with all we have to go through getting through customs and immigration, especially after 9-11. It was a different time, back then. Dad was Italian as well as Canadian, so he didn't need a visa or anything to board a plane home. Security officers didn't question whether we were his children or whether our mother was allowing us out of the country. We'd made the trip before, so I guess we didn't raise any red flags.

You may also wonder why none of us said anything, especially when it became clear we were being kidnapped.

It's hard to look back and think about what I was thinking at the time, but what I most remember feeling is numb. Dad had made us numb. He made sure we never questioned whatever it was he was doing. The thought about talking to the police, security people, customs officers, anybody, never entered my head because I was too busy keeping my head down, so I wouldn't become a victim of his temper again.

We could have made trouble though, as the flight had been diverted to Montreal due to bad weather. This was why Dad freaked out so, and probably why he'd gotten drunk on the plane, he must have thought Mom had called the police and they were bringing down the plane to arrest him.

But that didn't happen. The plane did indeed get diverted but left a while later with no incident. We were now flying over the Atlantic and out of Canadian airspace. Whether I liked it or not, a new phase of my life was about to begin.

Part 2:
Living in Italy

Chapter Nine
The New Home

Within a few weeks of my return to Kitchener after many years of absence, I made an appointment with Mr. James Sloan, then still a lawyer, now a Superior Court Judge. He was sympathetic when I told him who I was and why I needed to speak to him. He immediately remembered the case and said that he had only dealt with two kidnappings in his career. One was solved, but ours was never concluded. He wrote a letter at my request and told me that Dad would never have gotten away with what he did today.

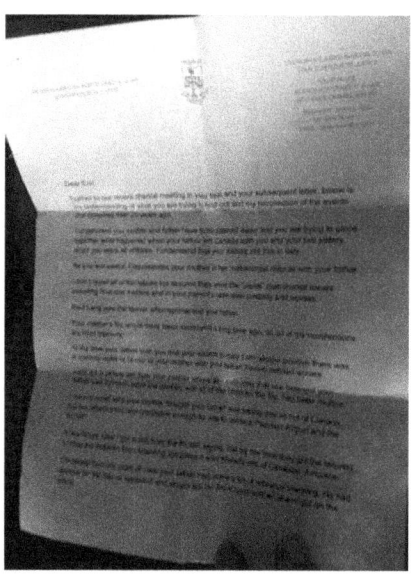
Judge James Sloan's letter.

Mom did call the police, and the RCMP were alerted, but as we'd already left Canadian airspace, there was nothing they could do directly. Mom sent $500 to a lawyer in Italy to retain his services, but the bastard never replied to her requests for updates.

As for Dad, he took all four of us to see this other lawyer and he forced us under his heavy hand to sign a document stating that we wanted nothing to do with Mom, and that this was our own choice.

Dina couldn't even print out her own name! But Dad put his hand on hers and wrote it out. The rest of us, Lydia, Jack and my-

Living in Italy

self, all signed it. Lydia was Daddy's girl and did as she was told. Jack was Dad's best little buddy and was always accommodating his needs. Myself, I knew what would be in store if I didn't do as I was told.

I learned later that Dad had bribed the lawyer to witness our signatures.

Nonna.

He made it clear to us that we were never to mention Mom in his presence. It would be thirteen long years before I would ever see her again.

Whatever you could say about Dad, he must have planned our exit from Canada meticulously. He'd arranged all the paperwork. He'd gotten passports for all of us. He'd sold his barber shop, sold his trailer, and gathered all of our things and brought us to Venice.

He must have had help, too. Or, at least, he must have known who to call when we came to Italy, because a friend met us when we arrived.

Mino di Toma owned the local grocery store in Dad's home town of Osoppo. Dad had known him since they were kids. I wonder if he knew he was an accomplice to a kidnapping or, if he knew, did he feel that his friendship trumped everything? Either way, he helped Dad bring us to Osoppo.

We arrived at the old house that had been in Dad's family since the early 1900s. I remember finding Grandma, sitting in the dining room as we entered. She was tense with anger but allowed us to settle in with our bags and bid Mino good night. As soon as the door closed, however, she gave Dad a tongue-lashing.

"What do you think you're doing?" she yelled. "These children need their mother, for Christ's sake!"

Grandma never usually swore, but there is a time and place for everything. This time, it was merited.

Dad looked embarrassed as he took his mother's rant on the

Eric Two Crowns (Supercabbie)

chin. He said nothing. And, in spite of Grandma's anger, in the end he got his way.

I remember being led to a room where Jack and I were supposed to share, and we went straight to bed.

Jack and I didn't say much when we were alone. I remember that it was cool in the room, as the house had no heating. Grandma had made the bed with three blankets, but I could see my breath fogging in the light from the street lamp outside the bedroom window. I asked Jack to move closer, so I could get some heat.

I thought about Mom and hoped she would come over and take us back. I was so upset, I couldn't even cry.

#

I woke to church bells ringing the next day. I remember thinking it sounded like the tune to a Rice-a-Roni commercial back home in Canada. Again, I thought of home, but when I opened the shutters, I looked down onto a road that was so narrow, the house across the street looked so near that I could jump over to it.

All the buildings around me were hundreds of years old. It was like going back in time. I have to admit, I was curious.

On my way down the wooden stairs, I noticed that they creaked when I walked on them. They also went up a level, and I looked up at the next flight and thought, *what's up there?*

So, I crept up, and saw a hole in the wall. Some of the cement had fallen away, and something was moving around inside. I touched the loose material and then jumped back as a scorpion fell out.

It wasn't that big, three or four inches long, and its tail had a nasty stinger. It hit the ground and ran at me, its stinger swinging back and forth.

I stomped on it! Thank God I had good thick shoes on. Then I rushed down the stairs to the main floor, calling for someone to come up and see it.

Talk about a wake-up call.

Grandma was in the shed outside, and I ran up to her, telling her what I'd just seen. She was wearing thick leggings, an apron and a headscarf, like what those Romani women wear. She had glasses and shuffled along in wooden clodhoppers.

Living in Italy

She told me not to worry as they were harmless. You didn't bother them, and they wouldn't bother you.

Well, not with those stingers, I thought. I decided then that if I encountered any more, I would give them a good stomping. That at least would lessen the population.

The family house had nine bedrooms. There was a small living room with a couple of chairs, a fire stove a couch for two and a television. When I say that the living room was small, I meant it. Four would crowd the place. We were more than four, actually six, and so that room was definitely crowded.

Not that we watched much television. Nonna only turned it on Sunday evenings around seven (for carosello), and we only got to watch about an hour. It was mainly advertising.

There was also a tiny kitchen, dining room and a pantry. Most of the space in the front of the house was given over to the shop. It had previously been my grandfather's barber shop, but it was now rented to a ladies' hairdresser, and so it was out of bounds. Of the nine bedrooms, one had been converted into a bathroom with a shower, toilet and bidet. Another was in use as a storage room, with a light-blue bicycle in it. I'd be using that bicycle to get around, but I was told not to touch it without permission.

The attic was huge, but was exposed to the elements, with only a tiled roof above it. Nonna told me that the "Cossacks and Germans" used it during the First and Second World Wars. Dad even mentioned that he'd once found bullets and a hand grenade in there when he was young.

Though Mom was always on my mind and I often cried when I thought about her, I had to admit that I was fascinated by my new home.

Chapter Ten
Leaving for Lignano

Lignano is a small peninsula in the northeast Adriatic. It's made up of four sections: Lignano Riviera, Pineta, Sabbia D'Oro (which translates to "Sand of Gold") and Lignano City, where most of the nightlife was.

Lignano was where I began my first real job, where I actually got paid. I remember, on my fifteenth birthday, my father came into my bedroom and saying to me, "If you can find a job, you can go to work." He had found out that I had been absconding from school.

What he didn't know was that I'd already been asking a couple of my friends about finding work. The summer season was just around the corner, and I'd had enough of failing at school.

It wasn't that I was a bad student. I'd been a good student in Canada, learning what Canadians learned. In Osoppo, I'd been thrown in the deep end. I didn't know Italian geography, the history, or the grammar that local students my age had been taught up to then. It was very frustrating.

Anyway, when asking around, I learned that Roberto (also known as Scai) needed help in his brand-new restaurant, the Ristorante Rubin. It was just 150 metres or so from the Lignano Riviera beach. I met with him and, after a quick talk, he offered me the job. He told me to be ready to leave on the morning of April the 1st.

I was determined to show Dad that I could work. By this time, I was fed up with his drinking and his neglect of my sisters. Lydia seven by this point, and Dina was just four. Grandma was nearly 76, and she'd suffered and sacrificed enough in her life. If I couldn't show my father what I could do at school, I could show him what I could do with a job.

Nonna wasn't too impressed, I could tell. She wanted me to stay. However, she didn't insist, and she knew I had to grow up sooner or later. Besides, we were not that well off, and I could help pay the bills.

Departure day came fast, but I was ready. My luggage was packed and all I had to do was say my goodbyes. The girls were at school.

"Nonna!" I called out. She was always doing something around the house, she came out as I stood there waiting. "I have to meet Roberto, Nonna!"

She just bowed her head. "Where are you going, Frute?" (Kid) "Where are you going?"

The way she said it saddened me. She'd been the biggest mentor to me. She loved me dearly, and I her. So, I just grabbed her and picked her up, twirling her around.

"Put me down, you little scoundrel!" she shouted. But it cheered her up. Then she said, "Tehn... Tehn," and reached into her apron. Out came her wallet and she handed me some money. I tried to decline, but she knew better, as always, and shoved it in my hand. With Nonna, I always knew when to quit and let her have her way. Within a few minutes, my ride pulled up into the driveway.

I knew I had to make this fast, as Nonna looked about to weep, so I picked up my bags, gave her a last hug, and got in Roberto's car. Off I went seeking my destiny.

We drove about an hour and a half south of Osoppo to the coast. When we arrived, I noticed the beautiful pines and other trees that decorated the properties all around. It was beautiful and clean. The restaurant itself had a navy-blue exterior with orange trimming, which I thought looked weird. It was a brand-new building with a swimming pool for the tenants upstairs.

We parked the car, where I noticed that there were about a dozen floors above the restaurant, and cars already in the car park. Some people had come early, the restaurant windows were still soaped down from the winter closure.

We went through the main doors and up a couple of marble

Eric Two Crowns (Supercabbie)

stairs to our apartment. As we entered, Roberto pointed at the couch and said, "Eric, that's yours." I didn't mind. Back in Canada, I'd liked camping, so I accepted the couch without complaint.

The apartment had only one bedroom and that was for the brothers. There was a small kitchen with a table for four, a small bathroom and a balcony so tiny, I don't think you could have placed two chairs on it. That would be our future emergency exit.

This would be my home until mid-September: six months of triple shifts, seven days a week (with a break here and there). I'd help serve breakfast from 6:30 to 10:30 in the morning before getting a half hour break. Then on again from 11:00 to 2:30 in the afternoon, then back to work by 5:30 for the dinner shift, which lasted until about 10:30 to 11 in the evening.

When I say "break" it was more like a pause, I would have to stock fridges, wash and clean cutlery, clean and fill salt and pepper shakers, wipe and check the dishes, et cetera. The list was long.

But the lunch trade wasn't that good, and that meant there weren't many tips. The beautiful beaches just down the road absorbed most of the people until the late afternoon. However, thinking this over, I came up with an idea.

What if I were to go serve drinks around the pool during my afternoon break? That way, people could lounge under the sun or under the umbrellas, with me at their service!

Roberto agreed, and the people around the pool loved it. Soon, I only had to appear with my bar tray, and people would call out, "Eric!", and I would quickly take their orders, skip to the bar, and return, *zip*, just like that. I started making tips! I was fast and full of energy.

Days were passing by, and after the first two weeks, I asked Roberto when we could go to Osoppo for a visit. He said that we would visit the next Sunday, as he was engaged to a really nice girl named Maria Rosa and wanted to "sow his oats".

Roberto was like a big brother to me. He was tall with short black hair. A scar on his lip enhanced his already model-like face, and he was in such great shape, his body was practically V-shaped. One evening he asked me if I wanted to go to a particular restaurant as it wasn't busy, and he was closing early.

I agreed, and we went to what he told me was the best seafood

Living in Italy

place in all of Lignano. He knew his stuff; it was indeed outstanding.

We both had a plate of spaghetti *alle vongole* (which means "baby clams"). Then he had another and finished with an eight-ounce steak and salad. Roberto had hollow legs or something, I don't know where he put it all! I thought I could eat, but he was just a hog, and I mean that in the nicest way.

If you love pizza, you know that you have to go to Italy to taste the best. There's just something about those brick and real wood ovens. Again, Roberto knew the best places to go. One evening he took me to a pizzeria called Il Delfino (meaning "the Dolphin").

It had a discotheque downstairs and that's where we eventually ended up. Their pizza was the best I ever had, and ever have had to this day (so good I had two!). Even now, I'm getting hungry thinking about it. We went there many a time during that first summer.

On our visit back to Osoppo, I arrived to see Nonna chopping wood, with an axe! She was a tough one; no flies on her!

Sometimes she would have a tipple of grappa, which was a northern Italian moonshine made by taking the skins and twigs of grapes after all the juice had been squeezed out, passing them through a grinder, adding sugar and water and distilling the mix. It's like fire water, and I knew when she'd had a couple too many when her glasses got worn crooked on her nose.

With Nonna, red wine was always on the table at lunch and dinner, along with the usual San Pellegrino mineral water. Sometimes we would run out of San Pellegrino and she would use this sachet of powder, stick it in a bottle of water that had to be closed quickly before the carbon solution would erupt.

Anyway, I was home again, however briefly. I dropped my laundry in the basket and went straight up to help her, but she was already wiping her apron and walking towards me. "Let's go in and have a drink," she said.

She got some coffee brewing and sat in her usual chair closest to the stove.

"So, tell me how it's going, *Frute*?" This was pronounced like "fruit" and means "young boy. "Do you like your work?" she asked.

Eric Two Crowns (Supercabbie)

"Yes, I do, Nonna," I replied. "Roberto is teaching me German. We have menus in German and Italian."

"Good, good," she replied. "And how are they treating you?"

"Everything is okay," I assured her, even though Lino was cuffing me in the head, and once had kicked me in the ankle to reprimand me, but I kept this to myself.

We chatted for a while, but time was getting on. I had agreed to meet Roberto at Missana's bar. I had just minutes to go. I said my goodbyes to Nonna and realized that I had seen no sign of Dad. So, I asked Nonna where he was, and she just shrugged.

"*Valla... valla... Lesse sta,*" she said. In other words: "Whatever. Leave it alone."

I knew what she was saying. Dad was drunk. He was in a permanent stupor by now.

Maybe it was better that I hadn't seen him.

After we finished hugging and said our goodbyes, I took off to Missana's. Later, Rob arrived, picking me up and taking me back to Lignano.

#

The earthquake happened that spring (May 6, 1976, as I said in Chapter One). Our home wasn't safe to return to. Il Rivellino, which is the area beside La Fortezza, was the site of a prefabricated housing complex called a barracopolli. This would be our home for a time while everyone rebuilt from the earthquake.

But we couldn't move in right away. Instead, we lived in an army tent that we shared with another family until Christmas Eve, when we could finally move into the barracopolli. We didn't have heat, and whose floors were gravel. When it rained, you had to wear boots. You wanted hot water, you cooked it yourself on the fire. The place had only eight shower stalls to accommodate hundreds of people and, of course, the showers were usually cold when you used them.

The military had built a wooden community centre for people to go and eat and mingle. Food was scarce, but there was something to eat at lunchtime and at supper for whoever turned up. They would always serve pasta, one of my favourites. Even in the army camp, I was impressed with the culinary skills shown by the soldiers in the community centre.

Living in Italy

There was work, at least. Fratelli Christ – a local heating and plumbing firm – was given the contract to do all the plumbing work in the reconstruction. I landed a job with them for a short time as an apprentice, and they had enough work to keep everyone busy for the rest of the year.

But the earthquake left many of us with scars. One day while we were eating, we felt another aftershock. I was just beginning to start my meal when suddenly I couldn't get the fork into my mouth because it kept going from side to side. Then I realized that everything was shaking. So, we all sat and waited for the shaking to stop. Though we were safe, the look of fear was still in everyone's eyes.

On another occasion, in September, I was sleeping, but woke to the noise of a great moan coming from the earth. The ground began to tremble. It was another big one. I was next to Dad, and I grabbed his hand and he extended his to me. I laid there, waiting for the shaking to stop. Dad told me to just stay calm, but I felt as though the earth was going to open up and eat me.

Finally, it stopped. I jumped up and looked outside towards Gemona, a town a few kilometres away that was built at the foot of the Alps and visible from our tent. The moon was so bright, it shone like the sun in the still of night. I could see dust rising above the town. It was obvious more structures had crumbled down.

Nonna woke up in the middle of the trembling and murmured, "When will this stop, Lord? When will this stop?"

That was the largest aftershock following the main earthquake on May 6th.

I believe there were something over 200 aftershocks recorded within a few months of the first tremor. Some five percent of the population of Osoppo had perished, including too many friends.

Chapter Eleven
Predator

On the day of my arrival back to Osoppo, after the summer of the Earthquake had ended, I found Nonna outside our tent, plunging and scrubbing away at the washing.

The wooden washboard had seen better days, but it still served its purpose. Nonna never threw anything away, and during World War Two she even kept the chicken feathers for use in pillows.

I remember, when we had our first Sunday dinner together in Osoppo, she served us all and then sat down beside me, and I stared at her plate in amazement. She'd served us beef, but her plate had only chicken giblets and feet. The feet looked like it would serve better as a back-scratcher than as food. But she just dug in, ripping at the skin and sucking the juice from the claws. Yikes!

She saw me staring, and she said, "You've never starved, have you?" Then she went back to eating.

That was one of my first lessons from Nonna. On the morning after we'd come to Italy, she'd asked me what I wanted for breakfast. "Bacon and eggs," I said, in Italian, as that was my favourite. She left the kitchen, then returned minutes later with a bowl full of pieces of yesterday's bread. She poured some coffee into it, along with some milk and sugar and said, "There you go! None of that other stuff around here."

That first breakfast was kind of like slop, but I got used to it, and I appreciate now how there was no waste or taking anything for granted.

So, when I arrived at the tent, that day, she ceased her chore and welcomed me with a hug. "Let's have coffee, Frute!"

Living in Italy

Her little red pot was always ready to brew. We sat down at the table, and I noticed that she'd set an extra placing.

"Do we have a guest tonight?" I asked.

"Yes," she replied, but didn't really explain. I left it at that, and after helping Nonna put things away, I told her I would be back for supper and headed off to see my friends at Missanna's.

Dinner was always at 6:30, and missing it would set Nonna off.. If you came home late, you ended up with cold dinner. If you didn't eat dinner, that's what you had for breakfast! I learned quickly to arrive on time. That night, however, I saw this guy sitting at the dinner table. He got up and introduced himself as "Grillo", a nickname.

I thought he looked a bit unusual, kind of scrawny, with these thick-lensed glasses that made his eyes look like they protruded from his face. He was friends with Dad and Nonna, and had done small chores for the family for no payment. He also said that he was a male nurse as well.

And he was Nonna's guest, so I gave him respect for his deeds. Dad was there as well, so I felt comfortable. At least initially.

After dinner that evening, Grillo offered to buy me an espresso coffee along with a glass of grappa – Nonna's drink – at the only bar on the tent site, just a few metres away. I liked the tipple, and as Grillo was buying, I let loose, and drank enough to get a little tipsy.

Grillo then said that there would be friends meeting at his tent in a while, and would I like to join him? I thought, hey, the party was on! So, I went to his tent, looking forward to making some new friends. By around 9:30 or so, as we drank and chatted, I got a little perplexed that his friends were taking so long to arrive. I asked him, "Where are your friends?"

"Don't worry. They'll be here soon! They'll be sleeping over for the night."

There were only two single beds where he was staying. I supposed the others had sleeping bags, though, so I didn't think too much about this.

We had a couple more drinks and, by then, I was getting tired. He offered to let me stay the night, but said he had only one large

Eric Two Crowns (Supercabbie)

blanket, and that he would turn the two single beds into one, so we could share.

Alarms should have gone off then, but I was tipsy, and I'd shared a bed with my brother Jack at different times in my life. I'd camped out, sharing beds with cousins on the reserve, so this was no big deal, surely?

With the bed now made, I climbed in. While Grillo continued to fiddle around in the tent, he said that there were magazines in the bedside cupboard if I wanted to read. Sure, I thought, and reached for drawer.

I immediately noticed that they were of the adult type. As a fifteen-year-old boy, my hormones were rampant, so of course I began glancing through the pictures. The next magazine, however, had nude men. That made me freeze up a bit and think.

Who did these magazines belong to? Were they his, or one of his roommates? But I didn't get up to go away. After all, Dad and Nonna knew this man and he'd done good things for them, so I trusted him.

I put the magazines away and told him I was going to sleep. Grillo continued to fiddle around the tent before climbing into his side of the bed shortly after. It was cold, and I was shivering, and Grillo said that our body heat would keep us warm in a few minutes.

That was when I started to feel fear. Things just didn't feel right. My mind began to race, and I tried to think of a plan.

I lay on my side and pretended to be asleep, snoring slightly, and I felt Grillo sliding closer, like a snake. Within seconds, he was snuggling close.

I pulled away and asked him to keep his distance.

"No problem, Eric! I won't hurt you!" he said.

I lay back and began to snore, and again he got closer. This time he put his hand on my hip as he cuddled up. I felt trapped. I knew I had to get out of there.

I jumped out of the bed and ran for it. I didn't stop until I got to my tent. Grillo, fortunately, didn't try to stop me, or come after me.

I told Dad what had just happened, and his response was to

laugh and to make a comment in Italian which translates roughly into "Bum Sergeant!". He didn't take my fears seriously at all.

I also told Nonna, but I don't think she really understood. She listened to me, but she didn't get angry on my behalf. She didn't promise to do anything to Grillo to stop him from doing this to someone else. I guess she didn't take my fears seriously either.

I suppose I was home and safe, and nothing had actually happened, but I still felt uncomfortable. I'd trusted Grillo, and he'd broken that trust. I resolved then and there not to have anything to do with him ever again.

Remember, I was only fifteen at the time, and quite vulnerable. I resolved that I wouldn't be that vulnerable again. My brother Jack and I tried out some martial arts classes. We only dabbled, but they came in handy a few months later.

It was Christmas Eve, 1976, and we had moved from the tent into a prefabricated house. It had snowed that evening, but we were warm inside. Jack and I shared a room, Dina and Lydia shared another, and Dad and Nonna each had their own room.

By this time, Jack was in culinary school, so I had the room to myself. I enjoyed this freedom, even though I missed him fiercely. I also had my job as an apprentice plumber and was bringing a cheque to grandma at the end of every month. I was bringing home the bacon because Dad wasn't working and he and Nonna were depending on their pensions. Dina and Lydia were growing up and needing things, and there were always bills to be paid, so I contributed. I felt good about that.

But it was also flu season, and I came down with influenza and on Christmas Eve was running a high fever. Lying in bed and sweating profusely, I heard a knock at the front door.

It was ten o'clock in the evening. Who could it be? I heard Dad talking to someone at the door, then Grillo's voice responded, asking where I was.

I froze up immediately.

Dad, like an idiot, told him I was sick in bed, and invited him in. I heard Grillo ask if he could see me, and Dad said it was okay. Then I heard Grillo's footsteps approaching my room.

I began planning my next moves as I heard him knock.

But then it struck me that, if Grillo did try anything, I could

Eric Two Crowns (Supercabbie)

prove to my Dad and Nonna what he had done. I could turn the tables, if he was stupid enough to take the bait.

He knocked on the door.

"Who is it?" I called out.

He opened the door. "It's me. Grillo."

"What do you want?"

He walked in, saying that he was sorry to hear I was sick, and wanted to help.

I told him I was tired, and just wanted to sleep. "No problem," he said, as he pulled up a chair. "I'll just keep you company for a while."

"Well, turn out the light," I said, and rolled over, putting my back to him. After a while, I began to snore, all the while listening hard and sensing what he was doing behind me.

He took the bait. His hand came between the sheets and he touched my hip and leg.

I whirled around, and punched him straight in the face, smashing his glasses. I jumped out of bed and turned the light on. I raised my fist to give him another punch, but he high-tailed it out of there as I shouted curses after him and warned him never to come back.

Dad came from the kitchen, shouting, "What's going on?"

I yelled right back at him. "I'm doing your job! You know, protecting me?"

I was disappointed he hadn't taken my problem seriously, but I had taken care of the predator on my own.

I never saw Grillo again, but I sometimes wonder if he tried what he tried on me with other people my own age. I sincerely hope not. The experience scarred me and has led me to think politically incorrect things about homosexuals. I understand, now, that Grillo was one person, a predator, and everybody is different. I have nothing against these people, now, just so long as they give me my space.

Chapter Twelve
Mona

That first season in Lignano went by quickly. It had been a hot one, and I'd had fun. When you are young, it's like you are like a sponge. You want to discover everything that is cool and suck it in. That I did with all the girls I'd met.

One girl in particular, Mona, was a couple of years older than me. She was from Germany. Rob and I met her in the disco that was below our favorite pizza place. I introduced myself, and she said "yes" to my company. I bought us a couple of cokes and we sat together, getting to know each other. That night we danced and had a good time.

She had curly brownish hair, a nice body with long legs, and she laughed all the time, which I found very attractive. Rob, meanwhile, was hitting on this Swedish chick. He was an old hand at the game already. When I told him that I was leaving that evening with Mona, he smiled at me and gave me a look like someone watching someone else growing up. I chuckled and left.

I asked Mona where she lived so I could walk her home. When she said, "Rubin apartments," I was over the moon! She was staying in the building where I was working, and I knew the perfect place to fool around, if we ever got that far.

At that age, that's all you ever think about.

We parted that evening, but we agreed to meet at the club the next Saturday night after I finished work. After dancing away the evening, and then smooching in our little corner, it came time to go, and again we walked for about thirty minutes back to the Rubin, holding hands all the way. Then, at the doors, she gave me that inviting glance that told me it was on.

Eric Two Crowns (Supercabbie)

I admit, I was a greenhorn. I was thinking about what I would do with her, being so obviously inexperienced in the art of making love. However, we went down to the cellar where we kept all the beverages (and where a friend named Walter would sleep if he was visiting; he wasn't visiting that day, fortunately). There, we got naked and laid down on the mattress. It was dark, but there was a glimmer of light shining through the crack of the shuttered small window, enough to see the shape of her milky white body.

I had snuck glances at a few pages of Playboy before, but this was the first girl I'd ever seen in the flesh. I began to kiss her and moved down to her stomach, kissing and gently licking her. We got sweaty and hot. She then said something very disappointing to this teenager: "I just want to fool around. No intercourse, okay?"

What? I thought. *After we've come this far?* But I kept on doing what I was doing. Perhaps she would change her mind if she were more aroused. Within a couple of minutes, she was shaking and I was on top of her. I removed my fingers and felt myself entering her. She didn't push me away. She just let go and accepted me.

I remember one thing that Rob had told me: "Don't get silly and forget where you are. You have to get out when the bell is about to ring, or you'll be sorry." I kept that in mind, as I didn't want to be a father at that age. I made sure I timed it right.

It was ecstasy. Afterward, Mona and I held each other for a long while before we got dressed and went outside. Her parents would be expecting her, and I didn't want her to get into trouble. We spoke for a couple of minutes and, after a long kiss, off she went.

I went into the apartment and I remember running into Astrid, Lino's girlfriend, who looked at me and laughed. I thought at first that she'd been spying on us in the basement, but she just pointed to my sweater and I realized that I'd put it on inside out.

She laughed and waved her finger at me, saying, "You little bad boy!"

I went red with embarrassment, but I smiled, and then beat a hasty retreat out of the apartment. I passed some time on my own by the pool, thinking to myself, *now I am a man!*

What a wally I was!

Living in Italy

Soon, the season was coming to an end. September 15th is the date many restaurants in Lignano closed. I'd learned a lot of German and, thanks to Roberto, had become proficient in my serving skills. I had many encounters with folk from countries all over Europe. I'd also met a few chicks and felt I had matured somewhat.

I had visited Osoppo every other week after the quake, I knew that, coming home, I'd have to find another job. Nonna wouldn't tolerate laziness now that I was working.

This is how I went from a restaurant worker to an apprentice plumber. I'd already put out some feelers, and my best friend Claudio had put in a good word for me at the *Fratelli Christ* company (which translates to "the Christ Brothers"). Mario Christ hired me on as an apprentice and assigned me to Edo, my journeyman. It was a new trade, and I looked forward to the new challenge.

Edo had a hare lip, so when he gave me orders, I had to listen carefully as, half of the time, I couldn't understand what he was telling me. He often had to repeat himself. Fortunately, he had a good sense of humour and was a really nice guy.

Sometimes Edo would pick me up on his orange Laverda 750 motorcycle and take me to the site where we would be working. There were about a dozen of us employed by the Christ Brothers. Our jobs were scattered around and sometimes we'd have to eat in restaurants, as we went far out of town.

My job as an apprentice varied from fetching tools to pounding concrete with a sledgehammer and chisel, tracing where the water pipes would go. I also measured and cut pipes to spec and wrapped them with fiberglass cloth (to make sure they wouldn't freeze in winter). Some jobs were monotonous, such as painting the heating pipes with orange anti-rust paint (days on end).

Sometimes my co-workers would play a few tricks on me. Once, when I was itching from working with fiberglass all day, they told me to take a hot shower as soon as I got home. What they didn't tell me was that hot showers open your pores. You want to take a cold shower after working with fiberglass to close your pores and keep the tiny fibers out!! After stepping out of the hot shower, I itched more than ever, the bastards!

Another time, the head journeyman handed me a plastic jug and told me to go down the street to the Osteria (bar) and get it

Eric Two Crowns (Supercabbie)

filled with Brule. Brule is a hot red wine made by adding sugar, cinnamon, cloves and bay leaves. It's a traditional Furlan winter tipple. I was given some to help warm me up, while I worked on the bare skeleton of the building tracing the cement for the pipes to go in. I appreciated that, as it was cold and the wind howled through the open house while I used a sledgehammer to do the tracing for the pipes. And when I asked for another cup of brule, and they cheerfully gave it to me.

Remember, it's hot red *wine*. Before long, I was hitting my hand more often than my chisel. The guys knew what they were doing. I was being broken in somewhat literally, but it was all in good fun.

I was eager to learn how to weld. Instead of taking a whole hour to have lunch when we were on a site, I ate quickly and practiced on scraps of piping, with the approval of Edo. I was getting better and he told me that the sooner I learned to weld, the sooner I'd get a raise.

After many hours practicing, I asked for a raise. Edo vouched for me, so I was pleased that my next pay packet showed I had earned extra money. My practicing had paid off!

In all, I put in about a year and a half learning the plumbing trade (leaving once and then returning) with the Christ Brothers. I did learn that it wasn't in me to be a plumber, but I did learn enough for my skills to come in handy throughout my life. It was really never in me to be a plumber but the knowledge came in handy. These skills would save me a lot of money.

Chapter Thirteen
Biker Gang

Hockey was my sport in Canada. In Italy it became difficult to play, simply because of how far I'd have to travel to play or practice. I would have to get a note from Dad to leave early from school. I would turn up with my hockey gear. Kids would stare at me and my equipment and ask what it was for? (They had little knowledge of what ice hockey was).

I would have to catch a train to Pontebba station, travel roughly an hour and a half north, towards Austria. My coach would be waiting to take me to his house and, after getting something to eat, we would take off for the rink to practice, or to Villach, Austria, for a game.

I was still a junior, I played in the so-called National "B" league. The other players were older than me by a few years, but they welcomed me with open arms, because I was Canadian. They knew the best players in the world were from Canada. The coach and the other members of the staff were excited to have a Canadian player on their team. They treated me well. In my debut game, I had two assists, which was a great start.

There was one problem, however. Starting our warm up, I jumped on the ice, and my feet went sideways. *What the hell!* I thought. I went back to the bench to check things out. My blades were blunt! I couldn't understand it, as I'd asked the coach to sharpen them before the game and, when I called him over and asked about it, he assured me that this is what he had done.

I asked if there was a sharpener on duty at the complex. There was. Taking off my skates, I headed for the shop. There, I found that my coach had used a figure skating stone to sharpen my

Eric Two Crowns (Supercabbie)

blades. Yes, that made a big difference. Fortunately, the guy on duty redid the skates to my satisfaction, and all was fine.

The open rink had no siding. There was just a roof covering. It was so cold, you could see the spectators' breath as they stood, watching and shivering. Vapour steamed from the players on the benches.

After the game, some guy came up to me and started asking me where I was from, and how old I was. I answered him, not thinking much about it but, the next day, when I arrived home, one of my friends showed me the *Messaggero Veneto* newspaper. I had made the front page of the sports section! The headline read, in Italian, *Italo-Canadian makes debut with two points*! I was flattered and honoured at the attention and the praise.

When I went with a couple of friends to the Cortina D'Ampezzo ski resort (which had been used in the 1956 Winter Olympics), I'd just happened to bring my skates, and decided to make my way down to the outdoor stadium to zip around the ring, dodging people and having fun. I'd stopped by the boards for a quick break when someone tapped my shoulder. I turned and saw a man asking me, in Italian, where I'd learn to "skate like that." I told him I was from Canada, and he immediately asked me to follow him to the other side of the rink and speak with somebody.

I skated along the boards and saw the man talking to another man and pointing in my direction. They both came over and the first man introduced the coach of the national team! He asked for my father's name and how to contact him.

Of course, I agreed to give them the details, and they said they would be in touch within the next few days. I was excited and looking forward to being recruited. I returned home and told Dad that someone was going to call. They did call, soon after, but Dad told them, "No!"

I was disappointed, but I took it in stride. I'd been denied by Dad so often.

They'd been willing to put me up, feed me, school me, and offer me a contract if it all worked out, but Dad said he needed me to go to work and pull my weight. Personally, I believe it was just a move to control me, as he'd always done, and dash my hopes for a career. Later that season, my Italian hockey career would come to

Living in Italy

Me and my cousin's Vespa!

an end, as the travelling and having to work shortly after I'd quit school made hockey impossible.

Fortunately, I found another passion: Motocross!

The friends I'd made in Italy were all motorcycle-lovers. One by one, we all bought dirt bikes, and would load them up in a van which would haul us into the Alps, and we'd find trails to race on.

We even built our own track beside the Tagliamento river, which flows down from the Alps. It would partially dry up after the spring meltdown had passed.

Our gang would sometimes be challenged by biker gangs from nearby villages, racing for bragging rights.

We had a great time. Unfortunately, some of the villagers didn't appreciate the noisy engines. That was made clear to me one day when I was fooling around on my street, popping wheelies, when I saw a man walking behind a bush, brandishing a pickaxe. He came out from behind swinging it at me as I passed. I swerved around him and raced off home while the crazy man cursed and swore at me about the noise and nuisance.

Needless to say, from that day forward, I crept home slowly and quietly when I went by his place.

In all, about ten of us hung out together in our biker gang.

Eric Two Crowns (Supercabbie)

Motorbiking in the Italian Alps.

Every weekend we would hit the dirt trails and make our mark on the land.

The foothills of San Rocco also had a piece of land behind it that, when the small creek that ran alongside dried up, made a perfect practice area for jumping. We took shovels and molded the ground to our liking. All of us had a small flag, each a different colour to mark where your back wheel landed. That was the mark to beat, and the exhilaration of flying through the air for a few seconds was ecstasy.

All of us wore the proper equipment, and believe me, you needed it. Sometimes things didn't go perfectly and the tumbles we took were scary. I remember one day in San Rocco, after it had rained, and the ground was slippery, I was racing to beat one of my buddies who was in the lead.

I went soaring into the air, but I landed awkwardly, losing control, and fell. The landing was so hard, I bent the whole frame of the bike. I hadn't broken anything, but my crotch had taken the brunt of the fuel tank. Ouch!

I lay there a minute before looking to the landing flag, and that's when I saw I'd beaten the leader. The pain all but disappeared, and I'd felt great that I had at least given my all.

Bumps, bruises and sore muscles, but great times.

My bike was still crooked when I sold her. I didn't want to, but after hundreds of hours with my pride and joy, the time had come to move on to other pastures.

Chapter Fourteen
Meesha

When I turned sixteen in Osoppo, I felt a bit adventurous and wanted to spread my wings. I noticed a want ad saying, "Help wanted for Italian ice cream parlour in Ellwangen, Germany." I thought this would be a great opportunity for me, as my experience in Lignano had taught me to speak some German to serve the waves of German tourists who came through the season.

I have to say, I learned more languages working than I did in school. At Lignano, Roberto taught me many German words, and the menus were in both Italian in German. Other jobs serving other tourists brought other learning opportunities. By the time I was twenty, I could speak five languages: Italian, Spanish, German, French, and English – six if you added Furlan, the language of the Friuli region in northeastern Italy. These have mostly stayed with me, though it's hard to keep them all in your head if you don't have opportunities to use them.

Anyway, back to the story.

Nonna seemed sad when I told her I'd answered the want ad, and they had accepted, but she knew I was growing up. It was time to go out and stand on my own two feet.

My new boss, named Bruno, booked my ticket for Ellwangen in southwest Germany, and I rode from Gemona through the Alps. I'll never forget that trip. It was easy and beautiful. We'd be in tunnels for kilometers, before suddenly reappearing in daylight among beautiful vineyards and farms surrounded by mountains.

On arrival at Ellwangen, Bruno approached me as I stood alone outside the station in a strange and new town. "Are you Eric?" he asked.

Eric Two Crowns (Supercabbie)

Ellwangen, Germany. Image courtesy Eigenes Werk.

"Yes, and you must be Bruno," I replied.

We shook hands. Bruno was a burly-looking man with a thick mustache. He had short but thick dark-brown hair and wore large-rimmed Rayban glasses with gold frames. His wife and his parents were partners in his business. I don't recall her name, but she always wore the most fashionable clothes and had on a fresh hair-do every day. She mainly handled the banking, though she would help out on busy days.

The little shop only sat about 15 people, even though the line ups out the door were long. One of our specialties was spaghetti ice, which was three scoops of hand-made vanilla ice cream pressed through a potato masher so it came out like spaghetti. We topped it with strawberry sauce and grated white chocolate to mimic tomato sauce and Parmesan. It sold like crazy. Kids loved it!

Bruno's father held the recipe for the ice cream. Bruno would inherit it, of course, but it was the old man who cooked it up, mixing in the flavourings and putting everything in plastic ten-litre pails. He would shout down whenever a batch was ready for paddling. This is when ice-cold water is moved around the large terracotta basin holding the ice-cream mixture. A machine would

Living in Italy

scrape the freezing cream off the sides of the basin. Bruno used a wooden paddle to shift the ice cream around, pick it up, and scrape it into other ice-cold Terracotta basins.

It was, and still is, the best ice cream I've ever tasted. Bruno only made four flavours: vanilla, hazelnut, chocolate and strawberry. He also made two sorbets: lemon and orange.

On my first day, I got up around 6:30 in the morning and went down to the ice cream parlour, which was two blocks away. The first thing I noticed was how clean the cobble streets were. I also noticed how cold the air felt that misty morning.

I walked into the shop and Bruno welcomed me, asking if I'd had a good sleep. Of course, I replied "Yes", like a good boy, since complaining is a sin. In truth, my mattress had an odor of horsehair and it was cold in my room, but I was still ready to work. I was on a mission to improve my German, and this job fit perfectly.

I was able to live and work in Ellwangen for about three months before I became homesick. I had fun in the meantime. I worked for ten hours most days, getting Sunday afternoon off around 3 p.m. I was used to being a gofer for my father with no pay or allowance, so getting a million Lira per month with room and board included was like hitting the jackpot.

A million Lira sounds like a lot, but it worked out to about $1,000 Canadian dollars. This was back in 1977, but it was for a 65-hour workweek. Still, that's $4.00 per hour, in 1977! I was in the money!

Bruno's family gave me no love, and they seemed a little brash, but they did watch out for me.

I also met some new friends. Dieter was a tall fellow with receding blonde hair. He'd had a hare-lip and surgery to fix it, and the scar was very visible. He intrigued me because he spoke in a real deep voice for his age. I wondered if it was because he smoked one of Europe's strongest cigarettes (Gauluois, no filter). Trying to be tough, I gave them a try. I gave them up very quickly. Yuck!

Meesha was another friend. She took a liking to me. We met in a local bar. Her real name was Michele, but preferred Meesha. She was eighteen, and hot! She had the bosoms every man dreams of — large yet firm – as well as a small bottom. Her hair was blonde and about shoulder length. Her styling was Egyptian-like, which only enhanced her already beautiful face. She had dimples on her cheeks and a great smile. After a few encounters, she asked me out on a date.

Meesha picked me up after work and said we were going to a party. I thought, *cool! I get to meet more new friends and hang out for a while!*

But we drove down a road that was gravel and heading towards a forest. I asked her where we were headed, and she said, "Do you swim in the nude?"

Well, that clammed me up. She noticed and said, "Don't worry. If you don't feel comfortable, you don't have to. Relax!"

So, I sat a while, trying to slow my heart down. Then I saw bonfires in the distance, about four or five of them around this big pond. As we got closer, I could see a lot of naked bodies and felt very out of place.

Meesha stopped the car, looked over at me, smiled and said, "At least take your shirt off, okay?"

"I can do that," I replied. I had a decent body, at least, as I'd always been active in sports.

As we went over to the bonfires, some of her friends called out, "Meesha! Meesha! Over here!" We sat down on a blanket she'd brought and she introduced me to her friends who were already standing around in their birthday suits! Sheepishly, I acknowledged them all.

Meesha was eighteen. I was sixteen; still very much a greenhorn, albeit an adventurous sort and not a bad-looking guy. Plus, speaking English seemed to turn on the girls I dated.

All of a sudden, Meesha just gets up and dives into the pond. Surfacing, she puts her hand behind her back and takes off her bra. She beckoned me to join her, her smile teasing.

I wanted to, but all these strangers made me feel chicken. Needless to say, I was quite hard, and quite fortunate to have only taken off my shirt! I just stood there. Finally, she came out of the water and walked towards me, like a goddess, or that scene with Bo Derek in the movie *10*, while I watched, mesmerized. I felt lucky that she liked me and looked forward to going a little further.

We stayed for about two hours before going back into Meesha's white VW and making our way back to Ellwangen. On the way, she looked at me with those blue eyes and we stopped to kiss.

Living in Italy

Her lips were like marshmallows and she was passionate. I was on cloud nine, and she knew I was thunderstruck.

We didn't have sex that night. We just kissed and spent some time together in the car. I felt we would go all the way soon.

Something puzzled me though when we were at the pond party. Meesha asked me if I'd been sending her flowers. I assured her it wasn't me and didn't think too much of it at the time, but I still found it odd.

Turns out Meesha's flowers came from Dieter. He'd had the hots for her and he was getting jealous because he would see us sitting together at the local bar. The flowers were a good attempt, but at least sign your name when you send them! I laughed inside when I'd learned it was him, thinking that I'd beaten Dieter and it hadn't cost me a dime!

As I said, I became homesick three months after my arrival in Ellwangen. I made up my mind to go home and I let Bruno know. I agreed to stay on until Bruno found a replacement for me, and then I would leave. I planned that, before I left, I would somehow make love to Meesha. If I failed, it would have been one of those that got away!

As usual, I saw Meesha at the bar one evening, and made my way over. She greeted me with her usual soft kiss and we made our way over to a table. Her manicured nails dug into my skin just enough to get my attention as she snuggled up to me. I told her, then, that I was going back to Osoppo. Bruno had found a replacement, and I'd made arrangements to leave Sunday morning.

I could see the disappointment in her face.

We spent the remaining evenings hanging out at the bar. I thought maybe she was just going to let me go and we would never make love. Finally, Saturday came, and my last shift. I had already packed most of my things and was ready. The day seemed to go on forever.

I was going to meet Meesha at the usual bar and spend our last few hours together. I was still feeling homesick, but I also wanted to stay and be with her. She made me feel good. She was always upbeat and happy.

Finally, six o'clock came and I was done. I went home and took a shower. After making sure of my ride back to Osoppo in the morning, I went down to Costa's bar. Meesha was there and she immediately took my hand and we snuggled in our usual little corner and began to kiss.

She was a little subdued that night. As we talked and sipped our drinks, she said she would like to go for a walk. So, we decided to go to this other bar that was never too busy and had more privacy.

There, she asked me why I was leaving. I told her I was homesick and had to go back to see my two little sisters and the rest of my family. She looked a little sad, but accepted my answer and said, "Let's go back to my place."

The sensual way she looked at me as she said it let me know that we would be making love that night. Needless to say, I was eager to get over to her place.

She had a small bachelor pad not far from where I lived. We made our way there, holding hands, stopping often to kiss. Shortly after we arrived, we opened the door like a pair of thieves in the night. Meesha did not want to disturb the neighbours. She asked me to keep quiet as the landlord did not allow overnight visitors. He was very strict, and if we were caught, she could get in trouble.

So, we entered quietly, and I sat on her bed. She came over beside me, took my hand, and looked me in the eyes. "Are you ready?" she said.

"Yes!" I replied, and she started to take her clothes off.

I watched in a trance. She approached the light switch and turned it off just after she removed her bra and revealed her magnificent breasts. I quickly got out of my clothes and into the bed.

The Venetian blinds let in a little light from the street, so I could see her as she walked towards me, brushing my face with her breasts as she climbed over. We were both getting hotter, starting to pant and sweat up.

As usual, I was nervous, but she guided me, and I entered her and soon after she was climaxing. Bugs Bunny would have been proud of how quickly I sped towards the finish line, but I was too nervous to get all the way there!

Meesha noticed, and she looked up at me and said, "Relax." She removed herself and disappeared beneath the blankets. Soon, she was performing oral sex on me and shortly after I was in ecstasy.

We lay there afterward in silence, absorbing each other's heat. I knew she was happy as we fell asleep.

Living in Italy

I woke later to hear her whispering at me. There was someone outside her window, she told me. I looked and saw a shadow.

It was her landlord! He was a bit creepy, apparently. Even though it was five in the morning, she motioned for me to get dressed, which I did, as quietly as I could, while the shadow moved off towards the front of the house.

This was not the goodbye I expected, but I still grabbed her in my arms and kissed her delicately. I looked in her eyes with a tear in mine and said goodbye. Then I jumped out the front window.

Meesha lived on the first floor, thank God. The landing was just a few feet down. No problem.

I headed home, finished my snooze, and woke to pack the rest of my things and say my goodbyes to Bruno, his wife and his parents. Then I headed over to the milk depot for my ride back to Osoppo.

My friends Caio and Zizza were waiting when my ride let me off about an hour away from Osoppo. We went home together as they pestered me about my adventure in Germany. Like most kids, I shared my conquests first, knowing they were eager to hear of any girl I may have "bonked". Boys will be boys.

At Osoppo, we stopped at Missanna's bar for a drink, then Caio and Zizza dropped me off home. I was tired from my long journey and it was late. Nonna was already in bed. The girls, it turned out, had been sent to a boarding school about 100 kilometres up the Adriatic coast. Dad was in bed, no doubt after a day of doing nothing but drinking.

As I made my way through the quiet house to my room, I heard Dad call out, "Who's there?"

I went to his bedroom and opened the door. There he was, in his bed, looking worse than when I'd left for Germany.

I felt so let down that he was slipping away. I could hardly think of how this must be affecting Grandma, since she had to live with it day after day. I got upset, and I started yelling, "Papa! Stop! Please stop this!" I grabbed his mattress and pulled it to the floor with him on it.

He laughed as he fell off and just lay there. So, I left, and began to sob as I went to my room.

That took care of my feelings of homesickness in an instant.

Eric Two Crowns (Supercabbie)

The next day I called down to Lignano to see if Roberto needed help in his restaurant. Roberto was happy to hear from me and said he had a job if I wanted it. It was June, and there were still a few months until the end of the summer season. He said he would pick me up in a couple of days while on his next visit and take me down, back to Lignano.

It's funny how things work out. The trip to Germany had been fruitful, bettering my language skills and putting another notch towards becoming an adult and man.

Chapter Fifteen
The Last Time

Later that year, I arrived home one evening, and found the front door locked. I knocked, and Dad opened it.

I was sixteen at the time, after months spent taking care of myself. But Dad still wanted to dictate his authority. When he smelt the cigarette smoke on me he said, angrily, "Have you been smoking?"

"Yes. So?" I replied.

He went to hit me, but I'd had enough. I was old enough, and I was big enough, and he had no right to dictate anything to me. I blocked his swing and shoved him back, standing ready. I told him in a firm, angry voice that he was never going to touch me again. I reminded him that I was putting money on the table to take care of Lydia and Dina, not him. I remember yelling, "Go and have another drink!" before pushing past him and going to my room.

I didn't like what I'd done, but it had to be said. Things changed after that, but not for the better for Dad. He'd lost his grip on me, and I could see he was losing his grip on his life. Drinking was taking its toll. I felt sorry for my sisters and Grandma, having to witness this bullshit. This was one reason both the girls were shipped off to a children's colony in Lignano, but that still left Nonna, who had to watch her son deteriorate and renege on his responsibilities.

I recall, years later, an evening when I was told Dad had not come home. I was in England at the time, but Jack had come home to visit. Jack informed me that they found him in a ditch with his bicycle. He'd been drunker than a skunk that evening and had totally lost it. He'd broken limbs and had been unconscious in the ditch all night. I was disgusted at the news.

The villagers had known him since he was a child. He had a reputation as being a happy-go-lucky kind of guy, always joking around. Now, the joke was on him, but we weren't laughing.

My main relief was that he was done bullying me and I was in control of my own destiny. However, it pained me to see such a strong-willed man turn weak and vulnerable. I entered his bedroom one afternoon when he was sleeping. The room smelled stale. He woke up and said, "what do you want, son?" but there was a look of stupor on him. He was, by then, permanently inebriated; just one drink was enough to put him back into a drunken state, it seemed. His eyes had turned yellow and his flesh was pale. His legs were swollen and, when I pushed my finger into his leg, it left a dent that took a while to return to normal. I knew he couldn't continue on this ride.

I began to think the worst and prepared myself emotionally for it. I couldn't wait for him to die, so I just carried on with my life.

Jack and his wife Titziana had been in England, living with me and my wife, when it finally happened. I arrived home to news that Dad was in hospital. This was back in 1987. Jack left for Italy to tend to him. Two days later he called to tell me Dad had passed away.

Despite it all, I felt myself choking up and asked if he had asked about me. I was hoping he had a last thought for me, but apparently, he hadn't. Instead, with his last breath, he howled out, "Alberta!" and died. He had only Mom in mind as his last thought.

It was a crying shame that his pride had led him to this tragic final scenario. I had admired him and despised him, but ultimately, I pitied him.

I recall that, for months, I would have nightmares, waking up in a cold sweat and shaking. Not having said goodbye, or even the chance to ask him why he had hurt me so, why he couldn't love me, or play with me like normal fathers with their sons.

Then, one morning, the feelings all disappeared. I woke up in a cold sweat, but this time I had been crying in my sleep. Somehow, that final nightmare had cleaned the slate once and for all. I dreamt I was at his funeral, standing by his open grave. All the

Living in Italy

black-dressed women whimpering and the priest giving his final benediction as they lowered his casket into the ground.

I wasn't crying, though. I couldn't get myself to shed a tear for him. All that went through my mind was how he had hurt me, emotionally and physically, for all those years, taking away my dreams of a happy life with Mom and my siblings. Taking away my life in Canada with my friends, and blocking any career I could have had in Hockey.

Suddenly I heard a voice, it was his voice. I looked to my right, it was Dad watching himself being buried. I could see he was crying, and he looked me in the eyes and said, "Sorry, Son. I'm so sorry. Please forgive me."

I burst out in tears and said, "Yes, Papa, I forgive you, and love you."

He smiled at me, then vanished.

It was the last nightmare I had about him. I was free again, and flicked the hate switch off for good. His belt, thrown into the sea of evil, never to strike again.

Part 3:
Going to England

Chapter Sixteen
Touchdown

I arrived in England with nothing more than one piece of luggage, an address, and a little money in my pocket. I was apprehensive, but excited. This was my chance to work and get more experience in the food industry, in a new country where I already spoke the language.

As the plane landed, I readied myself. I'd have to ask someone how to get to Streatham. There, I would introduce myself to a friend of Roberto's, who would set me up for a while. Roberto had said that these people were "Paesani" from Osoppo, who had helped him get going some years ago when he went there, for the same reasons as I was doing now.

Heathrow is a huge airport, but it's connected to London by the Underground, so I checked the map and made my way to Streatham by way of Brixton, South London.

I'd heard about Brixton from the famous Brixton Riots years before, and I thought the area was notorious for trouble. I was a little nervous on my arrival. After exiting the underground, I got a taxi and made my way to the L'Abetone Restaurant, only to find that it was closed. I'd arrived on a Sunday. I wondered, now what?

By fate, I found a taxi office nearby with people inside, and I asked if they knew the people who owned the restaurant. By a nice stroke of luck, they knew exactly who I was talking about and told me where they lived. Within a few minutes, a cab brought me to the restaurant owners' home.

I'd never seen, nor met, nor talked to Helena or anybody in the home, but Roberto was right about the Paesani. As soon as I explained myself, they invited me in out of the cold. It was a married middle-aged couple with a young son and daughter. The husband's name was Rafaelle, from Tuscany. The wife's name was Helena. They immediately asked if I was hungry or wanted a drink.

I soon learned that Dad had gone to school with Helena many years ago. She knew him well. They made me comfortable and asked what I was doing in England. I told them that I wanted to work. They shared a private word briefly and then said they would give me a place to stay. I could share a room with Oscar, a guy who was also the son of a Paesano from Osoppo. Grateful, I agreed.

Rafaelle assured me that they would help me while I looked for work, but I still felt a little insecure and vulnerable. Yes, I'd left home before and had been to Germany on my own, but this felt different. Perhaps it was because I thought that failure was not an option. There was no more safety net. It was time for me to get on with my life.

When we arrived back at Rafaelle's restaurant, which had the flat that I would share, he led me through the back door, up two flights of stairs, and introduced me to Oscar, another person who I'd never seen or talked to before, but who Rafaelle assured me was a good guy.

Oscar was a huge young man, six-foot-two, and built like a brick shithouse. On first impression, he seemed a gentle giant. Then I noticed a long scar on his left arm. It went from his upper arm all the way to his wrist. I pointed it out and asked what happened. He replied that he used to play rugby, and some guy had dug his cleats into him in a tackle, and that it had taken a hundred stitches to sow him back up.

Ouch!

Oscar was in London attending university, studying for a law degree.

It was about eight o'clock in the evening, I was hungry, so I asked Oscar where a good place would be to get something to eat. "Just across the street," he replied. "There's a burger joint."

Perfect, I thought. I hadn't had a burger in quite some time, as Italy isn't big on burgers; I'd only really had one while in Germany. I wanted one now though. My mouth was watering almost immediately.

Then Oscar mentioned that he was hungry too, so maybe I could get him some grub as well?

Eric Two Crowns (Supercabbie)

"No problem!" I said and made my way down to the street.

It was all new to me, a big city in a strange new country. I knew I had to be aware of my surroundings, as you never know what could happen. So, I was looking around at everything as I approached the crossing lights when I spotted the shop called the Charcoal Pit right in front of me. My target in sight, I looked to my left to check for traffic and I stepped out onto the road.

All of a sudden, I heard a blaring *honk,* and by pure instinct, I pulled back. I felt a breeze as the side-view mirror of a double decker bus missed my head by inches.

England was a strange country, all right. I'd forgotten about everybody driving on the left! Jesus, I thought. I haven't been here a few hours and I was already nearly roadkill!

I stood on the sidewalk a moment as I got my senses back. Then I gathered myself, looked *right* instead of left, and crossed. I ordered our food and went back to the flat and told Oscar about my little adventure. He didn't laugh too much. He just told me to be very careful until I got used to the roads.

Believe me, from that moment on, I was super careful. I'd dodged death a few times already in my short time on Earth, and Oscar even told me, "You're using up your nine lives in a hurry, Eric!"

That evening, after having wolfed down our food, I said goodnight to Oscar and went to bed. There wasn't much heat in the apartment, so I lay there awhile, shivering, wondering about my future.

I must be crazy, I thought, going on a journey to who knows where.

I had done it on a whim. I can remember the date, and who put the idea in my head.

Late in 1978, I was in Forni di Sopra, having fun with a bunch of girls visiting from England: Shelley, Ann and Brenda. I learned that they lived in Chelmsford, north of England. Shelly told me that her father owned a factory and could probably give me work if I needed it.

At the time, that sounded like a great idea. I said to myself, "why not?" and, in January of 1979, abruptly left Osoppo for England, with no real plan.

Going to England

Had I made a mistake? There was a lot more to get used to than I thought there would be; not just the people driving on the wrong side of the road.

Oscar was kind enough to take me around for the first couple of days. Then I packed my suitcase and made my way to Chelmsford. Navigating was a challenge. I'd never seen so many lines at once, with all so many colours. Still, I figured it out, found my way to Waterloo Station, and took British Rail for a short ride north. I walked through Chelmsford, looking for the address Shelly had given me. I found a modest three-bedroom house.

I knocked on the door, but no one answered. I knocked a little harder, but still there was no reply.

My fears started to rise. It was worse than when I found the closed restaurant in London. I couldn't see anybody to talk to or help me, so what the Hell was I going to do, now?

It had gotten quite cold. I decided I needed to get to the nearest warm place to plan my next move. I set off in a random direction, my suitcase getting heavier by the minute, and by chance came to a pub. I walked in, dropping my case beside a stool at the bar and sat down.

While I caught my breath, a man came out and greeted me, saying he was closed for the afternoon break. I thought this was a strange way to say hello. Then he peered at my suitcase and asked me where I was going.

I showed him the address Shelley had given me, told him who I was hoping to see, and asked if I could have a glass of water or something. He was nice enough to serve me a Coke and let me wait inside a while. School would soon be over, he said. She would probably be home shortly.

It was nearly 3:30 p.m. I waited until four before thanking the gentleman and making my way back to Shelley's address. She hadn't given me a phone number, so I couldn't call her. I knocked on the door again and, to my relief, it opened to reveal Shelley, looking shocked to see me.

"What are you doing here?" she exclaimed.

"This is the address you gave me," I replied. "You told me I should come here if I ever needed a job."

She started laughing. "I never thought you'd actually do it!"

Eric Two Crowns (Supercabbie)

That's when I really knew that something was wrong. Maybe I shouldn't have taken that leap of faith.

But, once she stopped laughing, Shelley invited me in, looking rather sheepish.

It turned out that she had a boyfriend. Also, her father didn't own a factory, he was just its foreman. To put it mildly, it was a blow.

Her brother came in a few minutes later and introduced himself, and Shelley explained the situation while I stood, feeling really awkward. Still, I'm glad to say that they seemed willing to help me out. They checked me into a bed and breakfast where I could stay overnight. It wasn't expensive, offering only a small room with a bed and a side table, but it was clean, so I was happy. Then we hung out at her place for a while, thinking about what to do that evening.

We decided we would go to a club Shelley knew and party with some of her friends. It was another awkward moment, as I was the "candle" as they say, while everyone else were couples. Not only did Shelly have a boyfriend, so did Ann. Brenda was single, but things didn't click between us; they hadn't really at Forni di Sopra, either. That's just the way things work out.

I remember Roberto telling me that, in England, the girls will ask you to dance – something unheard of in Italy. Roberto was right. Candle or not, that's exactly what happened as I sat there, pondering my next move. A girl on the dance floor gave me a look. We made eye-contact a few times, and I played it cool. Within minutes, the girl was in front of me, reaching out for my hand. *Wow!* I thought. *That was easy!*

Although I was having a good time, I was also worrying about tomorrow. Where would I work? What would I do? The adventure with Shelley and Ann had been nice, but now that I was in England, it was time for me to move on.

Chapter Seventeen
Die Hard

Though we think ourselves as immortal when we're young, the truth is, we're not. I learned that the hard way with my friends Ivano, Zizza and Dennis. At the time, they were 16, 19 and 17 respectively.

Ivano was one of the first friends I made after I arrived in Italy. We were in school together and, like most kids, had our interests. We both liked fishing in the crystal-clear waters of the streams that came down from the Alps, where we could catch rainbow trout.

Ivano and I also loved our bikes. As we got older, that love moved over to 50cc motorbikes. We would make our way, on these bikes, down to our favourite fishing spots and try to catch whatever we could. Ivano taught me how to hook the line and lots of other techniques to try and outwit the little creatures. The fish in these streams weren't large, but they always put up a good fight. I loved feeling the pole bend and tug as the fish snatched the lure. We'd toss the small ones back, but the larger ones were taken home to eat. They were sweet, and the waters they swam in were uncontaminated. In fact, we'd swim in these cold streams, and drink the fresh water.

Ivano was slender and not too tall. He had a dark hair and Beatles-style haircut. His nickname should have been "Trouble", since he got into all sorts of predicaments.

One evening, my family and his were heading out to visit friends in a town nearby. With the adults all partying, Ivano and I decided to play around, outside the house.

The house was on the Portebana Road. We mucked around in

Eric Two Crowns (Supercabbie)

a ditch by the field next door and came upon this pile of gravel. On seeing this pile, Ivano just looked at me and said, "Watch this!"

The Portebana Road was always busy, cars passing every few seconds. Ivano made me duck out of sight, and ducking himself, he took a handful of gravel and tossed it at an oncoming car. I heard the gravel smack against the hood and the windshield as the car passed.

"What the hell are you doing?" I shouted. But Ivano just laughed and picked up another handful of gravel, which he threw at the next car.

Suddenly the car swerved, pulled over to the side of the road, and screeched to a stop!

There we were, in the ditch, shitting our pants waiting and watching as the car did a U-turn and came back our way. Ivano wasn't laughing anymore. He was looking scared.

We bolted. We ran towards the house and jumped in my family's car and locked the door. We ducked back in the back seat and pulled a blanket over us. As we peeked through the back window, we could see the car pull into the driveway.

A man got out, came straight over to us and peered inside. We stayed as still as we could, but we could hear each other's heartbeat as the man tried to open the door. A few minutes of stillness and quiet followed, and then we heard the man get back into his vehicle, close the door, then drive away.

Slowly, we came out of hiding. We got out of the car, looking around carefully to make sure we were safe.

Ivano nodded to the ditch and said, "Let's go and see if he's still around."

I was thinking this was a bad idea. I became more sure when he passed the ditch and crossed the road.

"What the hell are you doing?" I asked, running after him.

"Let's go over by that bush and see if the guy's still around," he replied.

I knew we were pushing it, but even so, we crossed the road, and within seconds, we saw the driver of the car waiting by a building, and he spotted us.

Immediately he ran at us and grabbed Ivano, who fell to the ground, kicking and shouting. I ran up and kicked the guy right

Going to England

in the ass! The guy let go of Ivano and went at me, but I ran for it. As I looked back, I could see Ivano had gotten to his feet and was running in the opposite direction.

I managed to give the guy the slip, and eventually I made my way back to the house, wondering where Ivano was. I found him when I got there. The guy had gotten a few good blows on Ivano, and when I saw him back at the house, I could see the bruises. His mother Nicholina was scolding him, demanding to know what he had done.

Ivano said that he'd climbed a tree and had slipped and fallen to the ground. I just stood there quietly. He got scolded some more for being so reckless, but his parents bought the story, and the truth was never discovered.

On another occasion, I turned up at Ivano's house and found he had a new Great Dane puppy. I thought it was unsteady on its legs, looking kind of goofy, but I figured it was just a normal young pup. Then all of a sudden Ivano grabs a bottle of wine and opens it.

"What are you doing?" I asked. We never drank in Ivano's house.

"Watch this!" he replied. He poured the wine into the dog's bowl. The puppy started slurping it up! Within minutes, we were watching the thing wobbling around, losing its balance, flopping all over the place. We laughed hysterically at the little thing tumbling around all over the yard. That was Ivano.

Ezio, or "Zizza" as he preferred to be called, was the opposite of Ivano. He was very strong, but he was also gentle. I knew him because we were both apprentices with the Filli Christ Plumbing company and would often work on sites together.

On one occasion, Zizza picked up an oxygen canister and an acetylene canister, one under each arm, and climbed up three flights of stairs without stopping. They must have weighed 100 pounds each!

He always smiled and was a constant companion all of us hanging out as boys. Ezio never had a bad bone in him. Even when he bought himself a new scooter, he let us try it out. Usually no one would lend you their motorbike, let alone a new one, but Zizza would do anything for a friend, and that's what brought him to his demise.

Dennis, on the other hand, was a loose cannon. He was a stu-

Eric Two Crowns (Supercabbie)

dious type and spent more time at home than with us boys. His father was quite strict with him. He lived across the street from us, and we always heard his father shouting at him to come inside, but when Dennis was in our company, he could stir it up.

His antics were like Dennis the Menace. His immature, yet comical character made us laugh. We always liked having him around.

It was shortly after I arrived in England, calling Italy to check in with my family when I learned the horrible news.

Dennis had just passed his driving test. He told Zizza that he wanted to take a girl back to her village in the mountains and asked if they could go in Zizza's car. Of course, Zizza said yes. Dennis asked if he could drive the car, and Zizza said yes. Zizza just didn't know how to say no. Ivano went along for the ride as well.

It was early evening and it had been raining. The mountain roads of the Alps can be dangerous in the best of conditions. There are hairpin corners everywhere that test the best of drivers.

Apparently, they were approaching a downhill corner with a bridge that turned sharp left with metal railings as barriers. Dennis lost control of the car, then, and crashed through that railing. The car was later found at the bottom of the ravine, having landed on its roof. Everyone inside was dead, the impact having broken everyone's neck.

If I hadn't travelled to England on a whim, maybe I might have been in that car that evening? Who knows? Fate is fate, and again I saw how fragile and unpredictable life is.

I had nightmares about the incident and, on one occasion, I swear I saw Ivano walking down a street in London, only to suddenly disappear.

On my last visit to Osoppo, I went to the cemetery to pay my respects. I wept by each headstone as I looked at the photos that are displayed on each grave. I remembered all of the dear and cherished memories of our youth together. I couldn't find Dennis' grave, however, and when I inquired, I was told his family had buried him at his birthplace, a town further north in the mountains.

I will always remember my dear friends and I await the day when I will see them again.

Chapter Eighteen
John Virgo and I

John Virgo is a world-renown snooker player. At least, he was back in the 70s and 80s. He retired around 1995 from professional play, but he remains a celebrity, and quite a character. He still is a senior commentator for the BBC, and was a former Chairman of the World Professional Billiards and Snooker Association.

I met him, as fate would have it, in 1979. It was at the Fife Road snooker centre in Kingston-upon-Thames in southwest London.

I'd been playing the game from when I was ten. Mark Snyder and Gary Beech would pick me up from school in St. Agatha. Gary had a little green MGB sportscar with a black soft top. I could just barely squeeze in the back, as it was really just a two-seater. Yes, I should have been on the bus with the other kids, but we'd timed it carefully. The bus would take an hour or so, going past the other kids' homes and their families' farms before getting to my drop off. That gave us time enough to go into the city, park at Waterloo Square and head downstairs to the bowling alley, which had a few pool and snooker tables.

I was always excited to play. I didn't have my own cue at the time. The ones on the stick rack were always poor, but they served me well enough. If I brought a stick home, Dad would probably have told me to get rid of it. He might even have thought I'd stolen it, as I rarely had money, and Dad never gave me any.

Part of the excitement was also worry. I was afraid I would get home too late, long after the school bus would have dropped us off, and I would have to make excuses about why I had taken so long getting home. That didn't happen. What happened instead was that, one day when I got home, Mom said that the school had called telling her that I was being picked up by two guys in a car and not getting on the bus.

Needless to say, when Dad found out, I was given the usual beating. That stopped the pick-up arrangement.

But I still loved the game. On occasion, my family and I would visit the Cuzzi family, who had one of these tiny 3-by-2 pool tables we played on.

Tony and Carlo Cuzzi were about the same age as Jack and I. My Dad and their dad Giovanni were good friends from Italy. Their Dad came from Gemona, which is only a few kilometres away from Osoppo. I looked Tony and Carlo up the day after I came back to Canada. They helped me settle back into Canada when I returned from abroad. Carlo passed away at the early age of 39, a heart attack. I will always remember him. Tony is still a friend of mine today.

I remember that the house they had on Layton Street had a laundry chute that went from the main floor to the basement. We would slide down that thing, into a laundry basket full of clothes that would soften the landing. We loved that!

But back to John Virgo and I.

When I moved to the United Kingdom, I arrived with my own cue. Obviously, I had to find a place to play. I made a few inquiries and ended up in a town called Kingston-upon-Thames, near Walton-on-Thames, which eventually became my home.

I walked into the Fife Road Snooker Centre and was surprised by the clean and spacious hall. I'd expected it to be all smoky and drab, with shady dudes hanging around, but this place was classy.

There was a bar lounge called the Ray Reardon Lounge. Reardon was known in the snooker world as Dracula because that's how he looked. He also won the world championship six times. He is from Wales, and I had the pleasure of meeting him once.

Anyway, I asked if I could have a table. The manager said, "no problem!" and turned one on for me. I didn't know anyone, so I asked if anybody wanted a game, would he send them over? "Sure, no problem!" the manager replied, and off he went.

I practiced for a while, and then this short guy came over and asked me for a game. "Sure thing," I said.

He suddenly opened up a small case and started to screw onto

Going to England

his wrist a rake-type thing that was specially made for him. He'd lost his left hand, probably in some accident, but I didn't ask.

So, we played. And he was good. He really gave me a hard time, but his spirit was good. I could feel his wanting to win. I won in the end, but it was close, there is no mercy in competition. He held his own like a grinder in life.

He was a nice guy, who'd noticed that I'd been checking out the cues on display. He asked me if I wanted to buy one. I tried one – a "two-piece" – that he said was decent, and I rolled it on the table to see if it was straight. Just then, a tall man came along, picked it up off the table, and said, "That's not how you check it.... This is how!" And with both hands he held it like a rifle, turning it in his fingers, and pointing to the light on the ceiling.

Well, I wondered who this dink was, sticking his nose in my business, but I didn't say anything, and he just gave it back and said, "It's good!" before walking off.

I looked at the kid I'd played against, and he was in shock.

"Do you know who that was?" he said.

I didn't.

"That's John Virgo!"

I thought, well, who the hell is John Virgo? Remember, I'd only been in England a few months, and I had no clue that Virgo was the 1978 UK Open Champion, ranked in the top ten in the world. I didn't know it then, but we were to become good friends a few years later.

#

The "Walton Snooker Centre" opened around 1988. I was so excited that a real snooker hall was opening near my house, that I made it a point to be the first person to pot a ball in the place. So, on the Saturday morning of opening, I was in line with a few others, waiting for the doors to open.

Though I wasn't the first in line, I raced in, got to my table on the second floor and quickly picked up the white ball and a red and immediately potted a red without racking the balls up. I'd done it! I breathed a sigh of relief.

Needless to say, the Walton Snooker Centre became my second home. I would spend countless hours playing there.

Jim Bates was the general manager. The owner, Len Hurles-

Eric Two Crowns (Supercabbie)

Benson and Hedges Masters tournament. Canadian Cliff Thorburn (right) vs. Ray Reardon (left). Cliff won this match.

tone, ran a classy joint. There was no smoking, no drinking, no eating, and no placing your chalk on the tables. Doing any of these things would get you an earful. There were nineteen tables in total, always brushed, vacuumed and ironed, along with two fruit machines (what we call slot machines) waiting for suckers to waste their money (me being one of them).

I became an above average player and got the respect of my peers there. One year, I was asked by Jim to play a marathon of 24 hours for charity. Jim, Dave Young, Bradley Dodds and myself sought out people to sponsor us and we managed to raise around 2,500 pounds. We were exhausted after twenty-four hours of play, but it was great.

I remember going to the BBC studios in London with the boys, to present the cheque to Lionel Blair, one of Britain's famous dancers. We could see some girls there who appeared on Page Three of the British Sun tabloid. Dave in particular was in seventh heaven seeing those beauties. Back at the club, we were asked to pose for photographs by the Surrey Herald for an article that highlighted our efforts.

One day, around eleven in the morning, I was in the snooker centre, practicing on my own when, suddenly, John Virgo comes in.

By this time, I knew who he was, and I was in awe. He was still a pro, touring all over Britain as well as abroad.

He was on the other side of the plate glass window that separated the lounge from the playing area and he was talking to Jim.

Going to England

Then he came through the door and walked towards me, asking if I wanted to play with him? Yikes!

Obviously, I agreed.

As John went to get his cue, I began to shake. I was going to be playing one of the best in the world, the thought of it was just exhilarating. Of course, he won. He'd even spotted me forty points a game for five quid, but our friendship was born. After he'd taken my money, he asked if I played golf? I said that I did.

"Great!" he replied. "Do you want to play eighteen right now?"

"Absolutely!" I replied. I knew well enough never to turn down such opportunities. So, off we went.

The West Byfleet Golf Club was not far away, and when we arrived, John was recognized immediately and some people started asking him for his autograph. The guy on duty said, "No charge!" to John. Nothing beats free golf!

The deal was that I had to give him strokes, as I was better than he was, but it turned out that we sort of levelled out between the two games. He usually won at snooker, and I usually won at golf.

John would often phone me out of the blue and ask me to go with him on tournaments or exhibitions that he would either play in or commentate for. Along with his Mancunian accent, he was a natural laugh-getter, constantly cracking jokes. He even does impersonations, which you can look up.

I recall one time when he asked me to join him at the Benson & Hedges Masters at the Wembley conference centre in London. He was commentating, and he left me a VIP pass at the box office. Another friend, Rodney Hutton, would be waiting in the hotel next door. He was an Irish golf pro and a friend who ran the prestigious Thames Ditton Golf Club. He'd often let John and I play at his club for free.

As I walked through the foyer, I looked towards the bar lounge, and there was Rodney, sitting and sipping on his favorite tipple: rum and coke.

John was propping up the bar with two other gentlemen. John is six-foot-two, and these two guys were taller than him. I wondered who they were? John spotted me and beckoned me over, introducing me to Rocky Taylor and Alistair Ross. I didn't know those names, but as they were friends of John, they were friends of mine as well.

Eric Two Crowns (Supercabbie)

Turns out Rocky was, and still is, a respected stuntman in the movie business. I learned that he'd made movies with such actors as Charles Bronson, Roger Moore, Harrison Ford and Sean Connery, just to name a few. Alistair Ross was a retired professional rugby player and a snooker columnist for the Sun Newspaper.

After being introduced, I took a seat with Rodney at his table.

Within a few minutes, John Street (the referee of the just-concluded match), his wife and what seemed to be their granddaughter, sat down in an area cordoned off by a low wall made up of brown bricks with plants all around the top. Rodney nudged me and said, "Eric, look at that bloke over there." He was pointing at the entrance to the private area where some guy was staggering up, dressed in baggy pants and with his shirt hanging out. He looked drunk.

He shouted at Mr. Street, the referee, then turned around and dropped his pants, mooning the referee, along with his wife and the child. Then he pulled up his pants, walked away a bit, but then turned around and dropped his trousers again, full frontal this time, exposing himself at them. Rodney and I just stared in disbelief.

Then the drunken man picks up a pint of beer from a nearby table and throws it up into the air, sending a shower over the nearby patrons, who were dressed in top hats, tails or in fancy dresses.

By then, a waiter was rushing over, but the guy grabs another beer and dumps it over the waiter's head. Then punches were thrown.

Immediately, Rocky and Alister came rushing over, but the drunken man had friends with him, and they joined the fight. Within seconds, it was a melee. There must have been about twenty guys fighting. Rocky and Alistair were among the good guys; Rocky throwing punches and Alistair holding two guys in a headlock one in each arm and rushing them towards a wall. Tables and chairs started flying.

I kept out of it, as did John and Rodney. The last thing I wanted was to be thrown in jail and charged with something. Even if we were with the good guys, it would still be a problem. When the bobbies came, John, Rodney and I hightailed it out of there into another lounge.

Going to England

I watched the tabloids for the next couple of days, expecting to see the news. Alistair worked for the Sun, after all, but nothing was reported. Only the people I told at the club knew what had happened, and they thought it was hilarious. I'm sure it was hushed up. After all, John had a reputation to protect.

In the washroom later, I asked Rocky how he felt. He said that he was in some pain, and I later realized that an old injury was acting up. Apparently, Rocky had been in one of the *Death Wish* movies with Charles Bronson, doing a stunt that had to be planned with split-second timing. It wasn't. The explosion hurled him out too far, and he missed the boxes below the building that were supposed to cushion his body. He'd broken his pelvis along with many other bones. Apparently, screws and bolts were keeping him together.

He'd had to fight for compensation, and filed a lawsuit which he eventually won, earning himself a million-pound payout.

John would invite me to tournaments where I was tickled pink to mingle among the greats of the game such as Jimmy White, or the legend Alex Higgins. Alex sat beside me on two occasions, twitching away like his usual self. On one occasion John had invited me to the world championships in Sheffield. I'd been doing well in my businesses by then. The day I went, I picked up my newly bought BMW. I was feeling good about my life, feeling like I finally belonged. I'd even developed an English accident and thought of England as my permanent home.

Sheffield is known as the Steel City. I'd never been there before, so after a few wrong turns, I parked near the Crucible Theatre, where the tournament was held. My VIP pass was waiting at the stage entrance office. John was commentating for the BBC once again, and had a schedule to keep, so I kept to myself while he did his thing. The bar lounge was the usual place to hang out. John eventually turned up and we had a few drinks together.

He asked if I wanted to sit in the commentary booth with both him and Ted Lowe? "Absolutely!" I said. Ted was a legend by then, the voice of snooker, with a distinct, slightly raspy voice softly delivering every word. He was a pleasant man who liked white wine. I had to be the runner if I wanted to be in the booth, and he was a pretty thirsty guy, so I went on a few excursions to fetch his favourite tipple. It was my pleasure.

Eric Two Crowns (Supercabbie)

I witnessed Alex Higgins running around frantically, placing bets on the greyhounds, during his break. He had even asked strangers to lend him money! I witnessed it myself. He was an addictive person in character. Most geniuses are.

It was great watching the monitor. There was just one. The booth was raised high, looking down at the table. John and Ted had a microphone in front of them, on the desk into which they'd speak into, sharing facts and their opinions about the match and the players.

The evening match featured the flamboyant Kirk Stevens from Scarborough (Canada!) and another player whose name I couldn't recall — possibly John Parrot from Liverpool. I'm only guessing because, when I went out for a brief walk, I came back in through the stage door and was greeted with screams and cheers for "JOHN!! JOHN!!" Some of these girls were asking for my autograph, thinking I was him, as we looked a bit similar, so I just bowed my head and quickly went inside.

I recall that Kirk Stevens had a reputation for being fond of the "crumpets" (or, chicks, as we say here). He always wore light-coloured suits during his matches along with matching shoes. He had shaggy blond-brown hair and a handsome guy indeed. He certainly stood out amongst the other players, that's for sure.

The Sun tabloid was always looking for a story, and there were many things going on in the snooker world at the time, back in the early eighties. The boys were living it up, and the papers revealed that drugs were rampant on the snooker circuit. People were talking about it all the time. It was big news.

John Virgo himself was centre spread when he divorced his wife, Avril. I'd actually posted John's legal papers for his divorce. Frankly, it wasn't a surprise to me, as a photographer managed to get a shot of them sitting on a set of cement stairs, seated back to back, each looking away from each other. You couldn't have posed that nearly so well.

I saw a lot of it happen. I could have lengthened my stay in England had I revealed some of the dirt to tabloid reporters and gotten paid for it. But I am not a snitch. I would join John on many occasions, at tournaments and exhibitions. These were memorable times, mingling with the greats of the game.

Chapter Nineteen
Pay up or Else

There are ways to gain respect; you can do it by deeds, or by force. I preferred to use deeds as I am a softy at heart, but there was something to be said about having danger written all over you. You should never mistake kindness for weakness. People can turn on a dime into nasty creatures, depending on the circumstance.

Terry Burke called himself an "Art Dealer". He was a regular visitor to the Walton Snooker Centre. He came across as a clumsy dude, ducking and diving through life. His shoulders twitched continuously, like he was always nervous about something.

At the time, I was a handy snooker player, perhaps among the top half-dozen players in the club. Terry was always looking to wager his skills against other members, preferring of course to challenge the lesser players so he could make a "Quid or Two". We had butted heads on the table a few times, and though he wasn't that bad a player, I usually get the better of him.

One afternoon, I was practicing on my own when he came over, case in hand, asking for a money match. I was happy to oblige, knowing he'd crumble under pressure. We agreed to a duel (best of three) with £20 on the line ($50). I won the first match handily, but it was close enough for Terry to ask, "double or nothing?" Now we had £40 on the line (close to $100). I didn't have anything to lose, as I was up. Terry was already twitching.

As we started our second match though, my friend Neil Clift walked into the club and grabbed a spot on the sidelines, watching us. I gave him a thumbs up, letting him know we were playing for money.

Eric Two Crowns (Supercabbie)

Again, I tanned Terry's ass, and I could see he was getting into second gear with his frustration. Again, he asked me, "double or nothing?" Now we were at £80 ($200). Neil was cheering for me as we were good mates. Again, I won, again keeping it close to give Terry hope, and again Terry asked for another double or nothing. We were now at £160 ($400). That was a week's wages for the average person at the time.

I was in a groove, as cool as a cucumber. After winning the first frame of a three-frame set, I started pulling away in the second frame and, with one red ball left to sink, saw Terry unscrewing his cue stick. He started to put it away in his case, turning away from the table, which told me that he was conceding. I cleared the table, just to make sure, as he walked towards the bar, Neil still watching.

I thought, *Cool! An easy $400 in the bank!* I went over to Terry at the bar with my hand outstretched, expecting it to be soon lined with cash. Terry, looking really frustrated, did nothing and said nothing.

"Hey," I said. "Where's the cash? Come on! Cough it up, Terry!"

Terry shook his head. "I'm not paying you."

"What are you talking about?"

"You fouled the green with your sleeve," he replied.

"Ah, I don't think so, mate," I said. "If you saw it, why didn't you call the foul while we were playing?"

I called over to Neil, who had been watching closely, and asked him if I had touched the green. He agreed that I wasn't even close to the green. Terry was trying it on. He was known to be a bit of a "wanker" at times, so I assured him he'd be paying me my money, one way or the other.

Gary King was playing the fruit machine (slot machine), and he could hear the conversation. He made an off-hand comment along the lines of, "Ooo! Tough man, Eric!"

I'd never considered myself a tough guy, but I knew a friend who was, and he had offered his services to me, if I needed it. I shouldn't name him, so let me just call him MH.

Now, MH was intimidating, to say the least. He was a professional heavyweight boxer in his day, and an international rugby

Going to England

player for Wales. He was 6 feet, 2 inches tall and weighed around 230 pounds. He knew how to intimidate you.

I met MH on a golf course where he refused my invitation to a three ball with his guest, who turned out to be his brother. I wasn't offended, as I'd just wanted company. There were two women behind me I could ask instead. I asked them, and they said, "No problem!" and we were ready to go.

All of a sudden, as I was practicing my swing, MH came over to me and said, "Okay, you can join is if you want."

I said, "Sure!" then apologized to the ladies, asking to join the guys ahead, and they said, "No problem," again.

I asked MH why he changed his mind, and he said, "You have a nice swing, and we're just learning to play." So, we teed off, the three of us, and a bond was formed.

When we became closer friends, MH invited Marylyn and I to his home for dinner and to introduce us to his wife. I'd told him that I liked boxing and had dabbled in the sport in my youth. I asked if he had any videos of himself in a real boxing match, and he did. He pulled one out for us to watch.

I recall his demeanor in the ring, moving around his opponent with a nimbleness that made me think of the great Mohammad Ali. Needless to say, I was impressed. And the guy he knocked out in the video was Hughroy Currie! Hughroy would go on to become Britain's heavyweight champion. How had MH taken him out so handily? Apparently Hughroy had whispered something in MH's ear he didn't like.

"Why did you ever quit boxing?" I asked MH. "You could have gone far with your talent."

He replied, "I didn't want this handsome face ruined, that's why!" and he gave me a grin.

Anyway, back to Terry, the welsher. I was thinking of calling MH and taking him up on his offer. I wasn't about to get into a fight with Terry myself because I'd built a reputation as being a businessman and a gentleman, but I still wanted to teach Terry some respect.

Well, first, I made sure to give Terry proper warning. I told him that if I didn't have my money in the next ten minutes, I would have to make a call.

Eric Two Crowns (Supercabbie)

That's when I noticed the club going silent around me. Terry began to look worried but he didn't move to pay me. Ten minutes passed, and I said, "Okay, Terry, your ten minutes are up."

I took out my wallet and pulled out a piece of paper that had MH's number on it. I went to the phone and dialed. "Hi, 'M', it's me, Eric," I said when he picked up. "I need you to do me a favour…"

I told him about my problem, speaking quietly into the phone. At the other end of the line, I could hear MH's tone change. He asked me if Terry was still there.

"Yes," I said.

All I heard was, "I'm on my way. Try to keep him there."

I hung up, feeling a rush as I was now in a position to be feared, and not just by Terry. I looked around and could see people staring at me. People had heard me demanding my cash and saying my threat. So, I walked calmly over to Terry and told him to leave, warning him that if he was still there when MH arrived, he would be sorry. Then I made my way back to the table and invited Neil to play with me while we waited.

Neil leaned close and asked if I'd actually made a call, or if I was just bluffing.

"Wait and see," I replied.

He knew then that I was serious, and I noticed the change in his attitude right away. He became quiet and subdued as we started to play.

Out of the corner of my eye, I saw Terry picking up his cue case and leaving. I was actually relieved to see him go, as I didn't really want to see anybody get beaten up. I settled down playing more snooker.

Moments later, Neil called over to me. "Hey, Eric! The door!"

I looked over to the entrance and saw MH standing there, his fists clenched, in a semi-rage and pumped up, ready to do the business. I hurried over to him and told him that the target had left, I invited him to join me for a drink, to get settled down.

I knew then that if MH had gotten hold of Terry, he would have messed him up really bad. I also recall how silent the place was as MH joined me at the bar. He and I spoke for a few moments

Going to England

before he left, assuring me that he would come back if I couldn't settle my deal with Terry.

In that moment, with all eyes watching I felt the power, something I'd never felt before. It was the power to have someone physically punished if they insulted, welched or disrespected me. It was kind of addictive, and something I knew I shouldn't overuse.

Either way, MH's message must have gotten across to Terry because, an hour later, Terry came back to the club, obviously looking around for any threats that might be lurking around corners. Spotting me, he approached and asked if we could talk in private. There, he gave me a proposition.

"I'll be here tomorrow," he said, "to play you for double or nothing again." ($800!)

After a moment's thought, I agreed, but with one stipulation. Since he had 'tried it on', claiming my sleeve had brushed a ball, I insisted we have a referee to oversee the match, and it would be at his expense.

Terry looked at me. "Who the hell am I going to get to ref?"

I looked over at Gary King, who was still playing the Fruit Machine. I pointed at him. "That's our ref. Gary will do it. Pay him twenty pounds." That was a reasonable rate, since a best-of-five match would likely only take up to two hours to finish.

After getting Gary to agree to the job, I then asked Jim, the manager, to hold the prize money until the match was concluded. This was going to be absolutely official. With everything arranged Terry knew that at least, he wouldn't have to face MH. With relief visible on Terry's face, he left.

Neil was impressed with me at how I'd thrown down the gauntlet.

The next morning, I arrived at the club early, just to get some practice in. Again, I had nothing to lose and everyone knew that Terry had better turn up, or I'd put out some feelers to track Terry down. Still, I was a little nervous over whether MH would have to be called upon again.

To my relief, Terry walked in a few minutes later with his cue case, pulled out the money, and handed it over to Jim at the bar. Knowing that I was watching, Jim counted it up, and gave me a nod: £320 at stake.

Eric Two Crowns (Supercabbie)

Gary also turned up a few minutes later, asking us what table we were going to play on. After a little discussion, we decided we should head to the back room, where we could play away from the main room's noise. However, as we headed towards the back room, a small audience followed us.

I didn't mind. I was pumped up and ready for the challenge. A toss of the coin meant that Terry started, breaking off.

Already, he was visibly twitching his shoulders. His face was red. I had him!

I'm generally a fast player, but just to tick him off, I took my time. I methodically took my shots, sinking balls, watching him wince each time I hit the pocket. By the time I'd won the first two frames, he was sweating from the heat and the pressure I was laying on him. One more frame, and it was all over, He conceded with three reds left on the table. With people cheering and clapping, Terry made his way to the lounge with his tail between his legs.

I think Terry might have learned a few lessons that day: don't gamble with empty pockets. Don't pull fast ones.

At the same time, I learned something valuable as well: I had a dangerous weapon in my hand in the form of a phone number that could change someone's fate in a heartbeat. That didn't sit right with me. I told myself not to get into that position again, to always see the money before the game begins. Then I'd never have to stoop to darker methods.

At the same time, MH was a friend, and having powerful friends is definitely good security.

Part 4:
Marylyn

Chapter Twenty
For Better or For Worse

In hindsight, I probably should have said no to marriage, at least for a while, because I was way too young. Even back then, not many guys in my generation got hitched at only twenty-years-old.

However, it was a leap year, and Marylyn told me that, in England, a girl could propose to a man on a leap year, so would I marry her?

Of course, I said yes. I was in love. All it took was that pea that I threw at her in the kitchen of the Seven Hills hotel.

Let me explain.

I was working at the Seven Hills hotel in Cobham, Surrey, and the other waiters were buzzing. They said that there was a "hot new blonde chick" who'd started working as a chambermaid. Of course, I was intrigued, and I kept my eye out for her.

I soon found out who she was when I deposited dinner plates in the dishwashing area, one evening. There she was, her golden hair swaying as she walked, wearing a black outfit. She stood out like a shiny diamond. Her body was slender, yet curvy. She looked at me and our eyes met for a moment. Then she turned away.

Not knowing what possessed me, I picked up a pea off a plate and threw it at her. She spun around, saw my playful smile, and gave me a smile in return. At that moment, I was cooked.

I followed her up a few stairs as she went to her quarters, then she turned around, giving me a look that made me back off, but I think secretly she was as thunderstruck as I was. From that moment, I could only think of her and how I could make her mine.

The other guys gossiped about her, and so far as I knew, she was single. I also had competition, however, in the form of a fellow

Marylyn

waiter named Alfio. I could tell that she liked him, so I knew I had to get my foot in the door before it was too late.

As the days passed, I did my job, and I found myself in need of fresh linen. It was usually handed out once a week by the head housekeeper, but I'd forgotten to get my order in ahead of the Saturday noon deadline. I knew head housekeeper Maria wouldn't help me, because for her a deadline was a deadline. Then I saw Marylyn and asked if she could get me some fresh linen.

"Happy to oblige," she said. I thanked her and mentioned she could drop the linen off in my room, and that the key to that room would be on the frame above the door. As part of our job, we had quarters at the hotel.

Later, when I arrived at my quarters and let myself in, Marylyn immediately yelled from her room beside mine, "There's a spider in your bed!"

"What?" I yelled back.

I unlocked my door, she had tidied up my room and my bed was made. There was no spider on it, but, just in case, I lifted up the sheets and there it was: black, hairy looking but very rubbery. I laughed when I saw it, and I could hear her laughing through the wall.

That was the clincher. I knew that something had started between us.

Marylyn worked hard at the hotel, taking on extra rooms and then a night shift washing dishes. I kept my eye on her and played it cool.

One evening after work, however, I went back to my room to sleep, and could hear music coming from her room through the thin walls. I banged on my wall, asking her to keep the music down, and she shouted back at me to shut up, as she had company. She did, too; I could hear girls laughing through the wall. It made for a restless night.

The next day after work, I went back to my room and noticed she was in. I knocked on her door and she answered, inviting me in.

We sat on her bed and chatted. She asked me where I was from, and when I told her I was born in Canada, she became extra curious. She pulled out an atlas and had me flip through it. I point-

Eric Two Crowns (Supercabbie)

ed to Kitchener on the map, and sowed her my birthplace on the west bank of the St. Lawrence River.

Through all this, we were shifting closer together, and one thing lead to another, as they say. I began to kiss her all over. I was kissing her belly when I noticed some scars. I asked what these were.

"Stretch marks," she replied, then explained that she'd had children from a previous marriage. She said she was expecting her final decree of divorce within a few months.

I kissed the stretch marks and told her it didn't matter. Indeed, I remember thinking that she was obviously fertile, and she could bare our children one day. I was on cloud nine, knowing I'd found love and affection, something I was starved for.

In the following days, I brought her flowers after work. I'd take them from one of the dining room tables after the customers had gone. She knew my intentions were serious.

I was only eighteen. I was both mature and naive. My life had forced me to grow up fast. I'd gone to a whole different country and was supporting myself without any help from Dad. On the other hand, I was naive because I thought that I had to be serious. I didn't believe that I could just have a good time and enjoy my life as other young men did.

So, I put my nose to the grindstone, flambéing crepe Suzette and frogs legs for the rich. Roberto's lessons in the restaurant business paid off. I took on two assistants, Giovanni and Vincenzo, who were a few years older than me but who had much less experience. The manager assigned them to me for their training.

Being so young, it took a while for me to gain the trust of my colleagues. For the first few weeks, I ate by myself as I wasn't one of the gang, yet. The Spanish contingent in the place ruled, and as far as they were concerned, I was the kid from Italy. For some reason they had it in for Italians in general, I don't know why.

Friday and Saturday nights were always fully booked, as these were the dinner-dance nights for our customers. People would start coming in around 7:30, having parked their Rollers and Bentleys outside. Heirs and graces were flying all over the place, the restaurant manager and the head station waiters kissed ass accordingly, moving chairs, shifting tables to accommodate any

Marylyn

party who needed their attention. Menus were handed out and the wine waiters took the drink orders. Then the next act was to announce the specials for the evening, giving the customers food for thought.

Through it all, it was vital to keep your eyes on your station. As one mentor said, "Eric, take constant photographs in your mind, if you are leaving your station!" It was a good training technique, as it made you think of your table numbers and what stage of the performance each were at, coffee time, dessert time, first course, main course, and so on. I could memorize my station in a flash!

With my assistants Giovanni and Vincenzo under my command, the show carried on while I discreetly showed them the ropes. Within days, they were progressing nicely, taught well by me, a guy much younger than they were, to be great at their jobs.

Still, this didn't protect me from being fired for being sick.

It was a couple of months later. I'd developed tonsillitis and was sweating with a fever. Tony Gomez, the restaurant manager, was having none of it. He was a heavy gambler and a bit of a hot head. He sent a waiter to my room to tell me to report to work immediately, or to pack up my things. Do as I was told or pay the consequences. Workers didn't have as many rights in those days; at least immigrant workers didn't.

I refused, and so was fired, and turned out of my room. I was left wondering what to do. Should I go back to London and start again? Should I go back to Osoppo?

But Marylyn came to my rescue. She wasn't about to see us part, so she invited me to move into her room next door. We were in love by this point, so I accepted.

A couple of days later, there was a knock on the door. I opened it, expecting it to be Marylyn, but it turned out to be Mr. Morgante, the general manager of the hotel. He wasn't looking happy, and at six-foot-four, you wouldn't like it if he was looking unhappy.

"How long do you intend to stay here?" he demanded.

Before I could say anything, he cut me off, saying, "You've got two days. That's it." Then he left.

I told Marylyn what had happened, and she was distraught. She had to make a decision herself: keep her job and lose me, or quit her job and leave with me?

Eric Two Crowns (Supercabbie)

My heart already ached with the thought that she would probably choose to stay, so I was elated when she said that she'd follow me out of this place. I knew then that she really loved me.

But where was I to go? What was I to do? I couldn't go back to Helena and Rafaelle's; that would be a disgrace. I couldn't go back to Osoppo either, for the same reason.

Fortunately, Marylyn had some friends who could help. She called a man named John, who was an agent for the service industry, and he knew of two positions at the same hotel that would fit us perfectly. He even promised to make us an appointment for an interview with the manager of the Burford Bridge Hotel in Dorking, Surrey.

And so began the next phase of my life, but this one with Marylyn by my side.

Chapter Twenty-One
The Burford Bridge Hotel

John picked us up from the Seven Hills the next day at 6 p.m. and had us stay at his home for the night.

I was relieved to have another job prospect, but I was also nervous. I was still a young man in another country, a little guy in a big world. I was like a young eagle that knew how to fly but didn't know in what direction. Marylyn was my guide. Yes, I was eighteen and she was twenty-eight, ten years and three months apart, but it's true that love is blind.

Morning came and John drove Marylyn and I down for our interviews. That was an experience in itself, as we arrived in record time, wheels screeching at every bend we took. John, apparently, was a recreational race car driver in his earlier days, and he'd never changed his style. As if we didn't have enough stress that day!

The interviews were at the Burford Bridge Hotel in Box Hill, Dorking, Surrey. They were looking for a Chef de Rang (Head Station Waiter) and a head housekeeper, which would be perfect for us. Anxiously, we waited in the coffee lounge for the manager to call us in. Marylyn went first, so I was left alone to wait. You can only imagine how nervous I was. But, finally, it was my turn.

I was met by the general manager, Mr. White. He was a tall gentleman, impeccably dressed in a suit and tie, with silvery white hair; very elegant. He invited me to sit down.

"So, you're a Chef de Rang?" he asked, looking me straight in the eye.

I could tell from the look that he had his doubts, because of my age.

But he continued the interview, asking the relevant questions,

Eric Two Crowns (Supercabbie)

which I answered ably. After the interview, he said, "Well, if you will go out to the lounge, I'll be giving you an answer shortly."

Oh, the nerves! I couldn't think of what I'd do next if the answer was 'no'. I held Marylyn's hand, hoping desperately for a positive result. Finally, Mr. White appeared, and this time he was smiling.

"Eric, Marylyn," he said. "I don't usually hire couples, but you are both what we are looking for, so I'll give you a chance. Congratulations! You've got the jobs!"

It was like a huge boulder rolling off my back. He told us a bunch of other details, but I hardly heard them, that's how happy I was. He told us that the jobs were a live-in position, which saved us having to find a flat or a house to rent in town. The wages were good, and the elegant dining room would surely offer up a lot of good tips.

So, at eighteen, I was now the youngest staff member of the restaurant; everybody else was visibly older – lifers, they were called. They were professionals in the trade that had "made their bones" many years ago. I knew even then that I'd have to watch out for them, because they could get very defensive around a young buck like me. I knew my every move would be scrutinized and any example of unprofessionalism would be reported. In this industry, you don't get many chances to screw up before you are shown the door, so I had to put my nose to the grindstone again and focus.

The dining room was immaculate, with pure lead-crystal wine glasses, brilliant white linen tablecloths, King George silverware and expensive ceramic plates and service-ware. Even the cruets (salt and pepper shakers) and ashtrays were of the highest quality. My "dummy" waiter, which is a cabinet, cupboard and counter on wheels as well as your Flambé, follows you around as your assistant, stocked with supplies. Apparently, this four-and-a-half-star establishment only needed new carpeting to gain a five-star status.

I was excited to have a real shot at ruling my own roost, testing what I had learned with minimal supervision. I was proud to work in such an elegant environment. The hotel had a swimming pool, a tithe-barn on one side, and well-manicured hedges all around. Our living quarters consisted of a bedroom and a small lounge that no one seemed to use. Better yet, Dorking was just down the

Marylyn

road where we could pick up any personal items we needed, or just take a long stroll to stretch our legs.

There was also a car park across the street where bikers would often meet on a Sunday, and next to it a food kiosk which made some awesome hamburgers. This may surprise you, thinking that since I lived and worked at a four-and-a-half-star hotel, that I could need a break from hotel food, but I did. The staff budget for meals was only around 75p per person, so you couldn't get a lot for that price. A burger or two went down nicely once a week.

Being management, Marylyn got a larger allowance to order food off the menu. She kindly shared some of her food with me. If you played your cards right and greased the right people, you could get some favours, sneaking a decent meal here and there. But that was the game you had to play.

Apart from the meals, everything was going nicely. I enjoyed working on my own. But as summer approached, I began to notice something going on with Marylyn. She was on the other side of the fence between management and staff, and sort of segregated from me while on duty. For some reason, she decided to 'test' me, as she called it.

Mr. Deneuvaux, an assistant manager, was hanging around her a little too much for my liking. Being young, inexperienced and insecure, I started to think that maybe Marylyn wasn't as in love with me as I was with her. One morning, I was in the kitchen, counting linen napkins and tablecloths, when they both came in, all happy like.

To my surprise, and then anger, Deneuvaux grabbed a metal serving tray. Lifting it up, he shielded his face and Marylyn's and made it look like they were kissing behind it. Right in front of me.

I went into a rage. In a fit, I came forward, grabbed him by his lapels, and shoved him into a stock cupboard, ready to throw a punch. He started yelling that he and Marylyn were only joking.

Well, that stopped me, but I didn't see the joke. I was offended, especially by Marylyn's act. I stood over him as he lay and warned him to be careful.

While this was happening, Marylyn stood watching me. I walked past her and made for my quarters to cool off. A few min-

Eric Two Crowns (Supercabbie)

Burford Bridge Hotel. Image courtesy Andrew Bowden.

utes later, she came into the room, apologizing, saying she didn't mean it and she was only testing me.

Testing me for what? My love? My commitment? I was ready there and then to call off our relationship. I had never loved anyone the way I loved her. She meant everything to me. Why couldn't she see that?

I now understand a bit of why she got divorced, if she needed to test love like this. On the other hand, the English are a little like the Germans: somewhat cold in nature. Maybe that's why she couldn't see, or believe, how I felt.

Either way, I was in a quandary. Was this what I was in for if I married her? Would our love be superficial, without depth? Would I ever find a woman that loved me as much as I loved her?

To this day, it bewilders me. I have struggled with these doubts throughout our marriage. I believe that she lacks the inner softness to allow herself to be loved and to deeply love anyone back perhaps due to a lack of tender love from her family. On the other hand, her temper is deep enough to destroy or maim the goodness she has in her. Sometimes she confuses control with love.

This wasn't the only cloud to appear during my time at the Burford Bridge Hotel. We had to be on duty every single minute and second, with only a couple of hours as a break between shifts.

Marylyn

I was eighteen. I wanted to have fun, meet people, see the world and absorb all its wonder. Really, I wasn't ready to settle down.

Worse, in our few months there, Marylyn became pregnant. We had not used any protection. She told me one afternoon she was carrying our child. I held my head in my hands, thinking *what now?*

But I accepted this news for what it was and manned up for the challenge, as I thought I had to. I thought about fatherhood and, frankly, a part of me looked forward to it. I got excited as the days passed, until a few weeks later when Marylyn went to the doctors and I was told that she'd had a miscarriage.

I was devastated. I had gotten used to the idea of having my own son or daughter, sharing time and seeing him or her grow and being a part of their lives. I had planned on being a pillar for them when needed. I would do it better than my own father.

Unfortunately, this would never happen. After tests and other medical procedures, we eventually learned that due to complications, Marylyn had lost the ability to have children. When she told me this, she told me that if I wanted to part ways, she would not hold any bad feelings.

At the time, I thought that there were other channels we could explore. We could try artificial insemination, or even adopt when the time was right. I wasn't going to part ways.

But on the other side of the coin, I simply wasn't ready for that kind of responsibility. Let's be honest, here! Marylyn and I had no real security. We didn't have a home, and no savings to speak of. In a way, I am happy that fate intervened to leave me childless. At least I have nieces and nephews to love. I feel like a father to them when we talk, and I help them, or advise them on their voyage of life.

Anyway, we eventually felt that the time had come to leave the Burford Bridge. There was no acrimony in it. I felt, and still feel, that I'd put myself to the test and succeeded, and the time had come to find new challenges.

Chapter Twenty-Two
By Hook or By Crook

The Elizabethan Hotel was our next port of call. This was closer to Marylyn's neck of the woods, in Shepperton, Middlesex. Her father lived a few kilometres away in Chertsey, and most of her siblings were nearby in Addlestone and Guildford Surrey. We settled in Walton-on-Thames, in the area.

The Elizabethan hired me as a porter and Marylyn as a chambermaid. My new position gave me experience in handling large banquets and setting up venues for business meetings. We would cater functions for up to 400 people, usually weddings. The hotel was another elegant property set in a large park where deer and other wildlife roamed. There was even a bird sanctuary nearby.

I was no longer a Chef de Rang, and at the time I did feel like I'd been demoted, but it was really a step up, giving me experience in how to organize catering on a large scale. A new colleague named Nunzio, who hailed from Naples, taught me some tricks on how to make extra money, as well as how to handle the job. The salary wasn't the best, but with large weddings, your pocket could swell, if you timed things well.

The trick was in knowing that, midway through a large wedding, people would be jolly, having consumed their favourite tipple. They'd be switching tables, chatting with other guests, and wouldn't notice certain things.

During one such wedding, Nunzio came into the kitchen and headed for where the cases of red and white wine bottles were stored. The empties were beside them, ready to be placed back in the boxes. However, Nunzio was also bringing back half-consumed bottles, and pouring these into other half-consumed bottles, making them full. Thus, when the next bottle of wine was ordered, he'd simply stick the cork back in and sell it to the next buyer.

The key was, the open bar was usually closed by then, and the ordering customer, someone sozzled, would pay in cash and think nothing of it. There was no request chit made, and Nunzio got to pocket cash for a bottle that the hotel had already been paid for! The party would go on until the early hours, and along with your gratuities, you were assured a good night!

Another worker at the bar was doing something strange while he was cleaning up. People who had a chit for drinks would hand it over, and he would monitor what table had what. After people'd had a few, he'd take a toothpick or two and put it in an empty glass.

I learned what he'd been doing after the worker had been fired. I was told that there were always two bottles of each popular liquors on display at the bar: rum, vodka, whiskey and gin. He would water down one bottle and serve it in mixers to the tables that had drank the most that night. People wouldn't notice, he'd apparently said, and he could pocket the difference in cash.

Someone must have overheard his big mouth and ratted him out. That put the end to his schemes. Nunzio, however, worked in an area where people couldn't see us, so he kept on doing what he was doing

My only excuse was that, at the time, we were working hard, and we thought we deserved better pay for it. We got that better pay by hook or by crook. It was dog-eat-dog as management and staff were at odds on many issues, especially pay. Management took care of themselves, and we took care of ourselves, and that was that.

One great thing happened while we were there, though: my brother Jack got in touch with me. He wanted to come and visit, and he would be bringing Ciao, my best friend from Osoppo, along with him as well. I managed to arrange for a room for Jack and Ciao just down the hall from our quarters. They arrived a few days later.

I was delighted. I'd been away from Italy for a year or so, by now. It was a beautiful reunion for us both, as brothers and best friends, and at that moment, the hatchet that had been between me and Jack when I left Osoppo was buried that day.

In the meantime, Marylyn and I worked at the Elizabethan for a while until another opportunity came along at a place called Il Pagliaccio. By this time, Marylyn and I wanted a place of our own in which to live. I had my skills nailed down by now, and so an opportunity came along as I was headhunted by a Mr. Giuseppe Mele. He and his wife owned the prestigious Castle Inn, in Sunbury-on-Thames.

The Castle Inn was of the highest quality, with Mr. Mele an accomplished sommelier at the wheel — an expert in the field of wines and fine liquors. He served post and pre-war brandys that were the most expensive I'd ever served, with a shot going for £8. That's about $20, thirty-four years ago. Wow!

The vintage ports and sherries would have to be decanted to rid the sediment from the bottle — a sign of a vintage liquor, wines, ports etc. His clientele were rich. I remember one businessman, when entertaining, would ask for the whole bottle of brandy to be left at the table!

Mr. Mele would receive invitations to go to London wine auctions and he'd return with his car full of cases, licking his chops knowing the profits he was going to make. These were purely Vintage Wine and liquor auctions.

You had to know how to flambé at the Castle Inn, as frogs' legs, Mediterranean prawns, Steak Diane and Veal Marsala were all on the menu, along with Crepe Suzette. So, in hiring me, Mr. Mele made me the manager in charge of operations.

At least, that's what I thought.

Never work in a family-owned establishment if you can help it. Within a few weeks, I realized I'd made a big mistake. Mrs. Mele would stick her nose into everything, and then Mr. Mele would scold her. This would spark a big argument that made everybody uncomfortable, but resolve nothing, because later Mrs. Mele would stick her nose in again and they would fight like cat and dog. Billy the Cockatoo, in the foyer, would start squawking like crazy every time they went at it. It was intimidating to all.

Two months into this, I began looking for a different job. I hadn't stayed for long, but I did get some insight and finesse from

Marylyn

the experience. It wasn't long before I found a new position as head waiter in a place called Plage D'Or, in Walton-on-Thames.

This place wasn't as plush, but it was still a worthy position and it paid the bills. Salvatore and Pietro were co-owners, and they were easy-going guys, much more my style. Sal was Sicilian and Peter was from the mid-north of Italy. Both were in their mid-thirties. They appreciated my knowledge and energy and respected me enough to give me the reigns to do as I pleased without interference. I did a good job for them.

After working for them for a few months, I found myself head-hunted again, this time by two businessmen, Jim and Oliver, who were regulars at the Plage D'Or at lunchtime. I didn't know what they did, but they wore sharp suits and looked professional. They would regularly stay after closing, talking about their work over another bottle of wine, while I waited patiently for them to leave.

One particular day, they asked me to get a glass for myself and join them. The lunch crowd had left by this point, and I recall locking the door as I obliged. They were nice guys, always laughing, so I pulled up a chair wondering, *why the invitation*?

Jim then looked at me and asked me if I was happy with my work.

"Yes," I replied, because why wouldn't I be?

But then Jim said, "Well, I have a proposition for you."

"What is it?" I asked.

"Do you mind me asking you how much you earn?" asked Jim.

I didn't, so I told him, and I told him how many hours I worked to earn it.

"If I told you that I have an opportunity for you to put in half the hours for double the pay, would you be interested?" Jim asked.

I immediately said, "Yes, of course I would!" I mean, who wouldn't, right? So, I listened as Jim told me that he was in the insurance business. He told me the things he'd achieved there, and how he was now a branch manager.

I knew nothing of this industry. It would have been a complete change of strategy for me. I wasn't afraid of change, but it would be quite a challenge to learn something so new to me, and I said so.

"We can guide you and support you, if you'd consider it," Jim

Eric Two Crowns (Supercabbie)

replied. "We can even help with income while you put the effort in to get licensed."

There seemed to be no downside, but I told him I would think about it.

"That's great!" he said. "Let me know!"

Chapter Twenty-Three

Insurance

That afternoon, I mentioned my conversation to Marylyn. She'd taken a cashier position at Tesco's outlet store by this point, and she said that since she'd changed her profession, why not I, especially if the money was good enough? So, I pondered a bit, and then let a couple of weeks go by. I basically forgot about the offer.

A few weeks later, Jim and Oliver were at their usual table, and again Jim asked me what I thought about his offer. I was more curious, now, so I agreed to an interview at his office and showed up as planned a few days later. Jim was pleased to see me, invited me in, and got down to the nitty-gritty about the job. Before long, he'd convinced me that insurance was a good move.

Sure, I had no clue about the insurance and investment industry, but Jim assured me that as long as I put in the effort to learn, I would succeed. He signed me on that morning.

I returned home later that afternoon to share the news with Marylyn. She agreed that, since Jim's company was prepared to support me financially while I was training, I should take this chance. If worst came to worst, I still had my service experience to fall back on.

I gave my notice to Sal and Peter. The insurance classes started a couple of weeks later in the town of Sutton in South West London, in a "Toby Jug" Hotel. I was to spend five days there, come home for the weekend, and then return for a second week, whereupon I'd (hopefully) pass my tests and get my license.

This was the first time I'd been away from Marylyn and I missed her terribly. But in the end, it was worthwhile, because I

Eric Two Crowns (Supercabbie)

achieved my goal and returned home triumphantly with my certificate in hand. The Monday after would be my first day selling insurance.

Selling insurance was a far cry from what I'd been doing in restaurants. This new life had its own uniform of a suit and tie, and a spanking new briefcase. I had my own office. It was a pretty empty office, but it was mine.

After greeting the secretaries and talking with Jim, I learned the ground rules. One of the stipulations was that I had to have around two hundred contacts to approach. These would be my foundation to build on. I'd call them all with the hope of making an appointment and selling them on an insurance contract. If they answered no, then try to get them to refer me to someone else.

I was a bit scared about what lay ahead, but I had shone shoes in my Dad's barber shop, and had organized dances at the Breithaupt Centre. I'd always had a head for business. One restaurant owner once told me, "Eric, you could sell ice to Eskimos!" So, I took the bit between my teeth and went for it.

However, I'd only lived in Walton for a short time. I only knew a few people, not anywhere near two-hundred. So, I got out a phone book and started filling in my contact sheet that way. One of the guys at training told me that the company wouldn't care, just so long as I had four or five sheets filled in.

Before I made my first call, though, someone knocked at my office door. It was Gary Thomas, one of the reps. I didn't know him from Adam when he introduced himself, but he had a big smile and seemed an energetic sort of bloke. He had a strong, slangy accent. "Oi, Mate! Do you wanta come wiv us?"

"Where?" I asked.

"Me and a couple of the lads are going cauwd-cauwing in the Kingston Maauw," he replied.

Mall, I translated. Kingston was about twenty minutes away on the outskirts of Southwest London. I had nothing else planned, and this seemed like a good way to get into the selling mode, so I agreed. A few minutes later, I was on my way with Gary, his brother Clive, and Gary Warby, all of us rookie reps. We had different coloured pads to fill in as we stopped people and asked them if

Marylyn

they were interested in a range of products, from children's education funds to pension plans to life insurance.

To my dismay, most of the people I stopped were rude and stand-offish. At the time, I didn't know that the English were more anti-insurance than pro. None of us were having much luck and we soon called it quits. It was almost noon, and the boys decided to go for a pint.

"Is it always like this?" I asked Gary, later at the pub.

"You just have to get lucky once," he replied, "and that will make your day!"

He explained that one decent policy could be worth hundreds of pounds. All you needed to do was get in front of three or four people, and you should be able to convert one.

But that was easier said than done. I hated rejection, and the idea of being rejected by three people out of every four made me think I'd made a big mistake.

But back in my empty office that afternoon, head in my hands, the light went on: I could speak Italian, German, French, and Spanish. And English, of course.

I pulled over my phone book and flipped through it. There was a big contingent of Italians and Spanish in the area. I also knew many restaurant employees from those cultures. So, I just started searching the phone book for names ending with an "a", "e", "i", "o", or "u", revealing a lot of possible prospects. I knew I was onto something. Big visions of success filled my mind as I made my first call.

The people I talked to were very receptive. I was able to connect with them, and most didn't have an insurance agent. I introduced myself and my services and made appointment after appointment. I worked until eight that evening and booked myself up for the next two weeks. My only worry was my car. It was a vivid green 132 Fiat; reliable, but seriously rusted up. It wasn't exactly putting my best foot forward, like my suit and tie were supposed to do. However, I decided I just needed to make sure I parked up the road so that potential clients didn't see me getting out of that banger. In any case, I was relieved that I would never have to go back to the Kingston Mall again. I found some wings.

Later that week, Jim invited me into his office to talk about

Eric Two Crowns (Supercabbie)

how I was doing. It was something all agents had to do, going over your activities, how many appointments you made, and so on. Your performance would determine whether you'd get your cheque at the end of the week.

He was amazed to learn that I was fully booked for the next two weeks. I was way ahead of most rookies, many of whom would struggle for weeks before any success, or just quit or be let go within a few months. I'd already brought in three deals and made around 1,600 pounds! I'd tripled my usual restaurant pay.

And then I began to fly. The Italians I'd contacted started to recommend me to their families, friends and relatives. I stood out as one of their own although from the north of Italy, within an Australian company. I began getting inquiries about pension plans, tax saving products, and mortgages for themselves, or their soon-to-be-married sons and daughters. They were inquiring into sickness and accident coverage.

Those mortgages were always a little trouble to sell, as many would-be clients were self-employed, and tended to declare way less than what they made. At the time, mortgages were calculated at three times a person's yearly income, so under-declaring meant that they could borrow less, regardless of their ability to pay (and, trust me, they had no problem paying). Fortunately for them, a Mr. P. Jackson stepped in to help with that.

Mr. Jackson was an accountant who had his own practice. He was introduced to me at some function and, when I began to get inquiries for mortgages, I made an appointment to see him. He agreed that Italians were stand-up people, and he said that if I got them to switch accountants and go to him, he'd oblige with the necessary letters to the lender that would cement the loan.

To do this, he would "project" the current year's income by inflating last year's income by two or three times. This documentation would never be challenged by the lending companies and the mortgages would be cleared to go. All of this could be done for a fee of "a mere 200 pounds" ($500 Canadian).

Thus, we arranged a lot of mortgages, and a lot of Italians got their houses. Because of these small miracles, word got around in the community and, before long, I was invited to get-togethers. A good friend and golf partner named Don asked me to be his son's

Marylyn

From left to right: Don Faretta, Robert Tavagna, Rodger Davis, Me, Romeo Cerejo. The clients meet the pros.

compadre, or sponsor for his confirmation. I was honoured to be so trusted as a friend with this duty and commitment.

One Sunday, Don picked me up before noon, to meet up with a bunch of Italians to reminisce over a few drinks. It was an excellent opportunity to make more connections for my business, and make me a part of the "Southern Italian community".

Okay, maybe at the back of my mind I was worried that there'd be some kind of Mafia-style initiation. You see, these were southern Italians (Sicilians), and I was northern Italian. As a child, I'd had drilled into me the differences between northern Italians and southern Italians. Northerners were industrious and hard working. Southerners were cunning and would do anything to survive.

You see, we all have our preconceptions. Even part-Italian, I had preconceptions about Italians!

Well, this wasn't the case at all. Don's people greeted me and acknowledged the work I was doing. They were friendly. One preconception that was reinforced about southern Italians was that, once you did them a favour, you were a friend of theirs for life.

There were southerners in the community that weren't at that get-together, however, and everybody knew who they were. They were "the ones". I soon learned through my new friends that these were people to avoid. One individual had been busted, along with his boys, over a big drug deal gone bad. He'd made the television news, bringing a great sense of shame among the Sicilian community. Many knew some of the people involved, even though they didn't associate with them. They knew them because they'd grown up in the same little villages back in the homeland.

Through this community, I heard about and witnessed money laundering. There was a well-known businessman, who eventually became my partner, who turns out would charge "a point or two" to exchange English pounds for Italian lira, which would then be transferred from bank to bank in Sicily. Clients would ask to be paid in cash for services rendered, with some making fifty-thousand who would only declare ten-thousand of that to the tax man.

There was many a time I sold lump sum investment plans that would be paid for in "Reddies" (English for Cash). We'd shake hands on the deal, then the man of the house would vanish into another room and then come back with a big bag of cash, and that was that, another "bonding" handshake, and it was *finito!* Done!

Of course, this raised eyebrows back at the front office. My manager Jim once asked me why most of my deals were done in cash. I shrugged and said, "that's how Italians do business."

Jim left it at that. In the end, it was still money.

In my rookie year at the insurance firm, I tripled the previous year's rookie achievement record. Jim couldn't have been happier; I was making him huge bonuses. He treated me with great respect, and we blew the froth off many a beer together. I played golf with the boys on Fridays after work, basking in success.

#

I was reaching the end of my year-long probation, with all going so well, when my father passed away. His drinking had finally caught up with him. My brother Jack along with his fiancée Titziana were staying with us at the time. Jack left after we received information from Osoppo that Dad was in hospital.

I was devastated. Not at my father's death, but at the reasons behind it. And a fair amount of resentment rose up. Why had he

Marylyn

treated me the way he had? Why hadn't he treated me the way he had treated Jack and Lydia?

Nightmares followed for months afterward, waking up in cold sweats, reliving the beatings and neglect. Yet, I was grieving, perhaps over not getting a chance to ask him why.

Stranger still, Jack told me that, with his last breath, Dad cried out Mom's name, "Alberta!" I remember asking Jack if Dad had mentioned me. Jack told me that he had not. That hardened my heart with disappointment. He'd had sorrow and guilt about abandoning Mom, but not me.

While this was happening, my manager Jim had asked me to give a speech to the company about how I'd achieved my success. The event was scheduled for the next day. Somehow, I had to get up in front of a hotel conference room full of around two hundred associates, veterans and rookies alike, and give a speech to inspire the newbies to believe in themselves and work hard.

I told Jim about my father's death, and he was very sympathetic, asking me if I wanted to forget the speech. I decided to go through with it though. I figured it could be a tool to help me overcome some of my grief. Besides, it was possible Dad would be looking down at me, and I didn't want him to see my weakness. Jim kept on assuring me that I could bail out if necessary, but I would have none of it.

The day of the speech, I felt numb and confused. I hadn't slept the night before. The crowd gathering at the hotel was large and getting larger. Two hundred people is a lot of people to look out at, and I was getting stage fright. But, with nerves jangling, I took a couple of deep breaths and reached inside for strength. I had also downed a large brandy that Jim had given me earlier, so that may have helped. Either way, I made my way to the podium as the host introduced me and talked about some of my accomplishments.

I recall being humbled, yet anxious to get things over with. I started into my speech, but after a short while, I broke down in tears. I revealed to the audience that my father had died the day before. I carried on as best I could with the knot in my throat. I mentioned within my speech the need for insurance, as Dad had left us with nothing but debt. My sisters had no real financial security, only a roof over their heads. As I ended my speech, I began

Eric Two Crowns (Supercabbie)

to sob again thinking about Dina and Lydia and the hand they had been dealt.

Immediately, the audience stood up to clap as I dismissed myself from the podium. As I made my way through the middle of them to the seat next to Jim, people began reaching out to shake my hand or pat me on the back. Jim greeted me with a hug and whispered in my ear, "Great job, Eric! Great job!" For myself, I was just sobbing like a baby.

But, when all was said and done, mission accomplished.

Afterward, I went over to the lounge with Jim to gulp down a couple more brandies. I'm not ashamed to admit that I got a little sloshed that day. My colleagues came to offer sympathies and condolences, which I appreciated. It would be months before I could feel like I was at ease, or my normal self.

Chapter Twenty-Four
Brothers Again

So, this is how my brother Jack re-entered my life after I left Osoppo.

Jack had pursued employment in Germany. He, along with his fiancée Titziana, had been employed by a count or a baron in Italy who had homes in Germany, Italy and Spain. I was proud of him as he excelled in his profession. But while I was sitting at home one evening, the phone rang, and it was Jack. As he started to speak, I knew something was up. There was a catch in his voice.

"Do you think you could find me a job in England?" he asked.

"Why?" I replied. "What's wrong?"

He started telling me his story, about how his new boss had screwed with his salary (he had left the count for another opportunity), and Jack was having none of it. But quitting meant a lot of uncertainty, just as I had felt when I was fired from Seven Hills. What was he going to do?

As it turned out, Jack was supposed to get free room and board at his new job. However, upon receiving his first paycheque, he noticed the proprietor had deducted accommodation costs from it. Jack confronted him on it and got into a huge argument. That was when he decided to call me in England. With all of my experience there surely, I could help him.

I was certainly going to try. I racked my brains for a good restaurant he could work at. He was an accomplished chef and had been in culinary school for two years at Arta Therme in the Alps and, later, in Trieste near Croatia. He'd graduated in the top three of the sixty or so students in his final year and was headhunted immediately upon finishing school. Surely there would be

Eric Two Crowns (Supercabbie)

openings in England for someone like Jack, with his passion and talent.

As luck would have it, that very next afternoon, I was driving home from the office when I spotted Salvatore, my old manager at the Plage D'Or, on the sidewalk smoking a cigarette. I beeped a "hello!" at him and parked my car in front of him.

Just as I got out to shake his hand, he said to me, "Eric, I'm looking for a chef! Do you know of anyone good?"

Talk about a stroke of luck, eh?

I suggested to Sal that we sit in his restaurant a moment to chat. There, I told him about my brother, and how he was in Germany but wanted to come to England to work.

"Is he any good?" asked Sal.

"Absolutely!" I replied. "My brother is great!"

I told Salvatore about Jack's experience and credentials, and Sal agreed to take him on. We even discussed an appropriate wage amount to start with.

As soon as I got home, I called Jack with the news. "Jack, you're all set! I found you a job!"

"What? Already?!" he said.

Salvatore was happy to have his chef, and to have me as his agent. I was elated that Jack and I would be together again. We had spent a long time apart.

We had not spoken for a few years because of a gripe that I'd had with him due to the past, and our abduction. I'd put that past me, however, and now yearned to have him at my side. He said he'd be able to get to England in just a few days; he just needed time to book tickets and get his luggage ready. I told him that I'd ease his way into England by buying him and Titziana a bed and other supplies, and that they could stay with Marylyn and me until they felt comfortable enough to do what they liked.

For their part, Jack and Titzy planned to earn as much and save as much as possible. We had received some money to rebuild our house after the earthquake, but it was not nearly enough. They wanted to save enough to finish rebuilding the house and go back to live in Osoppo. It took a little while. In the end, he and Titzy stayed with us for about six months, and in England for about five years.

Marylyn

Jack, Joyce (niece), Fanny (another niece), Dina, Me and Lydia

Through that time, we spoke a lot, sharing our thoughts about what had happened in the past. We talked about our abduction, and his role in it. Perhaps I should have let sleeping dogs lie, as I could sense his discomfort as he talked about it, but sometimes you just need answers. At least I knew we loved each other deeply, and our discussions, while sometimes fraught, never pushed us away from each other.

We became close again. Sundays were often spent together along with our better halves. I enjoyed every moment of his company, often taking a ride somewhere together, or just hanging out at his place or mine.

Jack worked with Salvatore for two years, and then followed Andrew, Sal's restaurant manager, to a new place called the Greek Vine. He left on good terms with Sal and Peter, though they were sad to see him go. The money was better at the Greek Vine, however, and there was the added challenge of learning to cook Greek food.

Here, though, Jack would be mentored by the Greek Vine's owner, George Tsiripillis. George was a shrewd business man and

Eric Two Crowns (Supercabbie)

quite a cunning character. He was also meticulous and demanding. Jack sometimes called to vent a little steam over George's "dictatorship". I encouraged him to keep going, however, and he learned to endure the change.

On the other hand, George was getting to know me better through Jack, and decided he needed some advice on insurance. He was a wealthy man, so of course I wanted his business!

My brother Jack.

On the next trip to see Jack, I entered the Greek Vine and saw George tinkering around in the bar area. Seeing me come in, he greeted me with a big smile and beckoned me to sit down with him. He offered me a drink of Metaxa, a Greek brandy, and started asking me about fire and accident insurance to cover the flat above the restaurant, where Jack and Titzy were staying. I started writing down his needs, but he suggested that I come take a look at the flat. It was a decent apartment, though I could see that it could do with a revamping.

I pulled a proposal out of my briefcase and began filling in the necessary details and started talking about rates. George agreed to the premium without hesitation and pulled out a chequebook.

As he was writing out the amount, he asked if coverage was immediate. I assured him that "provisional coverage" would start immediately, and he would be fully covered once the contract was accepted. He liked that answer, poured us another brandy, and shook my hand to seal the deal. After finishing off my drink, I excused myself to go into the kitchen and see Jack, my mind filled with hope that this initial deal would open more doors with George and his friends in the future.

To my surprise, I found Jack on his knees, scrubbing the kitchen floor. I thought the dishwashers would be doing the dirty work,

Marylyn

but no, Jack was hard at it. His philosophy was, "if I pull the cart, then they will too." That's Jack for you.

As for George, he was cooking up his own plan that I was now a part of. I didn't know of his intentions at the time, but a week or so later, he called to tell me that the insurance contract had arrived, and he was now insured by Cornhill Insurance, one of the better agencies in England.

It wasn't long after that before George called me again, telling me that a pipe had burst in the flat (Jack and Titzy were out at the time) and asking me to come over and take a look, because there would be a claim involved.

"Jeepers!" I thought. The policy had only been in force for a week and already there was a claim! The insurance company wouldn't like paying out after only receiving one premium.

Arriving at the flat, I met George and he showed me the damaged pipe. Already I could see that things were a bit fishy. The pipe hadn't exactly burst so much as been cut. Had somebody taken a saw to it? I didn't say this out loud, though. I did my due diligence and took down some notes.

There was furniture under the pipe, and carpets and wallpaper, all damaged by the water. The compensation cheque would be in the thousands. I assured George things would be taken care of, although I had no real authority to say so. I did say, though, that an inspector would have to come in, assess the damage and make a report.

George didn't like this idea at all. He seemed to think that I could write out a cheque for him there and then! However, I told him that I was just the insurance agent, and not the claims inspector. I had to follow the protocol. I could see he was a little nervous about the whole thing, and this deepened my suspicions.

I don't know what the inspector did or said, but apparently a settlement cheque was issued, and the flat was fixed up, redecorated and refurnished, much to George's delight.

A few weeks later, I was again summoned by George. This time he wanted to tag onto the policy his expensive hearing aid, which he had just purchased. I again did my due diligence and submitted the attachment.

Eric Two Crowns (Supercabbie)

You're probably thinking, as I was, what was the old man up to?

Well, a couple of weeks later, he called me again, telling me that his hearing aid had been crushed, accidentally, under his shoe. Whoops!

So, the scene repeated itself: I went over and sort out the claim. While there, however, he sat me down and asked if I knew anyone who wanted to make some quick cash.

"What is it you need, George?" I said.

"Well, Eric, I went to Las Vegas to visit my daughter," he replied," and when I was there, I was just walking around the city when a woman approached me and asked if I would buy her fur coat!"

Apparently, it was a beautiful black mink that he'd got for a song and dance, but worth much more than what he'd paid.

"What do you want me to do?" I said.

"Well, I'd like to insure it on my policy. It's worth about 5,000 pounds!"

He even had an appraisal certificate saying so.

Again, I tacked it onto the policy with the certificates and all the proper forms and put the documents in my briefcase. However, George hadn't really explained himself fully, so I asked, "What's this about, if I knew someone who wanted to make some money?"

"Well, Eric," he replied, "That coat will be in my Mercedes at my other restaurant, in the car park next Saturday night. I wanted my wife to have it, but she doesn't like it. I'd be very grateful if you could find someone to make it disappear. A simple smash and grab?"

Now I was thinking that George was crazy. "You want me to arrange a theft?"

Without batting an eyelid, George said, "I'll make it worth your while!" Then he pulled out two fifty-pound notes and placed the money right in front of me. "That's for doing such a good job for me so far!"

I needed to back out, fast. "I can't take that, George! I'm happy just doing my job!"

"Nonsense! Consider it like a tip when you worked as a waiter!" And with that, he walked away. I was flabbergasted. He was a

Marylyn

millionaire, but he was still bending and breaking every rule just to make a buck!

But I did take the money.

I went into the kitchen and talked to Jack about George's proposal. "I think he's crackers, Jack! I don't think I'll be doing any more business with him. I'll end up in bloody jail!"

Jack and I laughed about it, but I was serious with my words. I decided that I would make myself unavailable for a while and hope he would eventually get the message. That meant that whenever I went to visit Jack, I would have to sneak in through the back door. Fortunately, I didn't have to deal with George again. He called me a lot, trying to convince me to come back, but it was never going to happen.

Finally, after five years in England, Jack had made enough money to rebuild the family home in Osoppo, and he told me he would be going back with Titzy. That broke my heart. I had hopes that we could open our own restaurant together in Walton. I knew we would have had a great partnership. Marylyn was experienced in running the bar and doing the bills. Titziana was a perfect server, and Jack was great in the kitchen. I could back him up, and also run the dining room. All we would need is a kitchen helper.

But Jack was firm with his goal. And, after all, there was Lydia and Dina to think about. They were still in Osoppo. Also Titzy had her family back home.

In the end they returned to Osoppo. They live there now in the old family home after buying the girls and me out, on the condition that I'd have a place to stay when I visit, and possibly if I wished to die there.

Chapter Twenty-Five
Opportunities Knock

By the time you get to your middle age, you might ponder and dream of "the one that got away." I'm talking about opportunities, not fish! Here's a couple that come to mind.

Shortly after my probationary year had ended in the insurance business, I was asked to attend a training session in the office along with my colleagues. We were being shown on how to use a new computer to illustrate projected payouts of investment plans at certain rates of interest. This was high end technology at the time, and we were impressed. I recall one of my colleagues saying that it was the way of the future. I thought about taking some of my bonus money and investing in this unknown company. I had other plans at the time though, like a new car!

The computer manufacturer's brand name was Microsoft.

Life is all about timing and you learn to be more patient as time goes on. If I would have taken that inspirational message from that little logo and taken a gamble like I have many times things would be much different now. I read some time ago that one thousand dollars invested in Microsoft in the early eighties would be worth millions today!

Not to long after, I was relieving Marylyn from her duties in our store. On Saturdays I would take over at noon, leaving her to do her chores at home. I was going over some paperwork when a young gentleman came in and politely introduced himself.

He wanted a few words with me regarding business. I had already made myself known around town as someone to talk to, so I asked him to sit down and explain what his proposition was.

He began to tell me that he and his father were owners of a

Marylyn

piece of land that had an endless supply of "natural spring water". He wanted me to invest five thousand pounds as an equal partner of one third share of his business. The joint capital of fifteen thousand pounds would provide a filtering system along with a start-up bottling facility.

In Italy, everyone drank bottled water, and had done so for years, but in England, bottled water was not even in existence, apart from imported San Pellegrino and Perrier. I told him that I would think about it. My own business was flourishing at the time, so I decided against investing. Shortly after, ITV News reported that the Thames River was infested with some sort of larvae. The reporter on the segment drank a glass of the infected water live during the broadcast. We could see the little critters wriggling around as the water went down his throat.

The reporter was assuring viewers that all was okay, and that the larvae weren't dangerous. Brave man! But I knew that wouldn't matter. It wasn't long before I saw the young man again, driving a new Mercedez Benz. His venture had paid off now that bottled water sales had gone through the roof! I was too late.

I could see a similar opportunity presenting itself after I came back to Canada. The Brita water filtering system was common here. Meanwhile in Italy, my sister Dina told me that some person or group of people were poking plastic water bottles in shops with contaminated needles. The public was becoming wary and on edge. On one of her first visits to Canada, she came shopping with me and saw the Brita filters. She immediately purchased one along with a half dozen filters to take back home with her.

I immediately did some research on how to export these filters to Italy. Unfortunately, it would have taken a $20,000 investment, and at the time I didn't have the funds. Now Brita and products just like it are in millions of homes in Italy.

I saw another potential opportunity visiting Italy in 2006, when I was grocery shopping with my older sister Lydia. I was intrigued by how the shopping carts had a device that allowed you to put in a Euro coin to unlock a chain that kept the carts together. Canadian stores have nothing of the sort, and these get scattered far and wide by people taking them off store property. I know these carts run about two to three hundred dollars each,

Eric Two Crowns (Supercabbie)

and there's even a business where people go around searching for them and hauling them back to the stores on the back of a pick-up truck for a $5-per-cart bounty. Surely this little device would save stores a mint, and if I could sell these devices to Canadian stores, I could have a piece of that mint!

So, after I returned to Canada and thought about it some more, I asked around, and my sources told me, "Sorry, Eric: we already have them on order."

Blast! My fault for not taking immediate action, I guess. As a friend of mine said, "Eric, you have such great ideas, but you keep on missing the boat!"

I did realize one success, though. In 1981-82, I started a small venture in Walton. At the time, there were no food delivery services in the town, or anywhere else, for that matter. I approached two brothers (Tony and Giovanni) who were from Naples, Italy. They owned a little food joint in Walton-on-Thames serving Donair Kebabs, Pizza, burgers and hot dogs. I asked them, "Why don't you sell submarine sandwiches?" I knew all about them, being Canadian (as far as I'm concerned, Big John's Subs in Kitchener are the best subs I have ever eaten), but the British hadn't ever heard of them.

At the same time, I'd been offered a deal to purchase a small sandwich business from a Scotsman named Bill.

The pieces were all coming together. I bought Bill's sandwich business for £5000 cash, including the goods and chattels, meat slicer, packaging machine, et cetera. Then I lined up ten or so buyers that would help me supply a lot of sandwiches to the London market.

I had great dreams for this business. Who knows where this could go, I thought. After all, McDonald's and KFC had just opened up in town, so I thought that Subs had to follow. It just made sense. The key, though – my secret ingredient, was Big John's secret ingredient.

Sitting at home, I got ready to contact Big John's in Kitchener, hoping they were still in business. I asked for help from directory assistance, and was relieved when the operator asked, "The Belmont Avenue location, sir?"

"Yes!" I was elated that they were still around.

Marylyn

I got the number, wrote it down, and dialed it. The line rang and someone picked up. "Hello, Big John's?"

"Yes, may I speak to Big John?"

"Just a second, please."

After what felt like much more than a second, I heard, "Hello, Big John, here."

"Hi, John! Have you got a minute?" I asked.

"Who is this?"

"It's Eric. Eric Comoretto. You may not remember me, but I'm Ferruccio's son. He was the barber next door to you a long time ago."

There's a moment's pause, then, "Oh, Lord, yes! I remember you! What can I help you with?"

"Well, John, would you consider giving me your sauce recipe?"

Silence.

"I'm not a threat to you. I'm calling you from England," I added. "I'm looking at introducing submarine sandwiches here. They don't have any. Look, I'll tell you what: here's my number, if you'd like to call me back, collect, just to prove it, okay?"

"Okay," says John, before he hangs up.

A moment later, my phone rings, and it's John. We chat for a little, and he proceeds to give me his recipe, complete with all ingredients and formulation. I thanked him profusely and he wished me luck before hanging up again. I yelled out loud, punching the air in my excitement. I knew I was onto a winner, and that the crucial link had been accomplished.

My next move was to select a local bakery and get them to try and copy the style of the bread I needed. Texture and shape had to be right and consistent. I contacted Mr. Heffernan, the owner of a bakery that was a couple of blocks away from home. After explaining what I needed, he said there would be no problem and to come back the next day to see his samples. I found he'd made a dozen samples of what the English called "rolls" but in a hot dog bun shape. I picked one that was fluffy, yet firm, and ordered five dozen, each four inches long, to be given out as free samples with every order from the Kebab Hut.

The next thing to do was design a simple flyer that would be inserted in every newspaper delivered around Walton, and then

Eric Two Crowns (Supercabbie)

ordering the six types of cured meats. Then we needed paper bags with our new logo and phone number on them. I named the business Yellow Submarine. I then ordered delivery bags that kept hot foods hot.

All of this required a lot of organization. Marylyn took charge of the delivery bags, sewing and stitching.

Now the ball was rolling. I arranged with my new partners to deliver everything on the menu. The small room at the back of the shop would be the prepping area, and I began to get things in order. The sandwich business I'd purchased from Bill required that sandwiches be made up at night and delivered to London stores by 8 a.m., Mondays through Fridays. We made these sandwiches in our house, using one of the bedrooms converted into a secondary kitchen, equipped with all the machinery and stock.

After getting approval by the health inspector, Marylyn and I set to work making approximately 200 sandwiches and rolls off different styles starting at 9 p.m. I'd load the car at 6:30 a.m. and drive to between seven to ten locations in southwest London to drop them off. It was all on a sale and return basis. If the sandwiches didn't sell, we'd have a lot of sandwiches to eat.

Even though I was juggling my hours between two businesses, everything was going great, until one morning in the Kebab Shop I noticed that, in the prepping area, there was a leak from the smoke extractor that led from the grill through the prep room and outside. It was dripping black grease onto the work surface, and had to be fixed, pronto! Looking for detergents under the sink cupboard, I opened the door and found huge snails crawling around the pipes. If the health inspector saw this, it would be trouble.

I removed the ones I could see and tidied up. Wouldn't you know it, but two days later we got a visit from the health department. Just as things were about to take off, he issued an indefinite closure order until the necessary work was done to his satisfaction.

The brothers at the Kebab Shop were weary of putting any money towards refurbishing the property, and decided to close the place down, instead, leaving me in the lurch. I had no option but to put my submarine sandwich business on ice, and continue with my London run, supplying the London stores.

I tried carrying on, fully intending to bring the sub store back

Marylyn

Delivering sandwiches on the job!

to life, when another bombshell dropped. It turns out the equipment I'd purchased from Bill hadn't been paid for. Bill had leased the equipment, not told me, and now the leasers were coming after me for the outstanding amounts. It was a total con job on Bill's part. He'd taken my money and run, leaving me holding the bag. My dream of success was crumbing down around me as the payments the leasers were demanding were crippling. All I could do was return the equipment and close up shop.

I made extensive inquiries after Bill's whereabouts, intending to take him to court, but he had vanished. The contact who had introduced him to me initially said that he'd gone back to Scotland, but Scotland's a pretty big place.

That bitter experience taught me some bitter lessons, like never to trust anyone when doing business again. Fortunately for me I had my restaurant trade skills to fall back on, which I did. Later, I learned to my dismay from a friend that Subway had opened outlets throughout England to great success. They'd finally introduced the English to submarine sandwiches. That could have been me!

So, those were the ones that got away. Here's a time that I did win.

I was never a big gambler in my life. This goes to show how

Eric Two Crowns (Supercabbie)

luck can pop up when you least expect it. Walter Maritti was a wealthy restaurateur who owned at least three restaurants in London, all of them 5-star. Each restaurant had the word Ponte (Bridge) in the name: Ponte Vecchio (Old Bridge), Ponte Vecchio Duo (Old Bridge Two) and Ponte Nuovo (New Bridge). He was a classy gentleman, always elegant in clothing and presence, tall and groomed. He also owned a few Group One racehorses which he named after his restaurants.

I'd been introduced to him during my first "London Italian Golf Society" tournament. My bosses Corrado and Roberto, after watching me greatly improve my game, decided to bring me along as a guest. The venues were at prestigious courses, such as Wentworth, Sunningdale, Kingswood, Walton Health, et cetera.

On the second year that I played, Walter came over to greet me as I was sipping some fine brandy. We began to chat about the Royal Ascot, which is one of the premier races on the calendar. It was just a week away. I asked Walter if any of his thoroughbreds were running, and he mentioned that he had a couple competing, but not to wager on them, as they were long shots. He also mentioned that he had sold one of his horses, as it wasn't performing as well as expected.

The next Saturday, I was back in Walton at the Snooker club, and I asked Jim the manager which horse he liked. He told me he was going over to the Bookies to look at the racing form, and make his picks for the day, so I joined him.

As I said, I'm not a high-stakes gambler, but I'm not above making small bets for potential big payouts. I looked at the card for the day and noted one of Walter's horses, Ponte Vecchio Due, right at the bottom of the list, number 32. It had gone six races without once placing in the top four, but I thought, "why not?" and I pulled out about six pounds in coins (about $15). I wrote out a ticket, placing six pounds for Ponte Vecchio Due to win.

That was bigger than any bet I'd placed before, but I had a gut feeling. So, we watched the race, and off the horses go, all 32 of them (In England, they have big fields). My horse had light blue colours with a white star on the light blue cap. The betting shop buzzed with people as the race came down to the wire, with Ponte Vecchio Due in the thick of it. The camera at the finishing line

Marylyn

flashed, and we had to wait for the announcement. I remember yelling, "Come on, my son! Come on!"

Jim looked at me, bewildered. "You didn't bet on that thing, did you?"

"I did!" I replied. "Six pounds on the nose!" I told him about my conversation with Walter.

We waited for the announcement. Finally, it came: "First: Number 32, Ponte Vecchio Due!"

I found myself the only one in the joint hollering "Yeah, Baby!!" Everyone stared at me in disbelief. Now we were waiting for the payout, and Jim mentioned that,

Connecting with a colt in Bamberg

before the race started, my horse was at 66 to 1. He added, "The longer it takes, the better for you, Eric."

I thought, great! Pool betting can get you better payouts in big fields.

Eventually, the announcer finally made the announcement, and my six pound bet raked in nearly $2,300! Now that's karma, if you believe in it!

My last story is probably the best one. By the time I returned to Canada, I'd given up on gambling completely. I did enjoy wagering on the three Triple Crown races in the US, just for fun, once a year. This particular year, my marriage was under a lot of pressure, so much so that I took a sabbatical from Marylyn and stayed a while on my own.

On the Saturday of the Kentucky Derby, I glanced through the sporting section, and saw a horse called Giacomo, spelt just like my brother's formal name. Even more interesting, it was wearing the number ten, and October – the tenth month of the year – was Jack's birthday. I decided that would be my first pick.

I looked down the list and spotted a horse named Closing Argument, which made me think of my separation from Marylyn.

Eric Two Crowns (Supercabbie)

That became my second pick. The third one I picked pretty much at random, and made a total investment of $19. I finished my night shift and arrived home around 4 a.m. having taped the race. I promptly grabbed a beer and a large scotch, and sat and watched as the announcer called, "They're off!"

Down the stretch the horses ran and, with 200 yards to go, Giacomo bursts into the lead with Closing Argument in second, and my other horse in fifth but closing fast. I couldn't believe it! The racing gods were smiling on me! I punched the air, shouting, "Yes! Yes! Yes!" as they crossed the line.

Unfortunately, my third choice finished fifth, but I nailed the winner and the second place finisher, and had bet the exacter. I was so excited as I looked at the odds: 50-1 for Giacomo and 71-1 for Closing Argument, the biggest exacter in Kentucky Derby history!

I immediately picked up the phone and called Dina in Italy, telling her the great news. My $19 wager had netted me over $4,600! I'd already booked a flight to Italy for a holiday the week before, and the win paid for my five-week stay and more! Now, tell me that's not good karma!

True, if my third horse had come in third instead of fifth, I would have been looking at a payout of over $300,000, but I was still very happy as I called the betting shop the next day and informed them of my large winning ticket.

You might think that, in the end, I gave all that money back through little bet, but you'd be wrong. In the years that followed, I've made fewer than a dozen bets, even missing my usual triple crown bets along the way. I know I got lucky with my gambling success. I'm not giving them a chance to get it back.

Chapter Twenty-Six
Down the Drain

My return to Canada in November 1991 wasn't by choice. I was chased here from England by Margaret Thatcher.

Well, by her policies, anyway.

The economy had been on a downturn for a while. Thatcher had proposed a pole tax that, in my opinion, was so damaging, it caused the recession.

How did it work? Like this: instead of paying, let's say, $1,000 a year in property tax, based on the value of the property you owned, they charged based on the number of people living within your property. Every son and daughter that was over 18, but not a student, paid the tax, let's say $600 per year. So, if you had four people inside a household, you paid $2,400 per household. It was a big tax grab.

My office was on New Zealand Avenue, right opposite the town hall. One afternoon I came out of the building and noticed people gathering at the back of the town hall. They began throwing rocks or whatever they could get their hands around at all the windows, shouting obscenities at the cronies inside, obviously angry at the pole tax. I watched from my car for about five minutes, then went home to tell Marylyn what I'd witnessed. I wondered what would the repercussions would be for me if this pole tax stayed in force.

I was doing pretty good at the time, with the three businesses I'd created in the fourteen years since I'd arrived in England from Italy, but it didn't last. Soon, sales began to slump, not only with our store, but also with the insurance business. It didn't take long for desperation to set in.

One of the worst blows came from a prospective client named

Eric Two Crowns (Supercabbie)

Nick Silbery. He'd been a millionaire at one point, living in a penthouse suite, owning racehorses and living a dream life in real estate. But he also had millions in development loans, and the recession killed development. His construction company had come to a standstill, and he could not sell any of his properties. He asked for my help in refinancing his projects at better interest rates.

This could have been a life-saving deal for me, giving me enough elbow room to ride this rough patch through until things turned around. I was excited as I arrived at his office for our appointment, but there I found movers hauling out furniture and clearing out the building. He had abandoned ship, fleeing to Spain, leaving everything he once owned behind, and leaving me without that life-saving deal. He could have at least called to tell me I didn't have to show up for our meeting!

I had a mortgage of about 1,400 pounds a month, Marylyn and I couldn't skip out on any bills, nor would we, even as they kept on coming in: rent, utilities, two staff members. I tried to keep going, seeking out all the possibilities and draining all the resources I had accumulated.

My last shot was with a gentleman from South Africa who played professional cricket and was a member of the national team. He needed refinancing on a project that was already underway: a nursing home with approximately 100 beds. It was nearing completion, but his current rate of interest was crippling his venture. I spent many hours contacting banks and other lenders to try and refinance the project, but there was nothing I could do in the end. All of the banks and financial institutions had run for cover. Money was difficult to borrow.

In hindsight, maybe I should have just let go of everything, like Nick had, and sought greener pastures. Instead, I struggled on, and I didn't tell Marylyn.

My nerves were shot. Marylyn could see that I was not myself anymore. She kept on asking if I was okay. I told her I was fine, thinking that something would go my way if I could just keep on digging. One good deal, and I could breathe again. But people were not spending. There were no mortgages to complete. I eventually sold our own house, taking a ten-thousand-pound loss.

I sold my BMW to cover the bills. I had no choice, but it didn't

Marylyn

help. I hated driving that older model Ford Capri, as seeing it made my clients wonder if all was well. Bad news travels fast, and I knew gossip would dampen my chances of getting deals.

As I had clients that paid monthly premiums in cash, I began to shuffle payments to use their money to cover my own expenses, and then use my monthly renewal bonuses to cover their premium costs. This is not something that one should do, but I couldn't see any other way out of this black hole.

It was quite a come down for me. I'd broken all of the probationary targets by a mile on the first year of my insurance career. I'd earned a bonus of nearly 20,000 dollars. I'd won awards and was flown to Glasgow to rub shoulders with the high fliers of the company. I was the Prince! Now I was the pauper. I was nose-diving towards self-destruction.

Finally, one morning, my manager Jim called me into the office. As I feared, they'd found out I had been stalling on paying the premiums for a couple of my clients. Jim brought the hammer down. "Eric, as of this moment, you are suspended." The ride was over. I was devastated and ashamed. I wanted to jump out the window.

But there was still Marylyn.

It was then I decided it was time to come back to Canada. Maybe that was an odd choice. I'd been gone twenty years. I could have taken Marylyn to Italy, where my family was, but Marylyn didn't speak Italian. She would have struggled to get a job.

Canada was also where Mom was. I hadn't seen her in years, and this decided the matter for me. Even though I considered England my home, it was time to come back to my original home.

I was still broke, but fortunately I still had good friends. Neil Clift lent me enough money to get by for a short while. I called him to tell him I was moving to Canada and to apologize for leaving so quickly. I told him I might not return. He was sad about that. He asked me to stay, and not worry about the loan. Another friend, Romero, gave Marylyn a place to stay for a bit, while I prepared to head off.

I felt a bit like Nick Silbery, running to Spain. However, I at least had tried to stick it out and not flee when the going got tough. My company had fired me; I hadn't quit.

Eric Two Crowns (Supercabbie)

Celebrating success in Glasgow, before it came crashing down.

But the company also didn't take any of the money they owed me and settle accounts I might have left outstanding. Instead, they dragged their feet. Eventually, I heard through the grapevine that someone had accused me of theft, and that the company might press charges.

That amazed me. I know I'd done wrong shifting money about to try and stay afloat, but the renewal bonuses should have gone to the company after I left, and that should have taken care of anything I owed. But the company had let me down on this and other promises. They'd promised, for instance, to help me set up my newly renovated shop for use as an insurance office. My landlords had been trying to muscle me out for another party that was willing to pay triple the rent, even after I'd put down £5,000 of my own money into renovations. I'd expected my company to intervene to force the landlords to stick to their lease, but instead the company's lawyers dragged their feet, which took out the last of my money.

Just before leaving for Canada, I put the house keys into an envelope and stuck it in the bank's mail chute with a note to manager Steven Hawkings, saying, "Sorry, Steve. Goodbye."

I left with a broken heart. As well as the disasters that had taken place with our business, my relationship with Marylyn took a

Marylyn

turn for the worse. I hate to say it, but it's true. Marylyn and I had been married for more than eight years when I learned that she'd kept a serious secret from me.

I knew that Marylyn had been married before, and that she'd had two children by her first husband, who were now living with their father. Simon and Nichola had been pretty young when their parents separated. But that was about all that I knew. Marylyn told me that I was to keep out of her past affairs and shot me down cold when I asked questions about it.

One Sunday afternoon, I came home after an appointment and entered our house to see a young girl sitting on our couch. I'd never met this person before, and asked Marylyn about it. She told me that the girl was a friend.

The girl was fifteen years old. Maybe it was one of Marylyn's friend's daughters or something? But maybe the look on my face did something, because she immediately changed her story, saying, "I'm only joking! It's Nichola, my daughter."

I didn't know what to say. Nichola was shy and timid and hardly uttered a word. I shook her hand, but she looked away, avoiding eye contact. I immediately felt for her, and saw a bit of myself in her reaction, because of my own experiences in my youth and the turmoil that goes with parents splitting up.

So, I made her feel welcome as best I could, and she stayed with us that afternoon. I drove her home and gave her some money, letting her know that she was always welcome to visit.

I'd never met Marylyn's ex-husband, nor did I wish to. She'd told me to stay out of her past, so I did. But the past still came back to haunt us.

After a couple of visits from Nichola, I took her home, and on the way back to her house, I noticed that she seemed a little upset. I asked her if she was okay.

"I don't want to go home," she said.

"Why not? What's the problem?"

That's when Nichola told me that she didn't get along with her sister, Julia.

Okay, I thought. Maybe she's referring to a step-sister. I asked her, "Your step sister?"

"No, my real sister."

Eric Two Crowns (Supercabbie)

I was confused. "You mean, your father's child with your stepmom?"

Now she got a little angry. "No! I don't have any step sisters!"

Dumbfounded, I dropped her off and raced back home. I tried to keep my cool and give Marylyn a chance to set the record straight. I met Marylyn in our kitchen. "Do you have something you'd like to tell me?" I asked.

"What do you mean?" she replied.

"Who is Julia?"

Marylyn immediately began to cry and ask for forgiveness. "I'm sorry! I'm so sorry!"

I could hardly understand what I was hearing, and what I understood, I could hardly believe.

Marylyn had lied to me about her past. There'd been more than two children. She'd lied because she was afraid that I would leave her if I learned that she'd had four kids. The fourth kid, named Spencer, had been put up for adoption. That took me into a dark place, because it was another kid that had been abandoned by his parents.

I demanded to know everything. I felt betrayed. I'd trusted Marylyn, and she hadn't trusted me with the truth. I left the house in a fury, and basically called it quits.

Marylyn's sister Shirley got in touch with me later that day, inviting me to her house for a talk. What could she possibly say to change my mind? But I went, and I listened, and Shirley said, "Marylyn has some problems."

"Oh, really?" I said. Well, they were not my problems, I thought. Except, I guess that they were.

That evening, Marylyn called me to say she was sorry. We met to talk about our situation. She played to my soft-side, and she coaxed me into having sex for "a last time". She wanted forgiveness, and that's how she got it. I stayed for the night and, the next day, decided to carry on with the relationship. The burden of that incident still lingers. It was a cloud over me as I headed back to Canada.

A philosopher once said, "You are where you are, and the main reason is *you!*" That's very true. At one point, I made an appointment with a priest to give Marylyn an opportunity to open up and

Marylyn

clear her soul of the burden she was carrying. Although Marylyn said she was an atheist, maybe the priest could help her find a sturdier path for herself. The priest gave Marylyn a Bible to read, but she hardly even picked it up.

Marylyn always struggled with her demons, in my opinion. At the time, I felt that it was my duty to try and show her the "light", committing myself to helping her live a better life. This was a hard struggle. She fought with temper tantrums that bordered on the ridiculous, fits of anger that demoralized me into making me think of walking out and never coming back.

In response, I wallow in self-pity. I struggle to understand the cards life has dealt me. I struggle with the fact that I wanted my father's love and he abused me. I struggled with the fact that Marylyn would test my love, and in her darker moments, attack what I stood for and loved.

I believe that the truth will set you free. I have come to believe this after seeing so many situations where the truth was withheld, before coming back to bite me.

Marylyn couldn't believe that I'd love her even if she'd had four kids. I found that really odd because, two, four, six, what does it matter? The only thing that matters is honesty.

And, of course, I'd failed to be honest with her. I lied to her when I told her that everything was fine, even as the business was going downhill. In that, I was also lying to myself, because I believed I could turn it around, without having to stress her out.

When I finally told her that I was up against the wall, she was lost for words. I could see that she was distressed and told her that we had to make a life decision. I've tended to look at life as a glass half full rather than half empty, when one door closes another opens, and all it takes is courage to change.

Nothing stays the same for long, so long as you can embrace the change.

So I embraced that change, with Marylyn. I would return to Canada.

Part 5:
Returning to Canada

Chapter Twenty-Seven
Finding Old Friends and More

I arrived in Canada in November 1991. I had barely £80 to my name ($200). I'd been away in Europe for nearly twenty years, so I had no friends in Canada to speak of. It was another long hill to climb.

Back in England, Marylyn took care of things while I found a place and a job here. Marylyn told me that my former employer was hounding her, asking where I was and putting pressure on her to reveal where I'd gone. Though she was shattered, she kept her cool. She told people that I'd left her, and she didn't know where I was.

Sometimes I think she would have been better off actually being rid of me. It would have given her a less stressful life back in England.

So, that's where I was: back in the country I was born in, but a stranger, married but separated by an ocean from my wife. All of this for many reasons, but ultimately because Dad had decided to run to Italy rather than be a responsible father.

Would things have gone better if Dad had been a proper father figure? I could have used some moral assistance, then. But at last I had my ambition. And I could still look up old friends.

Two in particular were Carlo and his brother Tony, the Cuzzi boys. Their father Giovanni had been a close friend of my father in Italy and Jack and I would always get excited when Dad said we were going to their place to visit. Tony was more my age, while Carlo and Jack were just a few months apart.

I asked for help from Peter, who was another friend of my Dad, and Lydia's godfather. I was staying at his place temporarily.

He drove me over to the Cuzzi's place the next morning. It was cold and there was a fresh dusting of snow on the ground. I saw no footprints visible, so I assumed no one was home, but I knocked on the door anyway.

All of a sudden, an old rusty green van came to a halt in front of the house and a burly, bearded man got out, walking briskly towards us. "Who are you? What do you want?"

"Carlo!" I replied. "It's me, Eric!"

He was startled, and his whole attitude changed. "What the hell?" He immediately hugged me, shook my hand, and opened the door to invite us in.

Carlo was so pleased to see me, and we began to reminisce about times past. Peter had left by then, leaving Carlo to drive me home when needed, so we hung out for a while until Carlo said, "Let's go and see some dancers!"

I had no clue what he was talking about. I wondered if he was referring to go-go dancers or something, which I'd seen a bit of in England. It didn't take me long after we got to the place to realize that he meant strippers.

I had never been to a "nudie bar" or anything like it in Europe. The closest experience I had was at a night club in a town called Spilimbergo, not far from Osoppo. There, they had a kind of cabaret show with topless dancers, but the place was high end. Not at all like this place.

When we arrived, Carlo promptly grabbed a small side-table for two and ordered a couple of drinks. I told him that I'd never been to a place like this, he said that he could break me in. "I'll get you a table dance later, okay?" he said, laughing.

"What the hell is a table dance?" I asked.

"Don't worry! You'll see in a bit!"

He chuckled. He had something in for me, the rookie, and to be honest I was a little intimidated. The former altar boy was to be baptized, but not with holy water.

The music got loud, and the show began. The blonde girl came out and began shedding her clothes in time to the music.

In hindsight, she was the prettiest girl I'd seen in the trade, so I was impressed with her body. When she was done, Carlo got up and made his way over to her. He whispered something in her ear and came back and sat down. I asked him what he'd said to her and he just grinned and said, "you'll see!"

Carlo was starting to remind me of the Artful Dodger in the movie *Oliver*.

A few more shows went by and then came another act by the bombshell feature. This time she was dressed as a cowgirl with a white-tasseled leather costume and hat. As she was finishing her act, fully nude, she approached the edge of the stage where we were seated and beckoned me to get up and get closer to her.

The stage was higher than the table we were sitting at and she squatted down and whispered in my ear to put my hand under her privates. I didn't want to wimp out, so I did it. I gasped as she deposited three ice cubes in my hand!!!

I shook them off and retreated in disgust, to the roar of the spectators. Everyone was laughing and shouting, "Green horn! Green horn!" I was embarrassed, to say the least, and tried in vain not to show it. Carlo was holding his stomach with laughter.

The announcer came on and said, "Come on, guys, give a round of applause for Angel Fantasy!"

I applauded along with the crowd and thought that was that. Little did I know what was to happen next.

Over Angel Fantasy comes, in her birthday suit, carrying a milk crate. She sets this down and starts to do a table dance on the crate, massaging her breasts and touching her privates while she puts her feet on my shoulders. I was frozen stiff, not knowing how to react. Carlo was getting his money's worth just watching my sad ass take all this in.

Apparently, he'd told her that I was fresh in from England and to give me a treat. How was that for welcoming me home? They all had a good laugh on me.

A few months later, I'd found a job and was outside my workplace having a smoke break when a delivery van pulled up and a woman got out. She grabbed a couple of boxes and walked past me through the main entrance. She looked strangely familiar, but I gave my head a shake and thought, nah, couldn't be. When she came back, though, I just knew. I threw caution to the wind and called "Angel!"

Returning to Canada

She nearly snapped her neck as she turned, hissing, "Shh! Not so loud! Where do I know you from?"

I asked her if she recalled the ice cube stunt and she laughed. "Absolutely!" she replied. I then asked her why she did dancing as a job, when she was working hard at delivering as well. She replied that she'd bought a house and wanted to pay it off as soon as possible.

I expect that mortgage was probably paid off in no time, as she was making a lot of money dancing and probably decent money at her regular day job delivering parcels. I wished her good luck, and that was the last I ever saw of her.

None of this was my cup of tea, but I still had to respect how hard Angel and others like her worked. Over the years, I've had to work some very hard jobs. And though I didn't know it at the time, more were on the way.

Chapter Twenty-Eight
East End Madness

I had taken a job on at a factory which manufactured skate sharpening machines in the nearby city of Cambridge. Unfortunately, the place was going down the drain due to competition with new technology. I was soon laid off with a bunch of other guys.

I quickly took on two part-time jobs, one as a bingo caller, and another as a part-time breakfast cook. I also found myself accepting a server's position at the East End Tavern. The place was better known as Tom's Kats.

This tavern was a strip joint with a twist. It had a reputation as a rough place frequented by losers and boozers, bikers and hookers.

By this time, Marylyn had joined me in Canada, but our marriage hadn't recovered. After our third split-up, she worked in the sister strip-bar, a male strip joint called Huggies. I was disgusted that we'd sunk to these depths.

The manager and right-hand man to the owners of these two joints was a man named Ralph. He took care of most of the managerial duties, and he'd hired me on the spot after I told him about my experience in the food and beverage industry.

The place was a dump. I recall my first encounter with the boss, a man named Brian. I'd put on my uniform that I'd worn for my previous jobs – black trousers, white shirt, and a black "Dicky Bow" tie. Seeing me, Brian called me over, saying, "You've never worked in a place like this before, have you?"

"Uh... no?" I replied.

He assured me there was no need for the bow tie.

He further told me that it would be a good idea, for the first few weeks, to look at him whenever customers came in. He'd shake his head 'no', if a person wasn't supposed to be there.

"Okay," I replied. "What do I do, then?"

"Well, you watch my back, and I'll watch yours," he said.

I was then introduced to the bouncers, Mark and Manny. Mark was an average-sized guy, but Manny was huge. He stood about six foot three and had to be about 350 pounds. He sure looked intimidating. Between Brian's instructions and Manny, I began to wonder if I was working in the wrong place.

Slowly, the girls began to arrive, heading to the dressing rooms to prepare for the night. They were the main reason guys came in; beer was secondary, though you had to be sure you were drinking something, or you'd be asked to leave, with assistance, if necessary.

I have always been able to take care of myself, but I sided towards discretion when I had a choice. I found that fighting solves few problems, so I try to solve things by intelligence. My first test came days later. When I arrived at work that afternoon, I saw Brian, looking disturbed. He called me over and pointed at two guys shooting pool. "See the guy shooting now?" he asked. "That guy has been barred for a year, and I've just let him back in. He's a bad one, so be warned."

"Okay," I said. "I'll keep an eye on him.

I took my serving tray and began to tidy up the lounge, which had bottles and ash trays left over from an earlier session. I was in the back seating area where the girls performed table dances, when I heard a loud bang.

I looked over to the two guys playing pool and I could see a chair was still twirling on the floor. The guy who'd been barred had kicked it after missing a shot.

I looked at Brian and saw him coming around the bar, heading towards the guy, looking intense. He shouted, and a scuffle broke out between them. Mark was standing buy, ready to help if needed, but Brian was skilled in martial arts. He was one of the toughest guys I'd ever met.

Suddenly, the guy grabs his pool stick and swings it at Brian, grazing his ribs, but then Brian grabs the stick and the two begin to wrestle. Brian wrenches the pool stick from the guy's grasp and smashes it on his back so hard, it shattered. Now the two were fighting freely. The punches flew. Mark stood by, waiting to pounce, and I just stood there, in the shadows, waiting.

Brian and the perpetrator both fell to the ground with a big crash, and that's when Mark jumped in. He grabbed the guy's legs in a bear hug, while Brian got the guy in a headlock. The guy was built like a brick house, though, and was slowly wriggling free of the chokehold. I prepared to jump in and help. When Brian jumped up, I rushed in and put the guy in another headlock

With Mark firmly holding his legs, and me holding on for dear life, Brian shouted, "Hold him hard!" He stepped back, and I could see him getting ready to kick the guy in the face! He took a big wind up, and came forward. I looked away as the first kick landed with a big crunch of cracking teeth.

"Keep holding on!" Brian shouted again, and with another wind-up of his steel capped boots, he delivered another crushing kick in the teeth.

The girls that were there started screaming at the sight of blood streaming down my arm. The feeling of the warm blood made my stomach churn, but the guy was done. I got up quickly, and he just laid there.

The next thing you know, Brian and Mark picked the guy up at both ends and plunged him head first through the thick metal doors and down the stairs. Another thrust through the main door with his noggin, then they dropping him on the pavement outside, his face split open and blood gushing from his wounds.

The adrenaline rush was evident as we all gasped for air. Girls were running for towels and began wiping me down. I started to panic a little as I realized that I'd been an accomplice to assault. They'd just left him there on the sidewalk, with people on the street watching in horror. I thought that if the guy died, I could be charged with being an accessory to murder! Holy shit, I thought, what did I get myself into now?

But Brian didn't seem to be bothered. He'd been through this kind of thing plenty of times and, if anything, he seemed proud of this achievement.

A few minutes went by and a policeman entered with the ambulance outside tending to the bloodied loser. There was a brief inquiry and, when all was said and done, the cop left with no charges being laid on anyone. I guess he thought that the guy had come in looking for trouble, and found it.

Brian later told me that he had the guy had some kind of grudge and wanted revenge. Instead, he'd ended up worse for the wear.

The East End Tavern was to serve me in my path of life. It showed me how far I could go down, and how to set me on a better path later on. I suppose we sometimes find ourselves in situations and predicaments that serve to teach us for the future. We make mistakes, but we get to make right our mistakes.

The seats around the main stage is called Perverts Row. That's where most of the action is, with money being slipped into bikinis and tops. Most of the dancers were not that attractive to be honest. There were a couple that stood out, though.

One was Jennifer, a university student paying for her own tuition by dancing. She had a beautiful face and body and kept to herself and went about her business with an air of purpose and confidence. She kept away from the drugs and her main focus was her education. As time went on, I found out that she was making way more money than the other girls. She told me that she could clear $2000 in a week for her efforts. Wow! I thought. To be beautiful and have the guts to walk around half naked and entertaining scummy characters took a lot of courage.

Most of the other girls did it for the drugs, booze and the attention. Some of them had bad addictions, and at times I witnessed a couple falling from the stage to the floor, drunk, drugged and out of it. Eventually I would get to know them all. There was a black girl who would get so drunk she would not only fall off the stage, but by the end of the night want to bed anything in sight, including me!

I also saw the other side of the strip industry. A month or two working for Tom's Kats, Ralph turned up and said he needed me down at the Grand Hotel the next night as someone had quit and they needed a body down there to help out. I agreed, but I soon wondered if I'd made a mistake as, as soon as I got down there, I was told that I'd be working on "the Huggies' side" as the bartender called it, showing me through to the adjoining male strip joint.

I wondered what I was in for; screaming women ogling guys'

Eric Two Crowns (Supercabbie)

meat and two veg? But, tray in hand, I started my job, putting ashtrays on tables, wiping them down, vacuuming the carpet.

The first female patrons started coming in as Marylyn took their cash and handed out tickets. They scurried to their favourite seats and sat down, giggling and acting as if they were true desperadoes, eager to have a look at what tackle was flopping around that night. One of the things they looked forward to was, after an act, to pay two dollars to kiss their favourite dancer on stage. The dancers would invite girls up with shouts of "Toonie time!"

Let's just say that this wasn't my cup of tea.

I recall one night, when I was asked to go upstairs to the dressing room and look it over for stray bottles and glasses, and I saw one guy sitting at a table staring at a Playboy magazine. I just glanced at him, when I noticed that he was pulling his "wire", shall we say. What the hell was he doing, I thought. Then I realized: he was getting his Wally ready for the show. They'd get themselves aroused, then tie a hair elastic around it to make sure they didn't go limp. This was before the time of Viagra.

It didn't take long for me to tell Ralph never to ask me to work there again, or I'd quit. If I was going to work in this place, I wanted to make good money, but that was never going to happen. The clients were terrible tippers, keeping their two-dollar coins for a kiss from the guys rather than good service from their waiter.

I tried to be like Jennifer and keep to myself. We hung out together because we had the same reason for being there: making money, paying our bills, and keeping our noses clean. Unfortunately, I couldn't always do that, as I had to get involved when fights erupted. Telling a guy who'd had too much to drink that he was cut off could be trouble, and more than often, was.

I remember once, at closing time, there was one guy left at Perverts Row. Brian was behind the bar and I was finishing cleaning up the lounge. This last scumbag was taking his time getting himself together. Brian was getting annoyed with his antics.

He then approached Brian saying, "There's a load of some guy's 'goo' where he jerked off on Pervert's Row."

Brian handed me a flash light from the bar. "Go over and take a look, Eric," he said.

Off I went on this ghastly duty and shone the light in the area the guy pointed at. There was nothing, and I said so, at which point the guy started to laugh. He was screwing with Brian.

Without hesitation, Brian punched the guy full force on the side of the head, putting him down like a sack of potatoes. "Take that for being an idiot!" he said.

The guy was dragged out on his butt and he too met the pavement with a crunch. There was no messing with Brian. He travelled with a baseball bat in his gym bag, and there were many people wanting to get at him, with grudges for being barred or kicked out. That led to me getting my tires slashed, because Brian and I drove similar cars. It cost me $300 for the tow truck and replacement tires, before I was back in business, waiting for another episode to happen.

All in all, I worked for Brian for two and a half years. Finally, the building was purchased by the city and torn down. It reminded me of a scene in the movie *The Ten Commandments*, where Charlton Heston stands on the side of the mountain holding up God's own tablets saying, "Those who will not live by the law shall die by the law," and throws them into the crowd of sinners. Purification of the corrupt in one swift move by the city.

I don't know the reasons for some things, but I understood why I spent a piece of my life toiling with the sinners. I think Marylyn, was also somehow sent there to learn a similar lesson.

Chapter Twenty-Nine

The Break-Up

Marylyn and I split up for the third time in 1996. I suppose the trial of life had become so much of a burden, I failed in my management of it. Sometimes life throws you curve balls you cannot hit.

I had been working hard, trying to support Marylyn, as she had fallen into a depression. Perhaps leaving her native England the way we did was the devastating factor. She had scabs on her head, and there was weight loss. I'm told she developed a condition called alopecia areata. She only weighed about 110 pounds soaking wet, and now she was hovering around 100.

I couldn't stand seeing her like that, and though my own depression was eating me up, I felt I had to stay strong for her. I couldn't tell her my real feelings inside me, so I just bit the bullet and did my best to ride the wave. I was the breadwinner, and I worked six days a week to accommodate our needs. I even went so far as to smoke roll up cigarettes to save money. Marylyn smoked only the best, because that's what she insisted on.

I suppose being ten years younger than my wife was a problem, after all she was older and wiser. I could not and have still not conquered that philosophy of her thinking. After all, what could I know? I had met Marylyn when I'd just turned eighteen. I married her when I was twenty. Perhaps my naivety and innocence were attractions to her at the time.

I was shocked how quickly things turned from happy and forward looking to hurt.

I remember one time early in our marriage, I'd come home and was in the process of making dinner. I'd seen our Italian landlady making some chicken dish, and it looked tasty, so I gave it a go.

Marylyn walked into the kitchen, and I suggested that she should watch me to learn how to cook the dish too. I was taken aback when she retorted, "Don't think you can teach me anything. I'm older than you!"

How could this come out of the mouth of my newly married wife who says she loves me? Something was going on somewhere inside her that I was unaware of. At the time I knew she'd been divorced and she'd had two children from that defunct marriage, but why take it out on me?

On another occasion, when we were courting, she showed me her jealous side.

I was in our quarters at the Burford Bridge hotel in Dorking, Surrey, and had just finished my lunch time shift, when there was a knock on the door. I was in my underwear as it was a hot day and we had no air conditioning in the room.

Mandy, a chambermaid, was at the door, asking for Marylyn, her boss. I poked my head around the door so as to not expose myself and told her that I hadn't seen her and that she was somewhere in the hotel. Mandy nodded and went to look for her.

An instant later, I heard footsteps in the corridor and the door flung open, revealing Marylyn. I was just turning to the bedroom door when she walked in and slapped me full force in the back.

Shocked, I turned as she began to scream at me, insinuating that I'd been up to something with Mandy. She'd caught a glimpse of Mandy walking away from our door, and had assumed the worst.

At first, I didn't know what she was talking about, and was just shocked at her rage. When I realized what she was accusing me of, I got upset that she didn't trust me, and that she'd physically hit someone she supposedly loved. I'd been through enough physical abuse from my father in the past, and this made me lose faith in her love for me. If anything, I should have been angry at her for all her flirtations with the hotel assistant manager, but being brought up Catholic, I always turned the other cheek.

I recall thinking that I loved her so much I could help to heal the anger in her. I believe that love cures the soul and heart, so I took it upon myself to aid her in her bitterness, but years later, af-

Eric Two Crowns (Supercabbie)

ter fleeing Britain for Canada, I couldn't get Marylyn out of her depression, so I decided to give her space on her own to sort things out. Having me around was just a constant reminder of our strife.

Susan was a friend Marylyn had made days after our arrival in Canada. She was eating junk food all the time, and was huge, weighing around 300 pounds. She was kind of bad news. I was told by an acquaintance that she was a 'school yard whore' years ago, performing fellatio on boys after classes. I warned Marylyn about her, but to no avail. Little did I know she was leading Marylyn down a worse road of destruction.

Shortly after Marylyn moved out to stay with this woman, Marylyn called me to ask for some household goods that we had split up, as she wanted to come and get them. I agreed, and she and Susan turned up at my friend's house where I was staying.

I didn't know why Marylyn would want the silly pots that she was asking for, but when she came over, I realized it was to show off the big hickey her new boyfriend had put on her neck. Not even a blouse to cover it up! All that in just two weeks. So much for loving and cherishing "till death do us part".

A few days later, Susan called me, telling me that Marylyn was pregnant and shacked up with some cowboy dude nicknamed "Psycho" of all things, and that she was happy. It was a deliberate attempt to bring me down, and it was working.

I can tell you that I was a mess for a long time. I went into a tailspin. I didn't eat. I didn't sleep. I had no will to live. I went back to harming myself by drinking and smoking weed. I lost thirty-eight pounds in a very short period of time, and I started planning my exit from this world.

Years before, my uncle Bertrand had given me a cut throat razor. It was Granddad Moreau's, similar to the ones Dad used in his barber shop. I had it in the wardrobe as a memento of granddad's life. That thing was so sharp you could literally split a hair.

I began convincing myself that I was no good and would best be gone. Yet it is a sin in God's world to take your own life. In native Indian circles, it's cowardice. But I was battling the demons and they were winning.

Laying in my bed one evening I decided it was time. Tears streaming down my face. I looked at the closet, knowing my fate

Returning to Canada

laid inside a little box, waiting. At the same time, there was a beer bottle cap on top of the cabinet near the closet. I picked it up instead and started to drag the jagged edge across my wrist. I did it again with pressure enough to draw blood.

I thought, that's not so bad. If I'd used the cut throat razor, I'd be gone in minutes.

I got up from the bed and moved to the closet, weeping. I stood there looking at the case and began to open it.

Tim, my roommate was in the house, in his bedroom, sleeping. I gazed over at the alarm clock and saw it was around two in the morning. I opened the case and laid back on my bed and continued to cry desperately, razor in hand.

Out of the corner of my left eye I saw something leaning on the bedside lamp. For some reason this book was there, just by chance, which I had never read or seen before. It took my concentration away from what I was doing. I wept even harder as the title read *The Light in Me*, with Jesus's image looking right at me. I was immediately inspired and knew he had come back to save me.

Most of my religious tendencies and beliefs had dwindled over the years, with Jesus the only person I actually retained in my heart. When I was being beaten, he was there. When I was in pain, he was there. When I was weak and vulnerable, he gave me strength.

I put the razor back into the case and gritted my teeth. I wiped the tears away and began to read this book. In my desperation, I had found the will to survive. I told myself that I would never let myself be dragged down by anyone again.

I started to pull myself together. I had applied for welfare assistance when I couldn't work, and I recall the worker who came to see me being so sympathetic. She said, "Eric, you speak five languages, you're young and have much to offer, you are not 'worthless'. I began to wonder whether I could save this marriage and made the decision to seek out "Psycho", the person Marylyn was seeing, and have a chat with him.

I began inquiring through my channels and found out where he lived and the places he frequented. Within a couple of days I knew where to go and what to say to this dude. His favourite watering hole was TJ's on Weber Street, and I went there one afternoon hoping to run into him. Unfortunately, he never showed. So I asked the bartender if she knew where the guy lived, as I was an old friend back in town, wanting to see him again. She spoke to a couple of guys in the back and returned, telling me his address.

The next day, I waited outside his place, my heart pounding. I had my *Rambo* knife taped to my ankle, ready for a fight with this "Psycho", ready to kill him. Suddenly, a guy looks out his window at me, not looking much like a "Psycho" at all, but still the person at the address I was given. I got out of the car and knocked on the door. He opened it, asking what I wanted.

"Do you know Marylyn?" I asked.

He jolted at my question, and asked me why I wanted to know.

"She's my wife," I replied.

He took a step backward.

"My name is Eric. I'm her husband."

Now he was looking really uncomfortable. I was ready to pounce and get in on it, but then he stopped me by saying, "Sorry."

He explained that Marylyn had told him that she was separated and getting a divorce. We had never discussed divorce; the separation was supposed to be something temporary, to give each other space. I further learned that "Psycho" was dating two other women as well as Marylyn.

I informed "Psycho" that Marylyn and I were just having a break, and he could see that he'd made a big mistake. I asked him how many times he and Marylyn'd had sex, and the answer left me boiling inside, but he seemed genuinely remorseful, and I left feeling that I'd brought an end to this charade.

Later, when I confronted Marylyn about this, I asked her how many times she and Psycho'd had sex, and she said, "Just once!", not knowing that I had the answer already. I did not like the lie. I was even more confused by the fact that she was upset to discover that I'd been smoking weed, and yet she'd been living with a guy who'd been dealing in drugs, had two daughters with no mother in sight, and was dating three women at once!

Maybe I should just have walked away and left Marylyn to her choices, but I held out hope that Marylyn would come back, and everything would sort itself out.

We made arrangements to see each other one evening. When

she came out to the car I was amazed that she looked so good. Her hair was coloured and cut, her clothes were nice; it was like the day we met. She seemed to be happy to see me. We drove around, talking and sharing memories, until I pulled into a car park, and she pulled out a condom suggestively.

I was surprised, saying, "Why do you have one in your purse?"
"You never know," she replied.

That wasn't the answer I wanted to hear. I just started up the car and drove her back as quick as possible to where she was living with Madam Susan. Eventually, she and Susan relocated into a house in one of the slummiest places in the city. Marylyn would mind Susan's kids and the door while Sue would perform "Tricks" for fifty dollars a pop.

I have to admit that, during our break-up, I had tried to get revenge. I'll call her "Wendy". She was an acquaintance that I'd known for a few years, and she just happened to be at the club I frequented. We were making small talk when a phone call came in for me. It was Marylyn, telling me that she was seeing someone else.

In the days that followed, I invited Wendy to my house. One thing led to another and I found myself in bed with her. It was all so surreal, and I felt that I'd lost my wife for good. Wendy was giving me oral sex and we were about to have intercourse when a bell went off in my head. I just stopped, laid on my back, and told her I couldn't do it. I was too in love with Marylyn and knew it was wrong to continue.

All Wendy said was, "that's the closest I've come to sex without having it."

I was relieved that I had, for myself, made a good decision. On the other hand, when Marylyn and I eventually did get together, it seemed that Marylyn had no regrets about her fling. As a matter of fact, after we got back together, when I got upset hearing about her antics, she poked me in the forehead and said, "Get over it!"

Why didn't I just leave? The truth is, I thought, "better the devil you know." That's a poor excuse, but I took my vows and I kept them, for better or for worse, right? I curse myself for being a believer and to uphold the rules of the Church. If there is Heaven, and I don't get there, there will be Hell to pay!

Chapter Thirty
Nutraceuticals and TW

In my travels, I've met all sorts of wealthy people. I kept many at arm's length as their aura felt false to me. They drove fancy cars, had all the material things surrounding them, but characters that were only self-serving. They believed they were better and deeper than anyone else, but they seemed shallow to me. What justifies their sense of entitlement or grandeur when they fail to open a door to the meek and needy?

In 1996, an opportunity came along. Marylyn had stumbled on an ad for "Nutraceuticals". I read that as medicines that were natural. I investigated further, making calls, and receiving a video. The gentleman who talked to me didn't know the specifics himself, but he said that one of the products had helped enormously with his wife's PMS symptoms. I began to get more curious and decided to give them a try.

At the time, I had a prostate condition, which my doctor had told me was rare at my age (at the time, 34). The drugs he'd given me were a Band-Aid solution, but also a catalyst for me to take my health into my own hands. I committed myself to these Nutraceuticals. I firmly believe that all our cures are out there in nature; it's up to us to go and find them. This meshes well with the native side of my identity.

Two weeks into taking these products, I felt a tingling in my body and a sense of euphoria. I was at work at the time, and my face felt warm and my mind felt refreshed, and I knew that something was changing inside me.

Vince, the gentleman who'd introduced these products to me, asked if I would be interested in helping him sell the products to others. I was more than willing to sell something I believed in, so I agreed.

But there was a problem: there were start-up costs I had to swallow — as much as $3000. Marylyn wasn't working at the time. I worked up to 55 hours a week at a circuit board manufacturing company just to make ends meet. We were just scraping by. My credit was non-existent. I wasn't willing to hit up my family, as I knew that creates animosity. So, what could I do?

Suddenly, I found a lifeline. I met TW, a gentleman that seemed genuine and kind. He was a highly successful businessman, employing about 450 people at his auto parts plant.

I'd met him not long before. He didn't look like much to see him but looks are deceiving. It was at the Legion branch 530 in Waterloo. As I got to know him, I could feel the openness within him. Most times, he was calm, but then we played cards, and he shouted so loud, he almost busted an ear drum. The first time we played, I put a card down, and he shouted, "What did you do that for, stupid!"

That doesn't look friendly written down, but when I looked at TW, and saw him looking back so sheepishly that I couldn't help but laugh. He didn't need to apologize, because I knew he was joking.

Perhaps TW could lend me money? Even better, I realized I had two portraits which we had purchased in England which I could offer as security. With the plan in hand, I called TW to arrange an appointment. He invited me to his office a few days later.

With paintings in hand, I approached his office and rang the buzzer. I was anxious and nervous as I waited for the door to open. He smiled when he saw me. I liked him. He had a demeanor of a wise and humble man, and yet he was direct and no-nonsense. His office seemed more like a party room, it was full of golf gadgets around a putting area. He had a bar that had dozens of liquor bottles from around the world. There was even a jacuzzi tub!

"Hi, Eric!" he said. "Come on in! What do you want?"

"I need some financing," I replied. "I have an opportunity, but no money."

He asked me what the opportunity was. Over a couple of drinks, I explained everything about the business opportunity,

Eric Two Crowns (Supercabbie)

TW's House.

and my offer of the portraits as security, if he was willing to take the chance. They were worth less than what I needed but they were still some security. I felt so uncomfortable asking for help, but I wasn't going to let it stop me.

After I finished my pitch, he thought for a moment, and then asked how much I needed? As I told him the amount, I was sure he was going to say 'no!', but he didn't. Instead, he pulled out a chequebook and began writing. Before I knew it, he tore off the cheque and handed it to me. I was relieved and amazed; not only could I give my venture a shot, but someone trusted me enough to invest in me. It was a good feeling after fleeing England. I was ready to hug and kiss him, but that wouldn't have been very businesslike.

He asked me to sign a promissory note, but told me, "Take your time and good luck!" The note said I had to pay him back at 10% interest, but there was no deadline.

Well, that was the start of a long friendship between TW and I. We were both passionate about snooker and golf. He invited me to a get together to play on the full-sized snooker table in one of his homes. He still lives on the outskirts of a small town close to the city in a house he calls The Farm. It's not a farm, it's more like an oasis in the bush. He loves his dogs, and I swear every one of

Returning to Canada

his hundred-plus trout in his pond have a name! There are also koi and bass. He has many bird feeders, and the place is visited by woodpeckers, blue jays, cardinals, orioles and more. Not long ago, he even had incubators to hatch blue eggs from southern-bred chickens.

It is peaceful there. For me, the Farm the closest thing to a spiritual rehab centre. I find myself recharging my inner battery whenever I go there. I grab a pot of feed pellets and sit by the rocks, feeding the fish, watching the water erupt and boil as if piranhas were attacking. I sit, pondering life and welcoming the solitude. TW would be inside, sipping a glass of white wine in the company of his beloved three Wheaton terriers. He also has thirty-pound bags of unshelled peanuts as well as cases of oranges for orioles, cardinals and blue jays to feast on. The sign above his entrance reads "Easy Street", which I think fits.

He is envied by many but loved by what seems like everyone. He is, by his own admission, "an Ayatollah of asshollery", as he'd crack jokes regularly, but he is generous, bringing snacks and edibles to the club to share with everyone, even strangers. He usually asks me to go around to hand out these goodies.

Eric Two Crowns (Supercabbie)

TW's Pond Oasis.

TW has shown me the good ways of life by being compassionate to all. I see him as a father figure, as he has always been supportive towards me. Others may have laughed at some of my ideas, but he has never said anything negative towards me in the over twenty-five years I have known him. He has even encouraged me to write down the words you see here.

It's good to have a friend that encourages you towards success. I know too many others who have been cynical, and had I been cynical, I would not have succeeded as often as I have. This is why we need more people like TW, who will encourage us through their optimism.

TW sometimes tells this story of how he got lucky. It was earlier in his business days, when he was approached by an automobile manufacturer. They were looking for a special part to be made, needing them quickly. He was already dealing with many auto makers on a day to day basis.

He was asked to give a quote on these special parts and headed to the US to try and seal the deal. He was going to ask for $50,000, but he asked his partner for his opinion, and his partner said the quote should be for $150,000.

Returning to Canada

He retorted, "Are you crazy?" Then he talked with one of his representatives, who suggested that he quote $300,000 for the job. He thought the representative was crazy too.

But he decided to take their advice and, upon arrival at the meeting with the auto maker's bigwig, noticed something in the man's office. From what I gathered, the bigwig was an African-American with a deep voice, who must have had a passion for pigs. There were pig decorations all around the office, from paintings to statues to ornaments.

TW Himself.

So, TW made his presentation to the man, who showed very little emotion. Finally, TW announced his price tag: $300,000. The man just grunted. But then TW thought of something. He asked to be excused and went out to his car where he'd coincidentally had a magazine entitled Playboar. The magazine was a satire of the Men's Playboy magazine, with pigs as the subject. It had been produced by a young man near Kitchener (Breslau), and TW had bought hundreds of copies of them.

TW came back in, placing the magazine on the man's desk, saying, "Here's a gift for you."

The man immediately said that gifts could not be accepted (company policy).

But TW said, "Well, could you accept a pen?"

"I suppose," said the man.

"Then pretend it's a pen and leave it at that."

Then the man looked at the magazine and flipped through the pages. He started to laugh. By the time he got to Miss Piggy's centrefold, he was roaring.

The man looked at TW and asked if he had any more "pens". TW said he did, and the deal was sealed.

Talk about opportunity knocking. That happy accident led to

Eric Two Crowns (Supercabbie)

many deals between the two. In TW's words, he says, "That's why I'm luckier than a dog with two dicks, on a street full of hydrants!"

I can only imagine how far I could have gone in life if TW had actually been my father. He's getting older, now (about eighty), and it's he that needs me. I help him any way I can, making a point to visit him at his home every Saturday morning. He always has something for me to do. And although his legs and his general health are not what they were, his mind is sharp and his wits are still intact. I know that, when his time comes, I will be devastated. I was there when he had a minor stroke not long ago, falling to the ground at our club. I cried as the ambulance arrived with the paramedics and, at that moment, I knew I loved him like a father.

We meet once or twice a week. He always has cheese or salami with crackers or popcorn for his buddies and anyone else that wants some. He'll ask me to go around and offer munchies to people he doesn't even know. He'll defend me when others attack and has helped me when others shied away. When I was sick, he's called to ask if I was okay.

That's why I would have loved him as a father. He is a considerate man with a huge heart and compassion. He also taught me something wise. He said, "Never mistake kindness for weakness." Some people might need to learn that phrase.

On one occasion, he called to ask me a favour. He was feeling ill and there was no one there to help him. "Can you come and pick me up?" he asked. "I need to get to the hospital."

Of course, I went, worried and fearful as I sped to his home. I have to admit I even shed a tear in the solitude of my car. But then I realized that he called me before anybody else. That feeling of being needed made me realize that we would be friends forever. I know this sounds weird, even as I write this.

I know he has been lucky, but I have been luckier finding him. We enjoy playing cards, golf and snooker. We enjoy drinks and laughs. He's one of the few people who help me play straight and fulfill my purpose.

Chapter Thirty-One
Forgiveness

Marylyn and I have been together for nearly forty years. There have been testing times. I think my lack of maturity in my younger days played a part in this, wanting to prove myself as a man, without the wisdom experience provides.

But through it all, we have managed to keep the flame lit. We have managed to come to terms with our flaws, our mistakes, and our indiscretions. I know that we love each other.

I know that Jesus installed in me kindness, tolerance love and forgiveness. I try to live up to these traits every day. Some people get bowled over by aggressors, people who think kindness is a weakness, who take advantage of love and the sharing of it. Many times, we have shown benevolence, and been disappointed. But love and caring for one another rules all. In the end, love conquers all.

Sometimes I have felt that we've bitten off more than we can chew in this marriage. Sometimes, we don't understand each other as well as we should. However, our fortieth anniversary is around the corner, and we're still here, till death do us part.

Maybe this is my purpose: to fulfill my vows and do all that I can to see it through. Not only because of the initial promise, but because of the unconditional love I have for Marylyn. I can't see myself without her.

I know it works both ways. Finally, as we walk hand-in-hand towards the horizon, I ask the Great Spirit to keep a place for her by my side in the afterlife in the company of the greatest Creator Manitou!

Eric Two Crowns (Supercabbie)

Be it any religion or culture, make no mistake, the life within you starts from our mother, Mother Earth.

And that is our other destiny, I think: to preserve and restore the planet. This beautiful Earth has been here for billions of years, and we've done so much damage in the last few hundred.

Our greatest task is healing the Earth, and I believe that it will be the Aboriginals of every country that will take the ultimate stand. When the calling comes I will make it a point to stand with them. Something must be done without hesitation! The challenge is here and now.

Chapter Thirty-Two
Kill the Beast

During that desperate summer before my reconciliation with Marylyn, I came very close to ending it all, and I stopped myself by seeing Jesus on the cover of *The Light in Me* and reading the book and finding strength through him. Also, during that summer, I had another dream, or vision, that I think came from a different source. Admittedly, I wasn't sleeping nights. I'd lost 38 pounds way too fast. I'd been drinking, and smoking weed.

But I had a vision of a vicious bear beginning to engulf me. The bear was the invader in the marriage between me and Marylyn.

Suddenly I found myself as an Eagle, flying high above a forest, searching for the bear. I knew I had to track it down. I had to kill it, to rid myself of its angry and evil spirit inside of me. I knew it would be a hard battle, to kill the beast or let it in my mind forever.

This vision came back to me as nightmares, night after night. I would twist and turn under the covers, feeling like I was in a straitjacket, desperate to free myself.

Finally, the time came. I was soaring, and I saw something moving down below. I spotted the bear scurrying through the woods, crashing branches as he strode.

The bear looked up, and I moved in for the showdown. He began to run faster through the trees, growling, as I began diving towards him. His growls grew louder than the sound of the wind. I made my first attack, claws extending as I landed on his back.

The bear snapped at me, turning his neck in both directions as I dug in with my talons. He couldn't get at me, as I was right behind him now, pecking and tearing at him. He rolled over, trying to pin me, but I flapped my wings and flew up, hovering over him.

Eric Two Crowns (Supercabbie)

The bear got to his feet and began to run, but he's moaning as well as growling, and the echo rumbles through the forest. I came at him again and attacked, this time aiming for his eyes. The bear let out a huge groan as blood began to gush from his face. I pulled back, hovering over him as he stumbled, disoriented and blinded.

I attacked again, burying my sharp beak and talons into his back. The bear groans helplessly as he realizes his time has come. With a last attack, I swooped down and buried my beak in his back. I burrowed deep into the body, digging for his heart, the only way to cleanse myself of this evil spirit. Finally, I tore it out.

The battle won, I flew back into the sky, with the bear's heart clutched in my talons. I squealed victory to the sky, and my cry echoes over the mountains. I am King of the Sky. The maker Manitou has proclaimed so.

I awoke in a sweat but feeling that I'd won a hard-fought battle. Another threat to my sanity had vanished. The intruder was destroyed.

Part 6:
Coming Home

Chapter Thirty-Three

Returning to Les Escoumins

Healing does not happen in a straight line, nor all at once. I actually first returned to Les Escoumins in January 1992, after many years of absence.

While I travelled on my way there, I remembered the times I'd spent there as a child. I remember, on one visit, suddenly coming upon a black bear pelt fixed to the wooden shack beside the original family home, a sign of a successful hunt.

I remember Lydia falling from her bicycle and scratching herself up badly.

I remember my uncle's gas station and garage where he and his son Serge repaired cars. I remember helping to fill up the cars, and my horror when I filled up my first car and couldn't figure out how to stop the pump. Gas started gushing out of the tank!

I also remember once, Serge asking me to move a car, so another car could get out from behind this orange muscle car. I got in the orange muscle car, put it in reverse, pressed the gas, and nearly took out the gas pumps as the tires spun up the gravel. I'd put the brakes on so hard! Serge laughed at me as I froze in fear, but he quickly reached in and shifted the gear back to Park. "Move over," he said. He was kidding, yet breaking me in.

I expected things to be the same when I returned. I expected to see the same houses, the same gravel roads. But the truth is, nothing stays the same. The roads were paved, and new houses had been built. There was a modern gas station with a convenience store and a tourism office all in one building. The bay below, where we used to swim in the icy cold waters, was now adorned with beautiful red and white chalets for tourists.

Coming Home

One thing that did remain the same, though, was the original family home, looking east out over the St. Lawrence River.

I didn't call my Mom right away when I got to Canada. Maybe I should have. However, Marylyn was still in England, taking care of some of the mess that I'd left behind.

If I had called Mom, she'd have been at my door in an instant, and I needed some time to organize and get things ready before I called her. I had just $200 in my pocket, and I needed a job and a place to live.

Within a few days, I found employment as a manager of a restaurant. I saved all I could from that job, to put a deposit down on a place and buy furniture for us before Marylyn arrived.

Finally, when Marylyn arrived at our place in December 1991, and we had a phone and everything, I picked up the receiver and called Mom.

But she didn't answer. I called again, but she wouldn't pick up. I started to think something was not right.

I phoned my cousin Claudio in Windsor to ask what was up? Surely, he would know. He told me that Grandma was dying, and her last wish was to see all her family, including children, grandchildren, great-grandchildren, along with cousins and all the friends who would undoubtedly oblige. She was not only loved by her family, but she was an elder, held in high esteem by all. She was the wife of a chief, or leader: my grandfather, who was renowned for his wisdom and guidance, and he had married a woman with the love and skills to keep the culture and its traditions alive.

Mom once told me that Grandma loved to be in the company of her grandchildren. She'd sing songs, play with them, and taught them how to play solitaire and cribbage. She'd rubbed noses with all of us in greeting. She never showed any favouritism. Mom, on the other hand when we were alone, would call me her "little Indian boy", as I was the one who most resembled her side of the family.

If Grandma was dying, I needed to be there.

I called my uncle Bertrand who still lived in the old family home in Essipit. He told me that Mom was there, but in the hospital at Grandma's side. I knew I had to get up there, quick, but I had no transportation. Fortunately, my childhood friend Carlo

Eric Two Crowns (Supercabbie)

Essipit Signpost

Cuzzi came through, offering to drive me. I left Marylyn in Kitchener with our cats and returned to Essipit.

As we drove, I could feel the bond I had to the place being rekindled. I felt a burning desire to rediscover and gain a better understanding of myself and my mother's people. I'd roamed the Earth for most of my life, and I needed somewhere to belong. Maybe then I could find peace inside me, and a place to call home, once and for all.

Carlo could fit in anywhere and was instantly welcomed by everybody there. They were impressed that he'd made the effort to get to Essipit, driving sixteen hours through some of the worst of Canada's winter conditions. Uncle Bertrand greeted us when we arrived and told me that Mom was with Grandma at the hospital. We quickly unloaded our things and, after a brief stop at Uncle Louis' place, I rushed over to the bedside.

Though it was a sad time for all, I felt that Grandma had lived a good life. She was nearly 92. The love she shared was deep, and she'd touched many people and she was about to touch me. I couldn't help but feel her aura, as though it was pulling me to her the moment we entered the hospital. I found my way to her room where some family members, mainly women, sat around her.

I was greeted by Mom, with a big hug and the usual tears. Others huddled around me and greeted me, before I made my way to Grandma's bedside and sat down.

She looked at me in the eyes, a little bewildered and asked who I was? It had been nearly two decades since she'd last seen me.

Mom asked, "Who do you think he is?"

Coming Home

"Jack?" Grandma replied, not sounding sure.

"No," Mom replied. "Try again."

Grandma looked me over again but before she could say anything, Mom blurted out the answer. "It's Eric!"

Grandma looked at me, and it was like she was coming back to life. She actually sat up and embraced me. She grabbed my face and we rubbed noses. I recall her exhaling straight into my face like a whale's breath, and I inhaled her. In a moment, she began to sing, and we all joined her in songs of youth and celebration. I admit, I mostly hummed along, but I was amazed at the love surrounding her in preparation for the journey to her next life.

I left about an hour later, feeling changed and closer to some peace in my life. Though there were still struggles ahead, it was still a big piece of the puzzle in making myself feel whole.

Carlo and I had been invited to dinner at Uncle Louis' home. I introduced Carlo when we arrived, and he was accepted as a friend of mine, and thus a friend of theirs. Everybody appreciated how he had made a personal sacrifice to help me in a time of my need.

As we entered Uncle Louis home, I noticed two plates of meat on the kitchen counter. I assumed it was liver as the meat was dark purple in colour. Uncle Louis offered us a drink and then, we chatted. Cousin Nancy and her husband Francis were also there. They told us that my cousin Serge would be arriving shortly to do the honours of cooking, as he was apparently the expert. We were also given a piece of traditional tourtiere (a meat pie), as well as homemade pickled beets to fill the hole as we waited.

Uncle Louis was now an elder and, although soft in nature, was wise and methodical. He was one of the most humble and loving people I have ever met. He sat in his rocking chair talking to us, making us feel at home.

Finally, the front door opened, in came Serge with ice and snow on his beard, letting in a gust of 40-below-zero wind that made your bones shake. "Welcome, my cousin!" he exclaimed, and we embraced. Then he shook his head vigorously, showering me with particles of ice and snow. "Take some of that!" he said, laughing.

We all had a chuckle as he tidied himself up and cracked open

Eric Two Crowns (Supercabbie)

a beer before joining us. After a few quick sips, he asks us if we would like to eat. "Absolutely!" we replied, as we were starving.

He put pans on the stove and began to prepare the meat. Serge is a very meticulous man, with many life skills, some of which he's taught me over my last few visits. He was taught by his father and grandfather in the ways of life and how to be a leader. In our culture, women didn't hunt, and men needed to survive while away hunting, so men needed cooking skills. Serge had mastered the art of making fire from a stick, rock and twine. Knowing this, I began to feel that my people were more in touch with the Earth and life itself.

Serge, my uncles, my cousins, all seemed much happier than the people I'd known up to then, in Italy, England, or even in Kitchener. I began thinking that I wished I'd remained in Essipit as a child. Maybe what had happened to me wouldn't have occurred. Maybe we would have lived a more valuable life, spiritually speaking, amongst the wonders of nature that can't be experienced in the city.

Serge had the frying pan hot, and the meat began to sizzle. Another beer, and it was chow time!

Carlo's eyes lit up as Serge placed the cooked meat on our plates along with some potatoes and carrots. We dug in.

The taste was fine, but I thought there was something awry as I chewed. I wondered if the meat was liver, but there was something in the taste and texture that puzzled me. Still, we polished off our plates and, when we were finished, Serge asked us, "Do you like?"

"Good," I remarked, "but different." I asked Carlo what he thought.

"Very good!" he replied, but he's staring down the uncooked meat in the other bowl by the stove.

"It's seal," said Serge. *"La Foc,"* in French.

I was a little dumbfounded as I'd never tried seal before. I asked what the uncooked meat in the bowl was.

"Foie de foc," he replied. "Seal liver! Would you like some?"

I passed, but Carlo asked to try some. Serge was happy to cook it up, and Carlo cleared his plate like a hungry dog. I was impressed. Maybe he was part Indian? Either way, our hosts were happy that we had eaten, and our bellies were full up.

Coming Home

As I understood, my mother's people had lived off the land the true way. Whatever was caught and consumed was a gift of nature. Nothing was discarded; even the claws, teeth and fur had a purpose, including clothing, decorative spiritual jewelry, and tools. This was true with any animal, be it bear, moose, deer or porcupine.

We returned to my uncle Bertrand's place, where we would stay. We were greeted by some of my cousins who'd heard I was there. Beers in hand, hugs and kisses, we toasted Grandma, and then passed around the "Peace Pipe". At the time, I'd consumed cannabis only once in my life, back in Italy. It must have been weak as I felt no effect.

I felt that we were celebrating life, even though death was around us. Everyone seemed happy as a new life would be waiting for Grandma. But she was battling on, grasping at her last few days on this earth.

After a couple of days, I had to make a decision. Grandma was alive and, although her time was running out, she was hanging in there. I had to get back to Kitchener as Marylyn was newly arrived and had no one around to look after her. She had called and was upset that I was having a good time with my relatives. I understood that she didn't understand our ways of life. She also didn't understand when I told her that it was snowy, freezing cold and that, on the day of our scheduled departure, we couldn't start the van, even though we'd plugged in the block heater. The ice on the inside of the van windows was an inch thick! In her innocence, she thought we were just partying. We were, but in the Native way. Eventually, she would come to understand.

Every day on that visit, Carlo stayed with my uncle while I spent time with Grandma and Mom, as well as my aunts and uncles. My cousin Claudio was also there and would share a ride on the way back to Kitchener before heading on to Windsor by train.

Whenever I think back on the trip, I feel it was enlightening. A big piece of the puzzle was filled. I began to feel a bigger purpose to my life, and a belonging. Maybe some of that purpose is to share it with others still unsure of theirs.

Chapter Thirty-Four
Pastel Coloured Friends

There are dreams, and then there are visions, if you believe in them.

Twice I have had what I thought were dreams, but they felt different inside. After consulting with my now departed aunt and Godmother Lissette, I learned that they were actually visions.

I would wake up in a cold sweat after these dreams, feeling like I'd just gotten off a wacky kind of ride. The first one occurred not long after we'd arrived back in Canada.

I found myself on a riverbank, under water, watching the flow of the current and listening to the ripples above. Everything was peaceful, and I could feel the coolness of the water in and around me.

Then suddenly a pastel-coloured yellow fish appeared in front of me. I tried to snuggle closer to the shoreline so as not to be seen. I didn't want to scare it off... I watched its mouth opening and closing, but then I realized that it was talking to me, asking me to go and swim with it.

Then another pastel-coloured fish arrived, this time blue, and both of them looked at me. Before I knew it, all sorts of fish in different colours were swimming and blinking at me, their mouths puckering. They were all telling me to come out to play. So, I did.

I swam out and joined them, and they began nibbling at my body with love kisses, brushing alongside of me. I swam and played, chasing each fish and being chased. They were tickling my feet. It was exhilarating!

I can't recall how long it all went on, but I was in a fish paradise and had never seen such beautiful colours before. It was all surreal.

Coming Home

I woke up feeling euphoric, still cool from the water and the sound of the ripples in my ears.

I called Mom that day and told her about it. She said that my dream was something special and suggested that I ask my aunt and Godmother Lissette to read it.

In our Metis circle, Lissette was the "go-to" person for this sort of thing.

I made plans to visit her in person at the earliest opportunity. I knew this was not something I could share over the phone. A couple of weeks later, Marylyn and I drove to Windsor, Ontario (About Three Hours)

Auntie Lissette was also my "Godmother". She was like a second mother to me when I was young. She and Mom were very close; they almost looked like twin sisters. She welcomed every opportunity to see me.

On our arrival, she was already preparing our favourite family meal, Sepot Pie, which is a traditional dish on the Reserve. It's a huge pot pie made of pork and beef, with a crusty thick crust on top. Although labour intensive, it's always worth the effort. I'm afraid the recipe is a strict family secret, so I can't give it to you, but I believe that the original recipe had bear, elk and any other meat that had been hunted.

Auntie and I greeted each other like the Innu do, rubbing noses before kissing on the lips. We gave each other a big hug, and I introduced Marylyn. This was the first time Auntie was meeting her.

Uncle Bruno was there as well. I didn't like him very much, as he had been heavy-handed with my aunt in the past, and a wannabe Mafioso, but I still shook his hand and gave him a hug to keep the peace.

After settling in, I asked Aunt Lissette to sit down so we could talk. I began to tell her about my dream and she listened intently. When I had finished, she said, "You are going to be in the company of powerful, important people."

"What do you mean?" I asked.

She said that the fish were a sign of power and influence and that I would be mingling with them in my future. (I'm a Pisces by the way)

Eric Two Crowns (Supercabbie)

I asked whether it was a vision or just a dream, and she asked me how I felt after having the dream. I replied that I felt euphoric, yet peaceful, like being suspended in air.

She agreed that it was a vision.

I didn't know what to think, but I decided that if it were true, I'd accept this destiny if and when it came.

Having been brought up in a white world dictated by Italian values and morals, this experience brought me closer to a more spiritual and earthly world. I began to see things in a different light, one that gives me a more solemn view about the purpose and meaning of my existence. Maybe I need to help others in their strife when life gets confused with all the materialism and egotistic values we all attain living the "white life". Maybe we need to abstain from selfishness and greed.

I had achieved financial success at a young age, and then fell into despair after losing everything. Today, I have little to show for all my previous successes, and yet I'm happier for not having to worry about losing anything more. Because there's nothing for me to lose.

In the old days, I'd scurry around, working all hours, so I could sustain my materialistic kingdom, with its BMWs, its new home, nice clothes, fancy restaurants, celebrity friends. Today, I have a twelve-year-old car. My wife shops at Value Village. We rent a modest apartment. Marylyn and I haven't been to a restaurant together in years, but fortunately I'm a pretty good cook, and Marylyn says, "why waste the money?"

There's no rat race anymore. When I travel, it's mostly to the reserve, where I cleanse all of the crap that's in my mind and body. It's the only place where I feel truly comfortable and accepted.

It rejuvenates me and fortifies me until my next visit, like a spiritual gas station. My cousin Catherine's boyfriend recently asked me when I was coming home. I suddenly thought to myself, *Yes, that is my home.* Who knows? Perhaps one day it truly will be....

Chapter Thirty-Five
My Cousin Serge

We get a good night's sleep as we prepare for the day ahead. The next morning, Serge gets up and begins his regimen of pills and medical gadgets such as his respirator, as he toils to breath and live.

Serge has chronic respiratory disease. It eats away at his fragile body, which now weighs about seventy pounds. Those closest to him are amazed at his tenacity. Most agree he should have been gone long ago, but he has a remarkable strength inside of him. I can't help but feel for him, but he deplores pity. He is a self-confessed self-abuser and requires no reminders.

Serge is another person who has never pulled any stunts on me or judged me. He is my first cousin and he calls me "brother". He always has wise words to share, and is loved by many on the reserve..

His wife, Francine, puts his ear-ring on, a claw of what looks like some kind of bird. She noticed me watching and tells me that it's an eagle's talon, for spirit and courage. She told me a friend gave it to him for strength.

My mind and soul soared up when I heard this, as the eagle is my guardian as well, I wish to return as one. I took stock of the aura and spirits around me. I mentioned before the feelings I get when I come back to my birthplace. It's a spiritual medicine, void of chemicals. I feel nature taking it's course and walking beside me on my daily quests.

I take it upon myself to relieve Francine of the cooking duties for a few days. I also make sure to bring some foods that aren't readily available in town (Les Escoumins). I make pasta e fagi-

Eric Two Crowns (Supercabbie)

Me and Serge.

oli, which is an Italian bean and pasta soup. They've never tried it before but are eager to do so. Francine sniffs, likes the smell, and lifts the lid to analyze the contents. I have to pass her nose test She nods with approval. There will be some for my aunt Micheline, my uncle Bertrand and my cousin Nancy, along with her family.

I also make lasagna, just as my brother Jack makes it, I have managed to perfect his recipe over the years. I know they will like it and more so they will admire the effort making it.

I suppose this is my way of expressing my love for them. Every time I go up to Essipit, I dish up something different and wait to see if the plates are clean, or if some is left. There is always some doubt, as you can't please everyone, but there are always smiles and I'm comforted by empty plates. I'm even asked for the recipe, which is an even bigger compliment; I oblige by telling them that I will send it by e-mail when I get back home.

My only regret is that Serge will try just a little, maybe a couple of spoonfuls. He hardly eats anything, these days. His main diet is a coffee in the morning, his medication, cigarettes and beer. The smoke begins to fill the room by mid-morning and, around noon, the beer starts. I can't help watching him and hurting for him, as his frail body battles on, day by day.

Serge tells me he is preparing for his next journey. He's unafraid as he awaits the calling of the great spirit Manitou. He's like a warrior scarred by the battles of life, he's fought well.

He lost his first wife, France, long ago, and laboured to raise three children alone. His new wife, Francine, is his constant companion as he requires full time care.

Coming Home

I wish I could be with him when his time comes, to embrace him as he is taken to the higher ground. I know I will dearly miss him.

Francine tells me that "I" will inherit a portrait that currently hangs on the entrance wall to there home. I loved it the first time I saw it.

It is a beautiful painting of a "Native chief", with a wondrous headdress, overseeing his tribe. Teepees in the background. It's an abstract, but it's a reminder of who I am and where I came from. Montagnais (people of the mountains). Innu. Descendants of the first Nations. It is to be mine when Serge is no longer.

My purpose becomes stronger as I come to accept and understand more, my reasons for being here. I share my experiences with my siblings Jack and Dina.

Uncle Bertrand, my godfather, welcomes me into his home. I have some food for him and he thanks me for it as we sit to talk. He's excited to see me and asks about my siblings and how they are doing. He tells me of his woes and health issues. Under his shirt, he has a multitude of scars from past operations. His legs reveal the stitches that run-down veins that have been removed and placed in his heart. Then he reaches to his left and hands me a brand-new fishing rod. "This is for you Eric," he says. "A gift so you may catch big fish!"

He wishes he could take me to some of his best fishing spots, but he knows he's not able to.

I ask him about the family and about my other aunts and uncles. He nods with approval as I show interest in our bloodline.

He hands me a piece of paper with all the birth dates of his eight sisters and six brothers, from oldest to youngest, and tells me that there are only six left alive. These are the elders that hold Essipit together with stories of the past and life-skills for the future.

I realize I'm on the verge of being an elder as well. Though I have no children of my own, and do not live there. I must endeavour to pass on all that I know to my Italian young cousins, nieces and nephews. Also the knowledge of a European nature to my Native kin as they are curious of my experiences in Italy and Europe. I want to remind both of my sisters' children and grandchildren

Eric Two Crowns (Supercabbie)

Me, flyfishing at the Rez.

of their Innu culture, and the beauty of the Innu nation. The people.

Journeys in life will present you with encounters that can set you on another path, this is so. I attest that my cousin "Serge" has done so to me.

His passing just days ago makes me reflect on his impact on me. His easy-going personality, his humane ways. His patience with life itself yet absorbing all that it gave to him. His son and two daughters, which he toiled for after the death of his first wife.

On my return to Canada, then Les Escoumins (Essipit), my encounters with him have left an impression that has only enhanced my life. Not only did he teach me lifesaving ways of survival in the forest, but ways of grace. His listening in patience to everyday issues that he encounters. Responding with wisdom and guiding words (sometimes harsh, so that the message gets across!).

On our last visit, on the eve before our departure back home. We partied, just the four of us, Serge, Francine, Marylyn and I, playing TV Bingo and sipping a few beers. It was in their basement, where I noticed painting gear. Lots of brushes in glass jars on shelves and a couple of easel's, with painted canvasses around, drying out.

Fun it was, as TV Bingo on the Rez is a huge pastime with just about everyone. It provides some enjoyment especially in the winter months.... After having played, Serge puts on some music; Acadian eastern songs with the kind of beat Natives love. Foot stomping, knee slapping tunes.

Serge begins to dance and invites us all to join in. His moves are unmistakably Indian. Stomping his feet to the rhythm. We all join in chanting and dancing. You could see him just let loose, having a great time. No inhibitions or judgments as we all move around to the beat.

After a good sweat session we are invited by Serge to paint.

All of us to depict something with a memory of our visit. He

Coming Home

Celebratory paining, by Serge.

does this to commemorate a special guest and a reunion of family and friends. The memories to be kept on canvas.

I recall and have a video and photos of that last evening we spent together. It was the last time I would ever see each other. Now he is amongst our forefathers and mothers his wife, mom and long gone friends and family....

Something strange happened though just a few days after his

Eric Two Crowns (Supercabbie)

passing. Dina my sister sends me a video from Italy of a "Pow Wow". She says to look at the winner of the male dance session. He is the Bear and dances accordingly to its Spirit. Dina's sign is coincidently the Bear as well.

Serge died on the 7th of January, he was 67. He had cut off his long braided hair and given to her as a Powerful spiritual gift.

The winners tag number was 767! I was taken back as my skin starts to goosebump. I know that messages are always around us but sometimes it's surreal when it hits you so clearly. It was Serge giving Dina a sign...

Francine, his now wife calls me to let me know she will keep for me the portrait that hangs on the wall, as promised. She had told me that when Serge had passed it would be mine. Francine being the artist she is, also has many other paintings, her talent plain to see.

Now though, she aches from the loss, it's evident in her voice. The minute I first encountered her and then saw them together, I knew she loved him dearly.

She catered to his every need, caring for him and working at the same time.. When Serge was well, they fished together on weekends in the lakes of the Laurentian mountains, mainly Lac Bernier. It is truly a spectacular scene. This Lake, which is fed only by the winter snow and ice melt and has been there since the beginning of time, is home only to medium size speckle trout. Fresh, sweet and uncontaminated. (Hickory Smoked it's like the "Caviar of smoked fish")

A case of beer, smokes and a couple of "spliffs" would last a few hours, enhancing our enjoyment. No cops allowed on the property as it's Solely Native land.

Serge had embraced me on my return from Europe after many years of absence. He welcomed me like a brother insisting I stay with him. The last few visits he would watch me cook. We talked, and we enjoyed each other's company immensely.

Now I look to the skies and know he is there among the stars watching us all, maybe sending messages that let us know his spirit is alive (767) in all of us, his people, "MONTAGNAIS!!" (and anyone who believes).

Coming Home

Tears are in my heart for you my brother, but my soul rejoices, knowing you love me as I love you... and the raven soars to the sun.

Chapter Thirty-Six
Chief Joseph Moreau

I would like to tell you a story about my grandfather, Chief Joseph Moreau, a tribe guide and visionary for 22 years.

Granddad Moreau had to provide for fifteen children and a wife as well as guide a tribe. He had been trading furs with representatives of the Hudson Bay company when he was summoned to a treaty signing in Ottawa along with other Chiefs and Leaders.

Never having visited a city, he got curious, and ventured into the downtown area, and saw what his furs were selling for. After calculating how many pelts went into making these garments, he became enraged at how his people had been screwed, paid pittance for all their hard labour, trapping and hunting. As I understand, when he returned to his reserve, he swore never to do business with the "palefaces" again.

On my last visit to Essipit, I found myself in awe of a pair of snowshoes my granddad had made. I noticed that these were not the kind you see in the movies or in a camping store. They were smaller and lighter than any I'd previously seen. They were all shaped from wood, which would have had to have been soaked, and a mesh made of gut of some kind. I could tell that it took great skill and patience to make them.

I asked my cousin Serge if I could buy them from him, and he instantly replied, "No way!" They were for his son, he explained, and no amount of money would take them off his hands. I left it at that.

Those snowshoes where too precious and sentimental to Serge. Actually, my memory of that moment is precious and sentimental to me now. I can imagine having to walk miles in those shoes,

Coming Home

My grandfather, Chief Joseph Moreau, moose calling.

hunting. They would need to be light, yet effective enough to be able to walk quickly over snow, in case you were chasing animals or maybe the animals were chasing you! My brother Jack would have loved them as he has a passion for native memorabilia and he has a small collection of artefacts in Italy.

Across the road from my cousin Serge's house, there is a sanctuary of artefacts that educate visitors on all the styles of tee-pees and tools. It has everything from large tents for community gatherings, to small one-man tents for hunting. There are tools made from stone, bone and wood, all displayed in glass cabinets with plaques explaining their purpose.

I marvel at the tenacity of the culture at Essipit, and the ingenuity of my ancestors. The winter is harsh there, and to survive it must have been a task in itself. The sanctuary also played a part in understanding my identity and my quest to belong.

Chapter Thirty-Seven
Paying the Piper

Sometimes you just cannot connect the dots about why things happen. There was a time when I had just left for Lignano, that I preferred to blank everyone out. Nonna was old. Dad was unrelenting in his drinking. The girls, at one point, had been handed over to a nunnery to be brought up, almost as if they were orphans. They kind of were.

Jack had been Dad's best pal for as long as I can remember. He was named after granddad Giacomo. He was the first born. Then came me, Lydia and Dina. And it seemed that Jack could do no wrong in Dad's eyes, while nothing I did ever seemed good enough. When we were kidnapped from Canada, I grew to despise him for being in on the deal with Dad. He knew what was going on, but did nothing to stop it, even if he was only sixteen.

As time went on, I began to distance myself from him, seeing him as much of a culprit as Dad was.

And yet I loved him dearly. We'd played together as younger brothers, rarely fighting or arguing. He watched over me and defended me. We'd walked miles together over the years, from church in St. Agatha to Petersburg on a Sunday. I even remember him beating up a bully that lived a few doors down from us, who was picking on me, when Jack intervened. I followed Jack to his house and before you know it, my "Big Bro" through him into a bush!

We would be together helping Dad on Sunday afternoon's in his beloved garden. I also recall us spending hours assembling "Airfix" planes and ships together, Spitfires, Thunderbolt's, Shtuka's, Mustangs, aircraft carriers and battleships, all complete with decals and delicate detailed painting. We had shared the same bedroom, in Italy actually slept together in the huge antique bed in our room. Jack was always the quieter of us two. Nonna would say, "You have to pull the words out of his mouth with a fork!", as he was so meek.

He had chronic asthma as a kid, as did Dina. Both of them gasping for air as their lungs bubbled with phlegm. Thankfully through puberty, they overcame the "Chronic".

Over the years I saw him become more introverted. I think as time passed, he felt more and more guilty. Maybe he was blaming himself? I blamed him to, and at one point I stopped talking to him completely. In fact, it would be a couple of years before I talked to him again, I had lost touch with him totally. Not knowing where he was or what he was doing.

I was now in England and as time passed, I began to suffer his absence. Still rejecting him, yet still loving him deep down. We were now men, both with our own destinies to follow. Dina just recently told me that he was suffering, I already knew why, and so did she. The decision to follow Dad's every command including helping him with the plan to secretly take us to Italy, was now haunting him years later. I believe it still does.

I remember one afternoon I received a telephone call. It was Mom. I was taken aback, speechless, as I had not spoken to her for nearly 13 years, the memories of her locked in a corner of my mind. Dad forbade us even to mention her name in his presence. The threats now stamped in my head, enough to blank her out, through the fear of him.

Mom, speaking to me as if a stranger, said she was going to Italy. My heart began to throb again as the old wound opened. I didn't know what to feel or say. I was dumbfounded. She wanted to see us, despite the danger as he had threatened to kill her if she ever turned up.

He had told his friends in Osoppo that she was in a mental home, that she had gone crazy. That was his blanket for his indiscretions. Now he was under pressure as she was perfectly fine except the dagger still in her heart.

All would be revealed. He was scared of the truth coming out, making him the guilty party. If anything, he was the crazy one. He

Eric Two Crowns (Supercabbie)

had committed a huge crime in our kidnapping. It was time to pay the piper.

I booked my ticket from England to Italy in anticipation of seeing her again. All the memories of Mom were flooding back to me, her gentleness and loving nature. I told Marylyn that Mom was going to Osoppo, and I would be flying down to see her. The only thing was, I needed to get there as soon as possible to protect her if anything went awry. I couldn't trust Dad to keep his hands to himself as something was sure to erupt, and it did.

With my flight booked I readied myself for the encounter. What would she be like? How old would she look? Was she going to try and stay in Osoppo? Could we rekindle what we had so long ago? A thousand questions must had gone through my head on the journey. I felt apprehensive to say the least, yet excited that she was back in my life again.

The 13 years had passed quickly, with me as a boy, now turned man at 26. I was married, had a career and living in England. Mother was now 49 years of age and no doubt scarred by the separation and by the betrayal.

As we turned onto *Via San Danielle*, I could see Mom peeking out of the front door, looking in anticipation. The first thing I notice was her hair, now greying from age. We stopped and I got out. She saw me, and the tears began to flow. She screamed out, "Eric!" and I dropped my luggage and ran to her, arm outstretched, shouting back, "Mamma! Mamma!" We had the long-awaited hug and embrace.

It was like I was suspended in that precious moment, not knowing what to say, just holding her, kissing her and rubbing noses. It was like a whale calf that was lost, suddenly finding its mother. "I've missed you so much, so much Mama!" I cried, the tears in my heart choking my throat.

I was near collapse as she whispered in my ear, "My little Indian boy; mon petit Indien." We held each other for a moment with Jack, the girls, and Dad looking on.

We entered the house and within minutes, I could feel the air beginning to thicken, something about to explode. The emotions all rampant with the past. Within moments I noticed Mom looking at my brother Jack, something had to be cleared in her mind.

Coming Home

She began to say through her tearing eyes, sobbing, "Why did you not stop your father, Jack?! Why did you help him take away my children? Why? Why? Why?"

Then, as they stood facing each other, Jack visibly embarrassed and distraught, Mom slapped him in the face. All of us were now trying to calm things down, wanting to just find some sort of solace. I could see Dad trying to come to grips with what was going on. His demeanor now subdued, finally paying the piper.

I think Mom did it knowing I would be there to defend her if things went too far. As children, any kind of confrontation between my mother and father was usually kept behind closed doors or away from us. We still heard, though.

This time, due to the anguish, heartache, anger, it was justified. Thirteen years of her life and ours separated through Dad's selfishness. He had used us as leverage, as pawns in his game.

I took Mom by the arm and guided her outside. "Mamma, I know it's hard, but you are here now, let's make the most of it and try to be calm."

She just kept on saying, "Why did he help him do that? Why didn't he stop it?"

"Mamma, shh, come on, stop crying. Come on, Mamma." I hugged her again and persuaded her to go back into the room with the others to try and come to some peace.

I know how incredibly hard it was for her over the years. Worse, she'd seen the news of the earthquake. It made her hysterical, being so far away and not knowing if we were dead or alive. Eventually, through the Italian connections, she would learn that we had survived. Those Italian connections had been the ones who'd paid for her trip. Her epilepsy kept her from earning enough money to support herself, much less fly across the Atlantic. I suppose, knowing that Dad had absconded and left her without her children, it was the least they could do.

We had conversations over the next few days, alone. We talked about what had passed in our time apart. She'd actually married again, for a short time, however, she told me she realized she could never love someone like she had loved Dad, and soon after had her marriage annulled.

I left, after a few days, leaving my door open for her to come to

Eric Two Crowns (Supercabbie)

England, once she was ready. She remained in Osoppo for a while, living in the family house that had been newly erected after the earthquake.

Two months later, back in England, I got a phone call from Mom. I was happy knowing I had not lost her forever. But again, we were apart.

Mom then told me that Dad had kicked her in the leg! Apparently he was upset that she didn't love him anymore. Are you kidding? I wonder why!

I was furious, ready to go back to Italy and teach him a lesson, but Mom just asked if it would be okay for her to come to England for a while, but she also said it would be best if she returned to Canada. There was nothing in Italy for her. The girls were young women, now, who could take care of themselves. Dad had also brainwashed them into thinking that she was the culprit, not him, and the static Mom was feeling from them was uncomfortable.

Marylyn and I had a two-bedroom apartment at the time, enough room for Mom to stay as long as she wanted, but would you believe that, when I started sharing some time with Mom, Marylyn started acting up? She never really had much compassion for my Mother, having worn out her battery within her first marriage. She didn't understand our complex situation.

Finally, after a little time in England, Mom told me she would be returning to Canada. I was saddened to know she wanted to leave, but there wasn't much I could say in the end, because she needed to be happy. However, although she'd stayed with us for only a couple of months, I felt we had bonded, or at least made up for some of the time lost.

It could never be made right, obviously; nevertheless Mom was Mom again. Over the years, until her sudden passing, I spoke to her at least once a week. Some people look at me weird when I say that I still talk to her all the time. I think, though, that if you believe in some kind of afterlife, it's not that weird.

I ask her advice and I always get a reply. She has now become my spiritual guide, always there when I need her, which seems to be often. I miss her dearly in the flesh, but now she walks next to me. That I know.

Chapter Thirty-Eight
A Father's Duties

Dad was an avid cyclist, I'm talking Tour de France style. I saw some old pictures of Dad on his bicycle, with his pals alongside.

From what I can gather, Dad was a spoiled son. Being an only boy and coming from a pretty privileged family, he had more than most kids. Having the skills of a barber and the only license to operate in a town of two thousand or so meant he didn't have to want for much.

Granddad Mino had secured that license long ago. Aunty Rosalina would help Nonna with the chores while Dad and Granddad took care of the barber shop which was part of the house facing *Via San Danielle*.

I'll say this for my Dad: he was never a showoff. After the World Wars, people had very little, let alone racing bikes for their kids. He was a prankster who always brought a party to life. He was a great dancer with a great voice. People in the town loved him and, when he died, my brother Jack said that just about everyone in town turned up for his funeral (I hadn't).

Perhaps Dad could have been an opera singer. He could definitely hold some air in those lungs and hammer out some great tunes. I'm proud to have some of those traits, as I can get some attention when I sing, especially after a couple of glasses of gods' nectar.

Dad had already passed when my sister Dina got married. She asked me if I would do the honours of giving her away. "Of course, I will," I replied. She was my baby sister and we were close as chil-

Eric Two Crowns (Supercabbie)

dren. She is also my soulmate in life. I always looked out for her as she does me.

The reception was held in a small town called Tarcento, just a few miles from Osoppo. It was in a restaurant alongside a river, and the room was decorated beautifully. We had a six-course meal, followed by desserts, coffee and the usual after meal *Digestivo* drinks. The wine was flowing, and everyone was having a good time.

I was so used to Dad livening up things that I gulped another *vino* down and went to a table where the in-laws were sitting and began to sing an old war song Dad used to sing. It was called *"Mazzolino di Fiori"*, or "Bouquet of Flowers". The song is about a soldier at war longing to see his girl, and the anguish of his separation.

I began to sing the intro softly and, in an instant, Tiziana's father Iacum and his wife Emillia joined in, followed by the rest. I was a little embarrassed at the attention I was getting as they all clapped and told me I had a great voice.

Dina's new sister-in-law, Lucia, was all over me, asking if I sang in a choir, to which I replied, "No." Actually, I had sang in the church choir as a child in St Agatha, but just for a short time.

That afternoon after the reception, my brother Jack told me we would be going back to Osoppo to get changed, then we were going into Austria to finish off the day at a casino resort.

We left in a stream of cars travelling north towards the border, towards a resort town in the Alps called Felden.

On entering the casino, I recall it was crowded. I remember waiting quite a while to play some roulette and, wouldn't you know it, just when I finally got to the table, it was nearly time to go. However, after a few plays, I nailed a couple of numbers straight up and won about a thousand bucks! It helped make up for the costs I paid taking my father's duties at the reception.

One of the traditions at the reception was for me to match all bids for a snip of my tie, with funds to go to the newlyweds. Little by little, the large bottle of proceeds was filling up, and half the money in the kitty was my own. I hadn't known about this tradition, so I had to ask Jack to cover me when I ran out of money. People had a good laugh at my expense, but at least I'd landed the

Introduction

right numbers in Felden. I also decided to give my sisters a chunk of that money as well.

But I was proud that Dina had asked me to be her sponsor. Her husband Paolo was a *Carrabinieri* cop, and he seemed a stand-up guy. They've been married for 22 years, and he has served eight missions with the U.N., including in Bosnia. He also went on one mission to Iraq. Dina told me he returned a different man...

Paolo did something special when Mom passed away. He paid all the necessary expenses, including three flights from Italy and hotels for Jack, Dina and Lydia. Again, a stand-up guy, sacrificing himself for others, on and off duty.

If I had a wish that I knew would come true, it's that I could be close to my siblings in Italy. Skype doesn't cut it all the time. I sometimes feel stuck between a rock and a hard place, not having the means to earn like I used to. It seems that time goes by so quickly, it's running out.

The last time I was in Italy, in 2005, I had a great time, enjoying the company of my old friends, reminiscing about some of the things that you now know. I recall making new friends and discovering a different way of life, compared to what I was used to here in Canada. I needed to fit in and it was the whole village that guided me and accepted me as one of their own. I'm sure the news had spread quickly about what Dad had done. Everyone knew everyone. You couldn't fart without someone making a comment.

The truth is, I believe the kids were told not to make a comment about our situation. Not once did someone ask me where my mother was. Not once did they poke fun at me or try to ridicule, like kids can do. Never did I have to divulge or explain anything. The friends that I had made in Italy are my best friends to this day. They helped me ease the pain of the loss of Mom and kept me busy with soccer, fishing, and motorcycling.

Nonna also played a big part in taking over the duties of our new Mom. She was probably my real best friend in a way. She kept me on the straight and narrow. Life was going fast and although Mom was not there, she was always at the back of my mind. I was stuck, too young to do anything and too afraid as well to mention her name.

I often ponder on the fact that, if it were today, there would be

Eric Two Crowns (Supercabbie)

an Amber Alert that more than likely would have halted his crazy attempt to take us away. But that was then, and this is now. Some say you can't live in the past, but sometimes it's hard not to want to change it. You have to have a kind of inner strength to switch off the pain.

I usually think of my sister Dina, Lydia, and my brother Jack and try to understand that they need me strong when I feel that they are reaching out to me as I do with them. Perhaps that's the key to the future sharing the grief and loving each other knowing that our bond keeps us together. I am realistic though, understanding that hurt will never totally go away, it's a wound that keeps on bleeding whenever I think of the past.

Part 7:
The Reasons I am Here

Chapter Thirty-Nine

Supercabbie

The life of a cabbie is very interesting. Your passengers come from all walks of life. Nights can be challenging with drugs and alcohol becoming a factor. To quote a famous movie, "you never know what you're going to get", and that's both good and bad.

I got into the taxi-cab business after working as a courier for ASAP Express. I loved driving, but courier work wasn't very lucrative, especially with gas prices increasing. So, when an acquaintance I knew who owned a taxi offered me a position as a driver, I thought, "Perfect! I could carry on driving, but this time my expenses would be covered by the cab owner!"

I still had to go through training, but it was surprisingly easy. It took just a few hours for me to familiarize myself with the communications system, and then I had to do some routine driving. When I took my final test, the manager of operations got on board and said, "Okay, Eric, take me to this address," and off I went.

As I drove, he asked me about where other addresses were. I answered quickly and correctly and, within five minutes, the manager told me to turn around and return to the office. Did I do something wrong? I asked why, and the manager said, "You're good to go. You know more than most drivers."

I guess the courier business had served me well, giving me knowledge of the city. My years of racing dirt bikes in Italy also gave me quick reflexes – a must if you want to survive the job. Accidents become nightmares to a cab owner, because all of a sudden the insurance rate soars, and your cab could be off the road for days, meaning no money coming in. But I knew I could drive safe, and I was ready to go.

The Reasons I am Here

Little did I know what was in store for the next few years. Marylyn didn't believe me. She said, "How hard can it be? All you have to do is drive people from A to B and that's it." No, that's not it.

At the start, I agreed to work nights, so Thursday through Sunday I'd be on the road from 5 p.m. to 4 a.m. the next day. Things went fine for the first few days until one night I was driving and I felt something in my gut. Working at Huggies had made me paranoid enough to tape a knife to my ankle, but not without reason. I did the same this night, and not long into my shift, I got a call to pick someone up at a local bar called Filthy McNasty's. I'm barely there a second when suddenly a scruffy-looking guy comes running out of the bar and jumps in my cab, screaming, "Go!! Go!! Go!!"

"Where?" I asked.

"Just go!" he shouted.

As I drove off, I glanced in the rear-view mirror and saw the bar's bouncer giving chase, on foot, and yelling at the top of his lungs.

"So... what's the address you want to go to?" I asked.

"Corner of Hickory and Hazel," he replied.

I knew where that was, of course, and I got into the right lane to make a turn when I noticed a police cruiser on the street I'm about to turn onto.

My passenger noticed it too. "Go straight! Go straight!" he shouted.

"That's not the way to where you want to go," I said.

"Keep going straight!" he screamed.

So, I did. And as I drove, I quickly realized that the man wasn't just drunk, he was an angry drunk. As I approached the next intersection, off the route I was supposed to be taking, I said, "so, which way now, man?"

"Where are you taking me?" the man screamed, his anger rising. I knew then I had to take the bull by the horns. "Shut the fuck up!!" I yelled back at him, and put the pedal to the metal. I screeched off towards the destination he'd given me, deliberately speeding, hoping to see a cop car. I didn't. Where are they when

Eric Two Crowns (Supercabbie)

you need them? It would have been great watching this idiot getting cuffed and thrown into a cruiser.

Finally, I turned down Hazel Street, and the guy opened the door, while I'm still driving, saying, "Stop the car now!"

I came to a screeching halt and, while he's getting out, he turns around and tells me he's not paying me and that I was a "crap driver"!

Okay, I thought, just let him go. But, as he walked away from the car, heading into a school parking lot, I began to follow him in my cab. Something wasn't right. And, sure enough, the guy walks up to the school building and starts ripping the screens off the windows. I immediately called the office and asked for police assistance.

That's when the man notices me watching him, and he begins to run towards me. I pull away and start doing circles in the parking lot with him following me. I could see him struggling in the snow in my mirror, slipping and trying to keep his balance. He then gave up the chase and headed towards the metal boundary fence. He climbed over but snagged his pants and fell head first into the snowbank. I was in stitches watching this fool scurry around.

He then headed between two houses, disappearing into a back yard. Minutes later I spot the police car and flash my lights at him as he approached.

The cop rolled down his window. "What's going on?"

I explained the situation and he asked me to follow him to show him where the culprit went. He got out and knocked on the house door.

Eventually two students appeared, neither of whom were the guy. The officer talked into his two-way radio and, minutes later, a van appeared with the driver getting out and opening the side door where a German shepherd dog is led out. They picked up a scent and off they went.

The original officer asked me for my cell phone number and sent me on my business. An hour later, he called and asked me to meet him at an address not far from the original scene.

I arrived to see two vans and three cruisers that had apprehended the perpetrator. He had walked into a house and the occu-

The Reasons I am Here

pants promptly kicked him out. He let himself into the next home and had fallen asleep on the couch where they occupants called the police. All in all, he was charged with a string of things from property damage to the school, breaking and entering two homes, vagrancy and other charges. The officer gave me the fare I was owed, and I left.

That was just the baptism. On another occasion, I was picking up a fare at a wedding hall at about 2 in the morning. I knew it had been a good night for the guests as they were more than merry as they boarded. The Lincoln Town Car that I drove as my cab is pretty spacious, but it got tight after all five passengers got in. The man and women were squeezed up front, so the woman decided to sit on the gentleman's lap for a more comfortable ride. It must have been really comfortable because, within minutes, I was hearing snoring in the back, and the two in the front were fondling each other. And I mean serious fondling, right beside me, with the guy tickling her fancy and her loudly expressing approval.

Needless to say, I put pedal to the metal and made sure this encounter was as brief as possible!

Friday and Saturday nights in particular can be wild. On this particular night, my pickup wasn't going too far – a guy and a girl going home from a night out bar-hopping. As we drove off, the girl, her voice slurring, says, "I need to pee badly."

Uh, oh!

I told her in no uncertain terms that she needed to hold on. "Hurry! Hurry!" she cried. Again, I put pedal to the metal. Finally, we arrived at the destination – some apartment building – and she quickly gets out. The guy hands me his credit card and I'm processing it when I just happen to look at a bush in front of the cab and see her pulling down her panties, squatting and peeing. She's standing in the lights of my high-beams!

The guy sees it too, and we both burst out laughing when the girl loses her balance and falls backwards into the bush, continuing to fountain. Just then, an elderly couple came out of the entrance and see the whole thing. The husband immediately covers his wife's eyes before hurrying her away, visibly disturbed.

The largest tip I ever received was $110.20. You might think it was for a long trip, but you'd be wrong. Instead, I got a call at

Eric Two Crowns (Supercabbie)

an apartment complex where this scrawny, jittery guy gets in. He looks like he's had a snort of something.

He says to me, "Come on, cabbie! Take me to where the action is!"

"What kind of action are you looking for, sir?" I asked.

"You know what I mean," he replied. "The ladies!"

So, I made a bee-line towards King Street.

As I was driving, he suddenly asks me to pull over at a bank machine. I do so, and he goes in to grab some money. When he comes back, he hands me $100 and says, "I'll take care of you, if you can hook me up."

"I'll do my best, sir," I replied, and off we went. Honestly, I didn't really know exactly where to go, though in those days King at Eby Street at the east end of downtown Kitchener was an obvious guess. Sure enough, when we get to the corner, I see a woman standing there, in a white fur coat with black spots, wearing long black-leather high-heeled boots, obviously looking for business.

I pulled up to the curb and pointed. "There she is." I was really hoping the weirdo would quickly be out of my car, but instead he rolled down the window to say, "Is it cold out there, honey?"

"Why, yes, it is!" she replied.

He beckoned her to my cab. "It's warm in here!"

This brings her over. She gets in the back. I'm getting pretty antsy by this point because I did not want to be involved with these characters. I turned up the radio to block out what they were saying, but not enough. Instead, I hear the guy talking about cocaine (I was right about the snort), and the woman asked me to "do a U-eee" and go up the street to a particular address. Well, I did, and pulled up to the stop.

I stopped the meter as the two got out. By this point, it read $19.80. The guy asked me to wait, and went off with the woman to the porch. I watched them standing and talking by the front door. Finally, the guy came back, handed me $30 and said, "We might be needing you soon, if you want to wait around."

By this point, I'd had enough. "Sure, no problem," I said. I waited as he walked off. When he was safely away, I revved the engine and peeled out of there, wheels screeching, as I hightailed it back to Waterloo. They couldn't pay me enough to stick around.

The Reasons I am Here

It was a generous tip for such a fare, but some trips are just not worth it.

I've had to deal with my share of runners in my time. A runner is someone that flees the cab without paying. It's also known as "transportation fraud". The perpetrator is usually a kid, either alone or in a group. Sometimes you nab them before they get away. Sometimes you don't. Once, though, I caught my runners, and made them pay in all sorts of ways.

I was flagged down by three young men. One stood out from the rest as he had a huge mass of curly ginger hair, a full "Afro". They piled in, gave me a destination, and talked as I drove. As I approached the drop off point, one of the boys says, "just drop us off at the corner."

That's a red flag, right there. And sure enough, as I'm pulling to a stop, I hear one of them saying, "My jeans are too tight. I need to stand up to get at my wallet." Still, I stopped, and sure enough, once they're out of the cab, they run for it.

Fortunately, I'd heard one of them saying that they were going to play poker at a certain address. So, I drove to that address and turned off my lights as I approached the house. There, I saw the guys standing by the garage.

I leaned on the horn. One of the culprits bolted for the front door and ran inside. One of the other kids came over. He wasn't one of the ones who'd been in the cab. Still, I explained the situation and told him that it was useless for them to hide, and that the culprits had better come out and pay me, or else I would call the cops.

The kid insisted that I must be mistaken, and walked away. I had no choice but to let it go. I wasn't happy about that, but karma repaid me the next weekend. I was driving, and I saw the same three kids flagging me down. Better yet, they didn't recognize me as I pulled up and they piled in. They gave me their destination (the same as the previous week) and I drove off.

As we approached the drop off point, I heard the same request: "Hey, just drop us off here at the corner."

"Sure," I said, slowing down. "That will be twelve dollars."

But I didn't stop. The street at the corner was a cul-de-sac, so I drove into it, circling slowly while the kids took in this new development. They were disturbed, but they tried the same excuses, including, "Sir, my jeans are too tight! I need to get out to get at the money."

Immediately, I pulled out of the cul-de-sac and drove back uptown. The kids are freaking out at this point, demanding to know where I'm going. I don't say 'kidnapping', but I do say, "I just received a message on my screen. My wife's gone into labour! I've got to get there, quick!"

They believed my story enough that they congratulated me as I headed uptown. They were even offering to buy me a drink and celebrate at a nearby establishment called the Silver Spur. I'd already pressed my emergency button, and home office was tracking me. I pulled up to our office and got out. I stepped into the office and told them to send the cops to the Silver Spur bar, and then I went back out with them.

The Spur was nearby, I went with them to the door and told them to go on inside while I had a cigarette outside. I'd join them a minute later. They did, and I saw the cops walking towards me. I told them everything, explaining about the situation that had happened a week before. I also suggested to the bouncer that he keep an eye on those guys and ask them to leave when we gave him the go-ahead. When we were ready, we sent the bouncer in, and he brought them out to where the cops were waiting.

Well, they came out, stunned, as police questioned them about skipping out on not one, but two fares. They were asked to pay back both in full. It was really satisfying. I hope they learned. If you mess with somebody's living, paybacks can be a bitch, as some people say.

This last story will confirm that driving a cab is not a job for everyone. Freddie Kropf was a veteran driver. I met him as a rookie and we became friends. We always sought each other out when we noticed we were in the same zone. He was a robust guy, with a powerful physique, He was always good for a laugh, but he eventually made us cry when he took his own life.

He'd been divorced for quite some time, living by himself. One day I realized that I had not spoken to him in a couple days. I thought he had taken a break, but then I was told that he should be on duty. I phoned him numerous times, but with no reply. Peo-

The Reasons I am Here

ple searched for him for two days, to no avail. Suddenly, the word was out that he'd been found in his neighbour's garage. He'd been taking care of their house while they were away, and that gave him the opportunity to do what he did without people noticing. He'd left the car running in the garage, and had killed himself with the car fumes.

Buddy, you're in a better place now and I always think of you.

This job can eat away at you and depression is a side effect. Freddie had obviously had enough. He gave us no telltale signs as he disappeared.

I have had to physically remove people from my cab. I've been spat on twice. I've endured threats and cleaned up vomit. But I kept driving. As Chief Dan George once said, I endeavored to persevere.

Eventually, being a night cabbie got so stressful, I decided to switch to days. These are nicer, because the people are nicer, and you do get a sense of making a difference. There are little old ladies going to church and elderly gentlemen coping with walkers and canes heading to doctors' appointments. There's shopping trips or runs to the community centre to see friends. I've helped elderly people with walkers and canes and assisted the blind. Once, I saw a lady who was struggling to help another woman into a van. Instinctively, I got out of the car and went to help. As I placed her in her seat, she said, "There are angels left in the world." It was humbling.

The rewards of being a day cabbie are not monetarily the same as driving at night, but they can be spiritually enhancing. I feel bigger in the heart and soul when I help those who are vulnerable. You realize that you are helping people stay active in their lives, now that they can't drive on their own. That feels good — as does the understanding that the worst that can happen to me is perhaps somebody accidentally clocking me with their cane.

Recently, I had a call-out to a blind gentleman and his guide dog. He was at Walmart with an accordion. I knew him from previous rides, and he was always pleasant and polite.

On that day, I knew the street he lives on was under construction, with new sidewalks going in. He was in unfamiliar territory around his own home, so I made sure to get out and assist him,

Eric Two Crowns (Supercabbie)

taking his arm gently and helping him secure his instrument. While his beautiful golden Labrador watched me, I helped him over the step and assured him that his path was clear to the door.

He thanked me, and his appreciation was very real. The good deed made me feel one step closer to my creator.

I am a self-analyst. I constantly try to mend my ways, so I can be worthy in the next world. I know that seeking perfection can be dangerous, but maybe it's not perfection I'm seeking, just forgiveness for the wrongs I have done.

Giving back is one way I hope to redeem myself. That's what I feel, anyway. It's a goal, and a purpose, and I think it gives value to others, and it comes back to you. A wise man said, "You have to count the figs at days end." The figs are what you bring home at the end of the day, whether they be money earned or deeds done. No deeds mean no figs!

No money also means no figs. But if that's all you go for, it means the tree is half full, yet you come home almost empty-handed. That's basically the world we live in. Yet, surprisingly, many only bring home the monetary figs, not the spiritual ones.

Chapter Forty

For the Love of Golf

My Dad used to tell me that you had to be a thief in life. No, not a thief with your hands, but one that steals with your eyes and your ears. The quicker you picked things up, he said, the more likely you were to succeed. I have done this learning to work at restaurants, and I have done this for the love of golf.

It was working at an Italian restaurant called "Il Pagliaccio" (the clown) in the town of Weybridge, Surrey, that I was introduced to the world of golf. On my first day, while I was stuck taking care of a couple of customers who were staying late, I noticed some of the waiters in the car park, loading their bags with what I thought looked like golf clubs. It was 2:30 in the afternoon, and dinner was just three hours away. Where were they going, I wondered, when there was work to be done?

But I was new, and the waiters were always skeptical of newbies, waiting for them to screw up and get fired for incompetence. I knew that the restaurant business has a high turnover. I needed to work hard, and I needed to stay on the older workers' good side. So I said nothing. And, sure enough, by 5:30, the waiters were back, ready to work. The next day, the same thing happened again. And again the day after that.

As the days went on, I noticed a lot of golfing going on with my peers. The St. George's Golf Club was just a few minutes away. Many golfing professionals would dine at our restaurant. Finally, Romero, one of the sister restaurant's staff who became one of my best friends, decided to take me under his wing. After my trial period was over at the restaurant, he asked me to join the others for a nine hole four-ball on the afternoon break. I learned

Eric Two Crowns (Supercabbie)

Romero was a very good player. I learned that he and his friends could fit in nine holes at St. George's and still get back in time for dinner service. I also learned that since the pros were dining at our restaurants, we always got a good deal, golfing at St. George's.

I fell in love with golf the first time I played it. I had played hockey, soccer, baseball and other sports, so I could handle myself athletically, but Romero showed me the ropes on the rules and the etiquette. He loved the game and so we played together at least once a week. With his help, I improved quickly, which must have been a relief to him. There's nothing worse than playing with a "hacker" that struggles, so I was fortunate to learn fast, and he and I had struck it off and become the best of friends.

It was after taking some golf lessons that Romero suggested I might try going pro. He said that I was a natural. I was playing once or twice a week, but with his vote of confidence, I resolved to practice at every opportunity. However, things changed in a hurry. Business demands and other commitments, so I never realized that brief dream. However, I did get to experience many special moments through golf not by playing it, but by carrying Professional bags.

While I was still in England, I decided to pursue my dream of playing professionally by caddying. Steal with your eyes and your ears, remember. I thought that, by watching professionals walk the courses, I could learn their secrets. I did. I even managed to bag (no pun intended) a few jobs.

My first job was carrying Peter Mitchell's bag. I was standing by the fairway, watching him during pro-am tournament, and he had no caddy, so I simply shouted out to him, "Hey, can I carry your bag, mate?"

He looked at me and said, "Alright, mate. Come on over!"

That was that, I went on over. I held his bag and watched closely as he prepared to execute his next shot. I was amazed at the pureness of the contact. I recall he used a 1-iron, and the ball soared high in the air and out of sight, before coming down to a blind green. WOW! What a beautiful thing!

I introduced myself and Peter and I hit it off immediately. He was such a nice fellow. I believe he was from London somewhere as he had that kind of slangy English accent that, if they speak too fast you will lose them. Either way, we finished up the

The Reasons I am Here

Winners of the London Italian Golf Society tournament. I'm on the right.

round and he thanked me for my help. For me, it had been more than a pleasure. I watched and sucked up all the mannerisms and routines that would help me progress. Things such as checking pre-shot routine and visualizing trajectory with maximum focus. I was hungry for more and wanted to see if I could somehow get between the ropes again as soon as possible.

I wondered if I could take some pictures of the pros in action, and that gave me an idea. Jack my brother had an avid interest in photography. He had all the equipment, from zoom lenses for his Canon AE-1, to the carrier back with all its attachments. I decided to ask Jack for his gear. With that and some of the red tape around my arm that pro photographers wore on their sleeves to identify themselves at events, I got in, incognito. The trick worked to a tee.

I went to the Wentworth Golf and Country Club where the Volvo British PGA event was being held. After gathering my courage, I got out of the car and made my way to the practice area and began to take pictures of the pros who were already practicing. I was on cloud nine and loving every minute. I had gotten a few suspicious looks from security, but not one stopped me to ask for my credentials.

Eric Two Crowns (Supercabbie)

That day I walked between the ropes alongside Sandy Lyle, Seve and Nick. I was working for an Australian company at the time and I was excited to follow Roger Davis who had those "Plus Twos" socks on and always stood out from the crowd just like the great Payne Stewart did. He was also sponsored by my company, AMP Society, the biggest insurance company in Australia at the time, I could take three of my clients to private clinics and days out to see Roger twice a year. Needless to say, none of my clients refused an invite. He was a party kind of guy, down to earth and very approachable. I had the pleasure of "Blowing the Froth" of a few pints with him and along with my clients who were also good friends enjoyed the times.

On that first invite, I had taken Romero, Don Farretta and Robert Tavagna to a club just outside of London. We had a ball and watched Roger play a couple of holes with each of the groups. On one hole they had set up a video camera and filmed all of the tee shots on the par four hole. That evening we were all having a few drinks with Roger cracking jokes, when we were summoned to a lounge where they were showing the video of all the participants.

There were laughs and jeers as the video was shown; we weren't professionals, that's for sure. Then it was me and as I sat there ready for my dose of razzing, the swing, *swoosh!* and I heard someone say, "Wow, who's that?".. "Nice swing!" and I was humbled. I had never seen my own swing on video and then I realized that I was actually natural and smooth. My friends would say that I could swing it in a telephone booth. I felt proud that I had put the time in and was now being complimented on my skills.

Still, I needed to get better and decided to try and be a caddy again but this time in a real professional tournament. My next opportunity would be again at the Volvo British PGA tournament in Wentworth, Surrey.(1991)

The Volvo British PGA Championship is always played on the "Burma Road course". I had decided to try to "land a bag" there if I could. It was a long shot. Most of the professionals already had permanent help so I would have to get lucky. I prepared my gear, cap, sunglasses, running shoes, t-shirt and a large towel so to clean the clubs after each shot.

Off I went that Tuesday morning, bright and early. When I arrived I looked for the caddy parking and found a spot not too

The Reasons I am Here

far from the practice area. I already could see some pros in the fenced-off area warming up. I didn't dare to hope about landing a job for the week; I was excited just to be there. However, I approached the boundary fence and noticed one player wiping down his clubs at the far left side of the grounds. There was no sign of his caddy. Maybe this was my lucky break.

I made my way over, only to have a security guard step in my way. I didn't want to miss this chance, though, so when he asked me where I was going, I simply pointed to the pro wiping his clubs and said that I was his caddy. "Oh. Go ahead," he said, and I was through, walking up to the player.

"Hi! Do you have a caddy"? I asked.

"Yes, but he's not here yet," he replied. "If he doesn't get here soon, you can have the job."

I got anxious and began to hope the caddy got lost or something. The pro's name was Stephan Hammill and he was looking a little upset that his guy had not turned up yet. Professional golfers, like all other athletes, are finicky individuals. They don't like it when you throw them off their game. As a caddy, you have to be on time, say the right things, never be negative, make sure to check all the equipment, and so on. The bag can weigh anything up to 40 lbs and you have to be fit to carry it the four or five miles of the course.

Stephan had been on a special invite to the tournament and was looking to make an impression, so he could seal a sponsorship deal with a man who owned a grocery chain. Stephan finished his warm up and told me that he wanted to play a few holes. Like a wally, I thought that he wanted me to play with him, and I said "Okay!" and went to get my clubs.

"Where are you going?" he asked.

Uhmm... "To get my clubs?" I said.

"No, not you! Me!" But he laughed. I had embarrassed myself, but we had a chuckle and he just told me not to worry and just stay close to him. Then, as we made our way to the first tee, he looked towards a tree where some guy was looking in our direction. It was his caddy. Stephan made his way over to talk to him. A few moments later he returned and told me that he had fired him.

Wow, I thought. The kid had travelled all the way from Ireland to get here, and now had to go back after taking a tongue lashing. That's how strict it can be amongst the pros.

Eric Two Crowns (Supercabbie)

Nick Faldo at the British PGA

Off Stephan and I went, and I suddenly realized I would be on TV, possibly, and walking amongst the best players in the world. I could see the Spanish contingent all around the chipping green, Seve, Jose Maria Olazabal, Manuel Pinero, Canizares, all joking around. Seve was hitting little chip shots landing and checking up at the hole. I stood in amazement at his deft touch and skill. He was one of the greatest player's ever and known for his amazing creativity. My heart was pounding with excitement, I had lucked out and would spend the next six days in golfers' paradise.

Friday morning was tournament start day as the British PGA finishes on a "bank holiday" Monday. I nervously checked the bag and made sure Stephan had everything that he needed. Food for the round, water, balls and don't forget to count the clubs! 1-2-3..14, perfect! Don't want to screw up on that one like Ian Woosnam's caddy had. He'd forgotten to count the clubs!. Woosnam incurred a penalty, the caddy was fired.

Time clicked down and then the announcer called out, "On the tee, from Ireland, Stephan Hamill!" The small crowd clapped as I handed him his driver and he teed it up. *"Swoosh!"* and the drive. The ball soared into the sky, right down the middle. "Great shot!" I said and off we went down the fairway. Stephan was already visualizing and prepared for the next shot.

That day I recall being paired with Ken Brown, who is now an announcer. Boy was that guy slow! He constantly fiddled around with his grip and began to get on Stephan's nerves. Ken would take forever, something like what Sergio Garcia went through, "grip, regrip, grip, regrip..."

"Come on, mate!" I heard Stephan mumble. Someone like that can get to you in a hurry and put you off your game! I don't re-

The Reasons I am Here

call the third player in our group but I can remember that both Stephan and him were getting agitated.

As the round progressed my guy was doing well. He had got himself within range to play for the weekend. The cut came on Saturday evening and Stephan and I were elated to that he'd made the cut at 3 under par. He was guaranteed a cheque and some of the pressure was off. Hopefully that would gain favour with his possible sponsor.

On Sunday, Stephan shot par, and although he was down the field a bit, it was still an excellent performance for a rookie. I was picking up little things along the way.

Composure was the biggest thing, I realized. Being able to concentrate and focus on things that mattered such as the set up and the whole pre-shot routine. Visualizing the trajectory so to transfer it to your body and "feel the shot", so to speak. That's what made Stephan's game so good.

The last day of the tournament is the "CASH" day. You either play well and move up the leader board and make a fatter cheque, or you tense up, miss a few putts, and move down. One shot can be worth tens of thousands of dollars, if not millions in the big picture. That morning, I was all fired up thinking that if we had a good day, Stephan would make more money. He was already guaranteed a cheque but the bigger it was, the better. A big paycheck to cushion Stephan for the rest of the year.

I wasn't in it for the money. I was there to help in any way I could. My cut would be nothing, Zilch. The experience alone was worth much more. I had spent the week absorbing all that I could. We were hovering at two under par and I was happy just to make the cut with him.

On the tenth hole (par 3) there was a hold up and the players were backed up. I sat on a bench and took out a banana to eat along with a can of coke. Stephan was talking to another player while we were waiting. I was near a bush and needed to go to the washroom but none were in sight. I looked around and as no one was watching I went behind a tree and did my business. When I came back, I wondered where my banana had gone? I looked around, and I found it.

Eamon Darcy, the Irish player who holed a putt to win the Ryder cup, was eating my banana. He looked at me and started

Eric Two Crowns (Supercabbie)

laughing. The bastard stole my banana and was chomping away nonchalantly. I began to laugh with them as they were "Taking the Mickey" out of me.

Finally we were ready to go again. On the back nine Stephan played steady. Nothing spectacular, but he did hole a bunker shot where I punched the air and yelled "YESSS"!

Stephan turned to me and said, "Eric, calm down! It's not to tie for the lead, you know!" I felt a bit embarrassed but I was excited and just reacted to the hole out. We were still at three under and as we got to the par five 17th dogleg left.

I pulled out the driver and gave it to him, "Remember to keep it down the right. Don't try anything fancy." I said. The last two holes are both par fives and you can pick up a couple of shots there. Stephan hit the ball sweet as a nut and crushed it down the fairway with a draw.

I lost it in the air and although Stephan hit it straight, I didn't see it land. I went towards where I had assumed it was, and couldn't find it. To my surprise, though, a spectator waved to me from the crowd, and pointing ahead, far ahead. I was amazed at how far Stephan had hit the ball. Usually guys are hitting three woods or 1-irons on their second shots, but Stephan had put a 5-iron in! Approximately 180 yards to the flag and downhill.

Stephan swung again. *"Swoosh!"* Again, great contact, but this time the ball went over the green by ten yards! The adrenaline was pumping, obviously, as the round was ending. We had both lost a little focus. A chip and, unfortunately, a two-putt followed for par.

Again on the eighteenth tee there was a another hold up, this time with two groups plus us waiting. I didn't mind so much. It had been a hot day and I was beat after five days of carrying a forty-pound bag, five to six miles a day and everything else in between.

In the group that was starting to tee off next was a tall lanky, dark guy. He didn't look familiar, Stephan said to me, "watch this guy, he's going to be one of the best in a couple of years. Just count the seconds the ball is in the air."

The man swung. There was a *"crunch!"*, and the ball went as high as a kite and seemed not to want to come down! I had 7 seconds on it. That's a long "hang time", as they call it. I didn't get a chance to ask what the guy's name was at the time, because it was time for us to tee off on the last hole.

The Reasons I am Here

Alas it was all over, but I felt good for Stephan. He had made one of his first cheques as a pro, and I was part of it. To tell the truth, he might have done better with a career caddie, but it was still a good showing. As I sat down in the locker room, Stephan said that I could take anything from his bag, like balls, gloves or tees, as a gift and memento. He also asked me how much money I wanted for the week's work.

I said again I was doing it for the experience, not the money. My financial situation was good. But Stephan handed me a dozen Titleist balatta's the best balls, as far as I'm concerned and a cheque for 150.00 pounds sterling. He insisted I take it, so I did.

The next thing you know the tall dark-skinned guy comes through the door. Stephan looked over at him, then turned to me and said, "Eric, grab a glove from the bag! Hurry!" I took out a glove and handed it to him. Off he went to the guy with the glove and came back with it signed. The name said "Vijay Singh". I didn't think much of it at the time but Stephan was right this guy turned out to be great. Me, like an idiot, used the glove and, because of the softness of the leather, it didn't last long. In hindsight I should have kept it as a souvenir and maybe today it might have been worth something.

Anyway, the tournament was over and I had accomplished my goal. The whole experience served me well and I had learned a great deal.

#

My favourite golf memory, however, was the time I caddied next to Lee Trevino.

I had heard, through the golf grapevine, there was a qualifying tournament for the first Canadian Senior Open in Ancaster, Hamilton (in the 1990's). The qualifier was to be held at the Westmount Golf and Country club in Kitchener, Ontario, not too far from my house.

I arrived early in the morning once again (early bird gets the worm!). I knew Rob Strahan, the pro at the club, and made him aware that I was available to caddy if anyone was interested. Not too long after, he found me on the practice area, there was an American player who needed me. I can't recall his name but I did my best to assist him in his quest.

Eric Two Crowns (Supercabbie)

He was not the most talkative man, but that was fine with me. I gathered my things, organized his bag, and negotiated the days rate.

This guy was wired different. He had twitchy habits. He would ask my advice and, before I was finished giving it, he would start addressing the ball. So much for listening! Being such a bag of nerves, he didn't make the cut. Not only that, but he also shafted me on my rate, as it is generally paid in US dollars, but paid me in Canadian. At the time, that made for was a thirty-dollar difference. Another reason not to remember his name. Nevertheless, it was a good day, because I found out when the Senior Open would be and made a note to be there...

The Ancaster Golf Club has a great layout. The tall trees and the lush green fairways stand out as you look around the valley-built course. The first Senior Open with all the legends was held in 1993. They might be "senior", but they still played great. It was a great opportunity for me, as many veteran pros had parted with their regular caddies by then, and often needed one.

I went in and made my way to the registration office and sat outside, hoping to land a job for the week. Unfortunately, things did not seem to be in my favour. Every pro that came out of the office went past me and, as time went on, it was obvious that my chances were dwindling away.

"Shit," I thought. "No-go today." But as I was there and it was pro-am day, I decided to try to get a bag just for the day, instead of a whole tournament. The fee would at least cover my gas expenses and pay for something to eat and I could get some leg work in.

The young lady at the shack was looking over the player sheet and asked me who I wanted to caddie for? I jokingly said, "Lee Trevino!"

She smiled at me and said, "Sorry, but I can put you in his group if you want."

"Are you kidding?" I asked.

"No, there's an amateur that needs a caddie. His name is Dave Lasorda." (No relation to the great Tommy) "Would you like to take him?" she asked.

I was flabbergasted! I was about to tread the turf with Lee Trevino, my favorite player! I had followed him throughout his years as a pro and loved his swing and his personality. In fact my good friend John Virgo told me that my swing was a lot like his. It happened when John wrote his first book called, *John Virgo's Snooker Sideshow*. He had autographed it, "To Eric (Lee). Best wishes! John." When I asked him why he had written "Lee", he replied, "Your swing is like Trevino's!" John knew how to give the best compliments.

Away I went to the practice area and began looking at the personalized signs with the names of the players. "There it is, Dave Lasorda!" I looked at the player, who was quite tall and athletic, I extended my hand and said, "Hi, Mr. Lasorda," I said, "I'm your caddie for the day!"

Dave acknowledged me and we had a brief chat before leaving for the first tee. I had noticed while Dave was warming up that he had a nice swing and was hitting his woods way out there. "Good," I thought. "Nothing worse than caddying for a hacker!"

This Dave dude seemed a little cold and pompous though, paying more attention to his handsome looks and garments than anything else. So, I did my job, more excited knowing Lee would be playing, even though his caddy, Herman, was on the bag and not me. I can only imagine what could have happened if Herman had not made the journey north. Perhaps I could have snagged the bag! That would have been wild!

There was a large crowd at the first tee at least a thousand people scrambling to watch Lee, the "Merry Mex". All of a sudden the crowd started clapping and cheering. A gap opened up as Lee came through and the cheers got louder! I was clapping along with the rest as the announcer introduced him. "Ladies and gentlemen, from the United States... Welcome Mr. Lee Trevinooo!!!"

The roar was loud and the adrenaline started pumping as he teed off. I could imagine the amateurs shaking in their boots. I would too, in their position. Lee lined up that classic swing and the ball clicked off the club head so sweet, flying right down the fairway. All of the rest teed off and the game was on.

I recall it was a hot day and the bag got heavier as the round progressed. My guy was driving the ball well, but the other two guests were struggling, slicing, hooking, you name it. Finally, on one hole, Lee watched as one of the other guys was about to tee off and then stopped him in his tracks. "No!" he said. "Not like that!

Eric Two Crowns (Supercabbie)

Like this!" He pushed the mans hands a little forward at address and then said, "Now, hit it!"

Swoosh! The ball went down the middle!

"See?" he said. "Just like that!"

The crowd laughed and the guy was amazed at the simple lesson Lee had just given him.

The next hole was a par three, about 195 yards. My guy asks me what club he should use to hit it? He hadn't really asked me for my opinion before, or listened to my advice, but I gave it anyway. I figured it was a four iron for him and handed him the club. He thought a moment, then puts the four iron back in the bag and pulls out his seven wood. He put down the tee-peg and started to get ready to hit when Lee said, "What are you doing?"

"Why?" Dave asked.

"It's a four iron for you!" Lee replied.

Dave switched back to the 4 iron and hit the shot. The ball soared into the distance and landed on the right side of the pin before rolling downhill towards the hole. The crowd got louder and louder as the ball trickled down and just missed the ace by inches! Dave looked over at me as people are clapping and cheering and said. "Okay, I'll listen to you from now on!"

Lee winked at me, knowing I had already told Dave which club to hit. I'll never forget that moment! Admiration from the "MEX"!!!

Off we went. Dave tapped his putt in for birdie and again got the acknowledgment from the crowd. A few holes later, there was a delay and as I sat down on the butt end of the bag in the middle of the fairway, pretty tired, Lee came over. I immediately stood up. He put his arm on my shoulders and said with a chuckle, "The bag gets heavier as the round goes on, doesn't it?"

I was almost paralyzed to have him there next to me, let alone touch me, an unforgettable moment. There was one thing though, I was puzzled why he wasn't signing autographs when asked by the spectators? I asked him, and he said, "There's thousands of them and they all want a piece of me!" I understood immediately and agreed with him. He added, "Right now, I'm working. When I'm done I'll spend time with them." That made perfect sense to me. Focus is the key to all professionals doing their job.

The Reasons I am Here

That same day, after finishing the round, I shook hands with the players and the caddies and Lee was surprised as I acknowledged him in his own tongue. "So you speak some Spanish?" he said. I replied that I did. He was impressed and I was honoured.

Dave, who I had helped, gave me the shaft, as he left me with no tip, but, I still had achieved something most golfers only dream of: being in the company of immortal figures such as Lee Trevino, Jack Nicholas, Gary Player, etc. That alone was priceless to me.

Back at the car, I looked over towards the practice grounds, I noticed a few people scurrying around trying to get a glimpse of someone. I decided to go over and check it out when I saw a few of the pros watching as well. It was none other than the (then) living legend, Moe Norman!

Trevino had said in the past that "Moe" was probably the best striker of the ball ever! I had to stay around and watch him for a while.

He was hitting a driver and I was mesmerized at the accuracy of every shot he hit. They seemed to be landing in the same area about 250-260 yards out. This man was not only extraordinary, he was respected by all pros that knew him. What a shame that he was a little mentally challenged, although still a genius. Apparently he had been hit by a car at the age of six, which left him with a mental ailment.

Moe once told me to "fuck off!" when I was watching him teach a young man, even though I was thirty yards away. Then again, Picasso was weird also, along with many other stand-out geniuses. Maybe that was the key to their existence?

I watched Moe for about half an hour and marvelled at his skills. In all, I caddied for seven professionals, including two female pros. Although all had been one day jobs, except for Stephan Hamill in the British PGA, I still gained the knowledge I wanted to be a better player.

That was my task. Having done that, I had the honour of paying it back one summer when I taught the fundamentals of golf at a local course here in Kitchener. 32 students signed up for my class. It was fun, and I enjoyed passing along the knowledge. I hope it has been of some value to them.

Chapter Forty-One
My Buddy Graham

It wasn't long after my return to Canada that I decided to rediscover my roots.

I had this burning desire to find my purpose and know where I stood and what I wanted from the future. I'd already lived a turbulent life full of drama — enough to make a movie, my friends had said.

First thing, though, is I needed some inspiration on where to start. I needed someone who could guide me, someone of aboriginal descent, a Shaman or Medicine man. Maybe I could use a sweat hut to cleanse my body along the way.

Then I thought, Graham Greene.

He was and still is a famous actor, (*Dances with Wolves*, *The Green Mile* just to name a couple). I knew he had a connection to Brantford, Ontario. I personally never spoke to or knew him, only through his career.

Yes, he would be perfect! If I could sit down with him for a while, he could see through me and chase away all the demons and restore them with spiritual warriors to guide and protect me. He could clear my fogged vision and restore my purpose in life!

So, I tracked him down.

First, I had to go to Brantford, Ontario and make inquiries. I got lucky my first go because the person I talked to knew where his mother lived: just down the road in the Six Nations Reserve. Great! I would simply ask her for his phone number and set up a meeting. I was sure, when I spoke to him and asked for his help, he would oblige.

As I drove onto his mother's gravel driveway, I felt an aura of

The Reasons I am Here

peace surrounding the place. The house was typical of native houses found on many of the reserves I've seen. As I got out, though, I started to feel a little apprehensive. But I went up towards the side door anyway and peered through the window to see a work table with a lamp above it. There were small handmade crafts on it, including baby moccasins, dreamcatchers and so on.

Pulling on my courage, I knocked on the door. A woman opened it and I quickly introduced myself.

"Hello, madam! My name is Eric. I am trying to get in touch with Mr. Graham Greene."

"What for?" she asked.

I explained my reasons.

She was more than accommodating. She invited me inside and went to fetch her phone diary. "Here it is," she said, and wrote the number down for me.

I thanked her and returned home, excited that this could be the break I was looking for. I called his number, unaware that was battling his own demons and had barricaded himself in his home.

"Hello," I said. "May I speak to Mr. Graham Greene, please?"

"This is he," he replied.

I began to tell him the reason for my call, when he interrupted me and said, harshly, "How did you get my number?"

"Your mother gave it to me, sir," I replied.

"Fuck off! Never call me again!"

I heard the crunch of the phone being slammed down and that was that. So much for blood, I thought, and abandoned any thought of getting together with him.

At the time I was dumbfounded by his reaction, especially after how helpful his mother had been. As I learned more, I sympathized with him. We are all human, and it shows how vulnerable and delicate we all are.

I've often thought how funny it would be if this book was successful and I found myself standing on stage receiving an award or something and he was in the crowd. Then I could say, "Ladies and gentlemen, thank you for this award. And special thanks to Mr. Graham Greene who, when I asked how I should go about on my quest, told me to fuck off, and so I did, and here I am!"

Even rejection can be a positive. I gained a stronger resolve because of it. Thank you, Graham.

Eric Two Crowns (Supercabbie)

Well, now that I've started dropping names, let me drop another one, thanks to my good friend, John Virgo the snooker pro.

John had called me one afternoon and asked if I wanted to go and see a comedy show. He and his girlfriend Diane were going, and he had a spare ticket. I accepted, and he picked me up that evening. We drove over to Cobham to pick up Diane, and then went on into London.

We arrived at Leicester Square and entered The Comedy Store. I noticed as we spiraled down the stairs a long line of photographs of famous comedians on the walls. They'd all performed here during their rise to fame and had thanked the club for their opportunity by signing their photographs as a thank you.

We arrived downstairs and immediately guests were recognizing John. The owner welcomed us and sat us in the second row from the stage and offered drinks on the house.

The place was a bit of a dive, to be honest, but it worked just fine for the show. People came out for a laugh, not to be impressed by the scenery.

The first act wasn't bad; it got its fair share of laughs. So did the next one, and the one after that. They were pretty good comics, and I was having a good time when they announced a break for a few minutes. We got up to grab another drink before returning to our seats, at which point the owner got back on stage.

"Ladies and gentlemen," he shouted. "When this gentleman comes to London, he always comes to say hello and gives us a few moments in appreciation. Put your hand together for... Robin Williams!"

The applause was deafening. People were shouting his praises. Needless to say, we were gobsmacked that this living legend happened to show up on the very night we were in the crowd. It was a million to one shot!

Anyway, Robin bounds on stage and the crowd settles down to listen as he goes into his improv. Of course, they didn't settle down for long before he had them in stitches. He's my favourite comic by far, and I know I'm not alone in thinking so. I was close enough to see the sweat on his brow, and you could see that this guy was born to make people laugh.

He was doing impressions, my favorite was his impersonation

of Jim Nabors, when he hesitated a split second, thinking about his next inspiration. In that second, I yelled out, "Do Gomer Pyle!"

He looked me straight in the eye and then just launched into his impression, and I started laughing like crazy. The only problem is, this being England, nobody else in the audience knew who Gomer Pyle was!

He quickly realized that I was the only laugh he was getting, and he quickly switched to something else, possibly thinking, "thanks for nothing, guy!" but it was a classic moment for me, even if I'd sort of derailed him.

He wasn't the last act of the night, either, and to this day I feel sorry for the poor guys who had to follow him.

Later that evening, as we made our way up the stairs, I saw Robin's photo on the wall. He'd autographed it, adding, "Thanks for the break!" It had been in the seventies when he'd gotten his break at the club, and he never forgot that. That's gratitude.

I was so sad when I learned of his death. He was one in a million. Rest in peace, Robin.

Chapter Forty-Two
Lightning Strikes Twice

I often think I've been given some special reason for being on this Earth. Of course, I haven't yet found out what it is. Maybe it's to share my life with as many people as possible, to help as much as I can, whether it's to show how to do something, or show how not to do something, from what I learned so far.

I've experienced a few near-death situations. One of the weirdest came on a Saturday morning when I was a young man in Italy, when Caio, Sergio and I were going to Udine.

A few weeks before, Caio had taken in his motorcycle engine to a garage there for a supe-up, and it was ready. Heading into this city of over 100,000 was going to be a treat — we would usually take in a movie or have a pizza while we were there. Sergio came along for the ride, but we had to pick him up at his place, first.

Caio was so excited that his little baby was getting a facelift and with that a lot more power. We were always trying to find ways to get more juice out of our motorcycles, tinkering with carburetors, using special spark plugs, and so on.

So, after picking up Sergio, we went off to Udine. We took the main drag down along the La Pontebana highway, a quick twenty-minute drive. I recall the sun was shining, it was a beautiful day. After we picked up Caio's motorcycle engine, we went for some food and hung out a bit.

When it came time to leave, Caio said he was going to take the back roads home. Udine was in foothill country, and there were some small villages along the way. It would be a nice scenic drive.

Sergio was in the back of our car, and I was in the front, with Caio's bike engine between my feet. Our car was a Simca 1000,

The Reasons I am Here

which is kind of a matchbox-looking car with its engine in the back. Caio was a good driver, but he could get a little aggressive, and we were young dirt-bikers, so nothing much scared us.

We sped down the back roads, encountering no traffic. Then, when we rounded a corner with tall trees on our left, out comes a car speeding towards us on our side of the road, the driver struggling to keep control on the tight turn.

Caio twisted the steering wheel, forcing us right and onto the soft gravel shoulder. The car zoomed past us, but that was the least of our worries. We were losing traction as Caio struggled to get us back onto the road. We were fishtailing and swerving all over. Before you could blink, we were on the soft shoulder again and then into a ditch.

I can still feel the breeze on my face as I was hurled through the air. The car had rolled three or four times, flinging me at least thirty meters into a corn field.

When I opened my eyes and looked through the corn stalks, I could see our car mangled up. Caio and Sergio struggled to open doors that were jammed closed. I was in shock and couldn't speak, so I watched as they struggled out and screamed my name. I could see them, but they couldn't see me. They were looking under the car and all around.

After a moment, I came to my senses enough to shout, "Over here! Over here!" As they rushed over, I struggled to get up and noticed that I didn't have my shoes on. I looked around to find them but no luck.

Finally, Caio and Sergio reached me. They were amazed to see me, still groggy but on my feet, and asked if I was okay. I was dazed, but except for some bumps and scratches, I was unharmed.

We started to laugh as I pointed to my feet and showed them my shoes were missing. The G-forces must somehow have claimed them. We looked around for some time, but we could only find one.

The car was a crumpled-up mess, but I could reach in and open the glove compartment and take out a pack of cigarettes. I sure as heck needed one right then. I stood in amazement as there were only a few cigarettes in it. *That's impossible*, I thought. *I had only just bought them before we left Udine.* Then I looked around

Eric Two Crowns (Supercabbie)

and saw a trail of cigarettes on the ground, leading to the car. How in hell did the packet remain in the glove compartment without flying out the window as I had, while still releasing a trail of cigarettes? The forces of nature I suppose? The motorcycle engine that was between my feet was still in the car, intact.

My mind ran over all that could have happened to me in that instant. I could have been pinned under the car or squashed while we were rolling. I could have landed on something much harder than dirt. Somehow, I was spared.

We gathered our things from the car and went back to the road hoping to flag down someone who could give us a ride home. The first car that did stop, was driven by a policeman — I saw the wand police officers used to stop cars at spot checks behind the back headrest — but though he asked us what had happened, he let us get in the car and brought us home without any fuss. After all, it was the other car driving on the wrong side of the road which caused the whole incident.

I was trying to figure out what I was going to say to Dad about my bruises and my missing shoe. Should I tell him the truth, or just tell him I'd been in a fight? The fight seemed an easier explanation, and Dad bought it. He gave me the usual cuff and told me off, but nothing more than that.

After I got cleaned up, and found another pair of shoes, I made my way back to the bar. Caio, Sergio and I met up again at Missanna's. While we were going over the events again, Caio mentioned that Trucha, one of our friends, was down at his mechanic shop, souping up one of his rally-cross cars, and that we should go down and check it out.

We heard the revving of an engine as we approached the shop. Trucha came out to greet us and said he needed to go across into a nearby field to test his contraption, so off we went. Caio and I watched on the sidelines as Trucha took Sergio for a spin. He was going full throttle, sending mud and grass flying all round, doing fishtails and spinning around the field. Then Caio was next, riding along as the car flew up and down, roaring away.

Finally, it was my turn. I slipped inside and Trucha shoved it into first gear, with wheels spinning and the engine blasting away. The ground was wet and slippery and, as we went into a

The Reasons I am Here

sideways slide, I braced myself. I saw a gravel path coming fast, and thought, "Oh, no! Not again!"

The car did indeed flip over onto the roof. The gas tank was in the back seat, with only a rag and a cork acting as a cap. There were no windows, just wire meshing. Upside-down, the fluid began gushing out of the tank.

Did I mention that Trucha and I were both smoking cigarettes?

We went berserk, trying to poke our cigarettes out through the mesh, kicking at the screen and panicking to get out, while the gas soaked our clothes.

But we managed to get out, and Caio and Sergio pulled us free. How the gas didn't ignite was beyond me, but I was lucky for the second time in just a few hours.

Talk about nine lives! Well, two of them anyway.

Last time I visited Caio, he remembered that day vividly. He was well aware that someone should have died that day. Someone was looking out for us, and was kind enough to keep doing so, as we pushed our luck.

Chapter Forty-Three

Soccer Days

In addition to hockey, I also played soccer left wing. When I was a boy in Canada, I played for the Rosemount Royals. Mr. Ingrams, an Englishman, was our coach. I always looked forward to the *KW Record* printing all the results from the many different minor leagues in town, watching the teams fighting for playoff berths. One year, as the season was concluding, we were right there in the mix.

Mr. Ingrams asked me if my father could take over coaching duties while he was off on a trip to England. I was hesitant to ask, sure the answer would be "no!", followed by Dad's usual excuses. However, my father surprised me by agreeing.

Dad was never really a Footy fan. He'd just enrolled me to get me out of his hair, but I still loved playing. I love all sports, from ping-pong to skiing. I was coordinated, fit, and could absorb things quickly.

Dad was in charge for about a month while Mr. Ingrams was away. Dad wasn't a brilliant coach. Basically, all he did was make us run a lot and practice passing. I think he just loved blowing the whistle.

But he and I would pick up a couple of my teammates on the way to practices and matches. And, on the way, Dad insisted on stopping at the local Italian store where they sold chunky dark mint chocolate. He told me that, in his cycling days, he would eat a piece before each race and it would give him energy.

I was skeptical but went along with the idea. After all, why turn down chocolate? The kids would huddle around, and he would give us all a piece of the stuff before we went out playing.

The Reasons I am Here

In our last scheduled game, we needed one point to make it to the league finals, but we were struggling through the match, one goal down. The field was drenched from overnight rain and it was heavy going.

Sometimes I wonder how fate works. I can recall the clock ticking down and suddenly destiny came knocking on my door. I was in the clear and one of my teammates passed the ball to me. I dribbled the ball, racing down the wing towards the goal, while the crowd shouted, "Shoot! Shoot!" — Dad yelling loudest of all as time was running out.

I hoofed the thing as hard as I could, and it sailed through the air towards the goaltender. I saw it losing speed and thought he could save it easily, but it landed with a splash in a puddle in front of him, and instead of bouncing into his outstretched hands, it went right between his legs and into the net. Goal!

The kids ran over hugging and slapping me on the back, yelling and shouting, "Victory!"

The game ended tied 2-2, which sent us to the finals against our main rivals whom we would play in the best field and stadium in the city (Woodside Park). I felt so proud that I had scored the goal that got us there. Win or lose, the finals were just gravy.

Which is a good thought, because we lost the final 3-1.

You've got to hang onto all your good memories. There's always more than enough sad ones to drag you down.

One of my friends, Tim Quirk, was a really good player. He actually went to England once to play in an invitational tournament. He and I practiced together in a field near his place, and he helped me get better. Many kids would shy away from heading the ball, but Dad told me to head it hard whenever it came my way. With Tim's help, I started practicing my headers and discovered that if you did it properly, it didn't hurt. The key was to pick the right moment, grit your teeth, and head it with a snap motion so that you hit the ball faster than it was coming at you.

I was a good all-round player in Canada. When I lived in Italy, it was different. The kids were playing at a different level. After all, soccer is to Italy what hockey is to Canada, with kids starting to play as soon as they could walk. I managed to make the junior team, playing *alla sinistra,* which means left wing. I could kick

Eric Two Crowns (Supercabbie)

with my left foot, which gave me an edge as most kids are right handed, and right footed as well.

On my last visit to Osoppo, in 2006, I wandered around the town, reliving my younger days and all that had passed. I wandered up to the soccer pitch, wondering if anything had changed.

It was around midnight and Jack had warned me to be careful as it was no longer safe. Since the war in Yugoslavia, people had moved into town, thefts and crime had gone up. He even showed me how to unlock our door with a special key that drove steel pegs into the concrete frame for added security. When I'd lived there, people just left everything open, knowing no one would ever touch anything.

As I walked to the locked gates and peered through them into the field, a car approached from behind and parked. I tensed, and readied myself for a confrontation, when suddenly a voice called out, "Picile!", which was our family nickname.

It was "Foofie", my cousin.

"How did you know it was me?" I shouted, and he began to laugh as he walked towards me.

"Your walk," he replied.

We immediately embraced.

We had played together as teenagers and he was our best defender, or full back. He was now head of sports for the town — or coordinator of recreation, as his title read.

He opened the gates and invited me onto the field. We went in and headed to the clubhouse where he brought out a bottle of red wine, which he uncorked. We began to drink and reminisce about old times. He asked me if I remembered a goal that I'd scored off a corner-kick. I couldn't believe he remembered!

It had been on a cold Saturday with the wind coming in from the north about 60 kilometers per hour. I had a corner kick and made a good feed to the middle of the crease where I'd hoped that one of my teammates would knock it in, but the ball soared past the awaiting players and met a huge gust of wind. The ball seemed to hover in the air for a moment, then bent left, right over the goalie's head and into the net.

That was a weird one, to say the least. Scoring a goal off a corner-kick was and still is a rarity.

The Reasons I am Here

Then there was the day we had a match with Trasaghis, a town a few kilometers away. I had bet Moreno, our best striker, a beer if he scored three goals. I figured I'd win either way. He was an excellent player with great skills and, by the second half, he'd already scored twice. His third goal was pretty sweet. I was coming down the left, crossing the midfield line, when a quick pass from my defenseman brought the ball to me. I spotted Moreno making a run right down the middle.

I crossed the ball at him and he chested it down and, after two quick strides, he yelled out, "Picile! La Birre!", which is to say, "The beer!" And he stuck the ball right into the top right corner, game winner!

He was poetry in motion. He could have made the big leagues if not for booze and girls. What a waste.

That day though, just to spoil the victory we felt another big earthquake. The match had just ended, and we were making our way into the dressing room when it happened, and of course we ran straight back out onto midfield where guys were already lying down, hoping the earth wouldn't open up and swallow them. It's weird, but it's what goes through your mind when the ground seems like it's alive and groaning.

We didn't bother changing once the shaking stopped. We just got our stuff from the dressing room, jumped into our cars and made our way home along twisting mountain roads. We passed a huge boulder in the middle of the road that had fallen down the mountainside — we just managed to squeeze by it and drove on, watching for more threats, but we made it home all right.

"Foofie" and I chuckled over our memories and, after another bottle of wine, we closed up shop and went our separate ways.

We would see each other a few times in the five weeks that I was there. Usually in the company of some other friends at the local Santa Colomba festival and in the bars. It was good times again, but as usual it passed too quickly. Now, thanks to Facebook, we still keep it touch.

Chapter Forty-Four
A Final Message

My friends, I am honoured to have shared my 55 years plus on this beautiful Earth with you. I have seen and walked through the darkness and discovered light. I have fought my battles, yet the fight is not over. Looking into the future I have many tasks still to accomplish. Tasks that lie in wait, hidden, perhaps just to suddenly appear and challenge all that I have learned, my patience, my wisdom, my character, my beliefs. Most of all my weaknesses so I can challenge all that I have said to you.

Who knows? Maybe our paths might meet some day, so our spirits can mingle and dance for a while, cry for a while, rejoice for a while, but forever strengthen our lives with the understanding that you must pass it on, your strength and all the good you have inside.

A wise man once said to me, "Remember Eric, that when you close your eyes to reflect, you can be sure of one thing, each of us need all of us." From the tramp that you point and snigger at, he is here for you to choose that reaction. From the many that are helpless what can you do? The many who are lost in their wealth, how can you make them see? The sick that toil to just live, how can you help? It's all inside of you. You have the choice.

For all those who choose to be blind, help them see. As I am here sharing these final words with you, I hear my mother's voice. She's saying, "Thank you, my boy, for fulfilling your promise to me. I love you!"

Her wish has been granted as she wanted her life shared as well, hoping that our lives would shed some light to yours. To

The Reasons I am Here

grasp life and all its sacredness and to use all of your wisdom to spare sorrow to all that are in despair.

The task has been a cleansing and an unshackling of many demons that have lived inside of me. I am endlessly grateful to you for your company as I have concluded this huge mission thus far in my life. The wounds that were open and bleeding not so long ago have ceased to bleed. My mind full of doubt and insecurity now conquered, passion and purpose now my engine. The bruises all vanished, but scars remembered, to serve me into the future as a guide and not a club to beat myself up with.

From neglect, physical and mental abuse, abduction, financial ruin and depression, guilt and anxiety, to freedom and peace within. On the verge of suicide to living and loving life. This my message to you. If your unhappy with your life, change it. If your hurting, tell your best friend, rid yourself of anyone negative or undermining. You don't have to be a goose! You can fly north, south, east, west, whichever way you want! Listen to the voice inside of you, and pay attention!

If your struggling with all the pressure, I'm here waiting for your call. Kuei-Kuei for now.

Acknowledgments

To my Mother for giving me life, love and the chance to live it.

To my sister Dina, for her unconditional love and the support only a Soul mate can give.

To my wife Marylyn for standing by me in the midst of despair, and illness.

To my brother Jack for every moment we shared together, for always being straight. The laughs we still share.

To the Creator Manitou and Jesus for the strength and enlightenment to my life.

To all my Taxi customers, who after sharing some stories, encouraged me to "go for it!" and not give up.

To all my "True" friends who never compromised my will and dreams.

To TW, who has been a true friend and comfort to my life.

To my Editor, James Bow, for being patient and guiding me through this accomplishment. Sacrificing his time, because he believed in me.

And the last thanks goes to you, the reader. I thank you for your interest in my life and story. Your support will help in my endeavour for children, parents and people in despair.

My sister Dina, in Essipit